Contents

Introduction

Shrubs and climbers are essential to any garden design, they provide structure and an ever-changing tapestry of colour throughout every month of the year. Their variety is both a delight and a dilemma – with so many to choose from there's almost certainly one to suit your garden, but the choice is so vast it can be totally bewildering.

Enjoying plants

Even if you stick to the basic fare offered by most garden centres, you may have 400 varieties of shrubs and nearly as many climbers to consider. So where do you start?

Well, not with an empty trolley at the garden centre, because impulse buys almost always lead to disappointing results. If you are planting a new border from scratch, buying all the plants in this way at best leads to a border that looks good at one time of year. The safest way to buy the right plant for your garden is to ask yourself the following questions while standing in your garden viewing your plot:

Climbers can be grown up walls and fences or to hide eyesores. Here, the pale pink, richly scented flowers of *Clematis nontana var.* rubens 'Elizabeth' brighten this garden fence in late spring.

Where is it to be planted?

Consider the amount of direct sun the plot gets; the type of soil and its condition; and the plot's exposure to wind, rain and cold.

What will the plant's role in the garden be?

Is it to fill a gap, add height and/or colour, extend the period of interest, cover the ground or a fence, hide an eyesore, act as a barrier or backdrop or a specimen or focal point?

How quickly must it perform?

Do you want results in a year or two, or are you prepared to wait a little longer? Bear in mind that many fast-growing plants will continue to get bigger and so will either need regular pruning or moving. Others, such as *Lavatera*, are short-lived and will need replacing after a few years.

Any special requests?

In certain circumstances you might want to avoid certain plants. For example, if your gardening time is very limited or unpredictable, you might want to avoid high-maintenance plants that require a lot

Low growing hedges can be successfully made out of lavender bushes. Here, two rows of lavender border a narrow path. As you brush past, the aroma is breathtaking.

of pruning or training. On the other hand, if you have young children or young visitors, you should avoid or remove any poisonous plants that you have in your garden. With this information in mind, you are then in a position to draw up a shortlist of potential plant candidates. You can follow the same procedure when planning a whole border from scratch. The first three questions apply to the border as a whole, then the last can be considered for each individual element.

Working with colour

Many beginners are worried about combining colours, but the key is simply to go for plants and effects that you like, without worrying about what other people do.

You can find ideas and inspiration in garden magazines, and there is nothing more enjoyable for the

Elegant hybrid tea roses (above) are essential plants for any cottage garden scheme, here combining well with phlox and other border perennials.

enthusiastic gardener than being able to wander around other people's gardens, horticultural displays or the grounds of stately homes in search of new ideas and planting schemes.

Choosing your plants

Plants form the basis of all good gardens, and none more so than the shrubs and climbers. We have produced two directories to introduce you to the best shrubs and climbers available today.

Each entry gives a description of the plant, with useful information on its growing requirements, how to keep it in good health, and advice on propagation, to help you decide which plants best suit your needs and the conditions in your garden.

An enticing vista (left) has been created by training *Rosa* 'Seagull' to drape over a hanging structure made of rope to provide a stunning focal point.

How plants are named

Although many garden plants have familiar common names, most are just local names that are not recognized universally. Some plants have many different common names, while other common names are applied to quite different plants.

Confused?

All the different names for the same plant can make life a bit confusing. For this reason, a Swedish naturalist, Carl Linnaeus (1707-1778), suggested that every plant should be given a two-word Latin name that would uniquely identify it. This would allow scientists and growers to talk about and trade in specific plants with the confidence that others would know exactly what they were referring to.

These days a Latin name still has two main parts: genus (first name); and species (second name). The genus refers to the general group of related plants to which an individual belongs, while the species sub-divides this group into collections of plants that share a range of particular major characteristics but differ in one or two minor ones. A third name, either variety or

By convention, plants have their Latin names in italics, with a capital letter for the genus, lower case for the species and their cultivar name in a roman font surrounded by single quote marks – hence the plant above is called *Viburnum opulus* 'Xanthocarpum'.

cultivar, is then applied to the plants to show how they differ from others in their species. Naturally occurring variations are given a variety name and those that are selectively bred are given a cultivar name.

Latin names do actually mean something, too. However, knowing this isn't always that helpful. For example, the Latin genus *Fuchsia* commemorates Leonard Fuchs, a famous 16th-century herbalist.

Species names are generally more informative for the gardener and usually indicate a major identifying feature of that particular group of plants, examples include: 'purpureus' (purple), 'macrophylla' (small leaved), 'nana' (dwarf), and 'glauca' (blue). Variety and cultivar names are extremely variable, often commemorating breeders, their family members and friends or famous people, but some are more helpful because they emphasize a particularly desirable feature of the plant, such as 'Golden Showers' – an excellent description of the flowers.

Hybrid species

When a plant species breeds with another, the result is a hybrid. Rare in the wild, crossing is very common among plant breeders and it is done in order to produce plants with desirable qualities, such as larger or double blooms, variegated foliage and greater weather resistance. An 'x' figure indicates a hybrid, with the name often giving a clear idea of the hybrid's origins.

Viburnum plicatum 'Mariesii' is so named as '*Viburnum*' is the genus name, '*Plicatum*' is the species name and 'Mariesii' is the cultivar name. Its common name is Japanese snowball bush.

How to use the directories

With so many thousands of varieties of shrubs and climbers to choose from, selecting the right plants for your garden can be a bewildering exercise. To help with this selection process, this book has been divided into two directory sections: Plants are arranged alphabetically, by genus. Each main entry features a general introduction to that genus, plus specific useful information such as tips on propagation and which hardiness zone the genus belongs to. This is followed by a selection of plants from that genus, also arranged alphabetically according to their most widely accepted names. One of these entries might be a species, a hybrid, a variety, form or cultivar. Each has a useful description that includes height and spread.

Caption

The full botanical name of the plant in question is given with each photograph.

Genus name

This is the internationally accepted botanical name for a group of related plants.

Common name

Sometimes a common (non-scientific) name applies to a whole genus, while some individual species also have common names.

Cultivation

This section gives the level of sun and shade that the plant either requires or tolerates, advice on the best type of soil in which it should be grown and other helpful tips, as appropriate.

Pruning

Pruning details specific to each plant are included. The type of pruning and the correct season in which to prune are given.

Propagation

This section gives essential information on how and when to increase the plant – from seed, cuttings or layering.

Individual plant entry

This starts with the botanical name of the plant in bold. This can refer to the species, subspecies, hybrid, variant or cultivar. If a synonym (syn.) is given, this provides an alternative name by which the plant is known.

Sarcococca confusa

SARCOCOCCA
Sweet box

A genus of around 15 species, including the dense-growing, evergreen shrubs featured here, grown for their neat habit and sweet vanilla-scented winter flowers. An ideal choice for a dark, shady corner where nothing else will grow. Well suited to urban gardens as it is pollution tolerant.

Cultivation Grow in a moisture-retentive, well-drained garden soil that is reasonably fertile and in dappled or deep shade.

Pruning No routine pruning is necessary. Remove any damaged growth in mid-spring.

Propagation Take hardwood cuttings in mid-autumn.

Sarcococca confusa
A dense, evergreen shrub with glossy dark green leaves that bears clusters of sweetly scented white flowers from early winter to early spring.
H 2m (6ft) S 1m (3ft).
Aspect: semi-shade to deep shade
Hardiness: ✤✤✤ Zones: 7–8

Photograph

Each entry features a full-colour photograph that makes identification easy.

Genus introduction

This provides a general introduction to the genus. Other information featured here may include general advice on usage, preferred conditions and plant care, as well as sub-species, hybrids (indicated by an 'x' symbol in the name), varieties and cultivars (featuring names in single quotes) that are available.

Plant description

This gives a description of the plant's key features, along with any other information that may be helpful.

Size information

The average expected height and spread of a genus or individual plant is given, although growth rates may vary depending on location and conditions. Average heights and spreads are given as H and S.

Plant hardiness and zones

The plant's hardiness and appropriate zones are given at the end of this section (see page 96 for details of hardiness and zones, as well as a zone map).

A directory of shrubs

This directory offers a comprehensive array of shrubs – including all the familiar favourites plus some rarer specimens. The selection here will help gardeners of all levels find the shrubs that will make the most of their garden space. The initial introduction for each entry is either for the whole genus or the main species grown. Beyond this, the entry is split between more common species and cultivars and those that are less common. The advent of the internet has meant that it is often possible to obtain rare shrubs from around the world. Growing rarer species can be rewarding, as they are often particularly beautiful.

However, there is also a joy in growing less exotic plants. If your garden centre does not have the ones you want, you can always try mail-order catalogues – and the internet – to find the perfect plant for your garden.

Shrubs are often viewed as the backbone of the garden, allowing other plants to look their best. However, shrubs in their own right make a delightful addition to beds and borders, with their stunning blooms, fruits, foliage and scents.

Abelia x grandiflora

ABELIA

A genus of about 30 species with a long flowering season that make excellent compact, garden plants. Their pretty, trumpet-like flowers are produced on arching stems throughout summer and into early autumn. Although hardy in milder areas, they will need protection elsewhere.

Cultivation They will grow in well-drained garden soil that is reasonably fertile. They need full sun and protection from cold winds. Most are not reliably hardy in colder areas and need the protection of a sheltered, south-facing wall or fence.

Pruning Prune established plants after flowering to encourage new growth. In colder areas, treat as a herbaceous plant and cut down the whole plant in autumn and protect roots with a layer of dry leaves or bark chippings held in place with wire netting.

Propagation Take softwood cuttings during early summer, semi-ripe cutting in late summer or hardwood cuttings in mid-autumn.

Abelia 'Edward Goucher'

Purple-pink trumpets are produced from early summer to early autumn along arching stems. The glossy, bronze-green leaves mature to dark green. H 1.5m (5ft) S 2m (6ft).
Aspect: sun
Hardiness: ✿✿ Zone: 9

Abelia x grandiflora (syn. A. rupestris)

Scented, trumpet-shaped, pale pink and white flowers are borne on arching stems from early summer to mid-autumn. Vigorous and long-flowering, this semi-evergreen shrub with glossy leaves makes a perfect focal-point plant for a well-drained border in sun. This plant is borderline frost hardy. H 3m (10ft) S 4m (13ft).
Named varieties: 'Confetti', with very compact, pink-tinged white flowers. Frost hardy. H 1m (3ft) S 1m (3ft). 'Francis Mason', variegated, glossy, yellow-edged leaves. More tender than other varieties. H 1.5m (5ft) S 2m (6ft). 'Gold Spot' (syn. 'Gold Strike', 'Aurea'), bright yellow foliage. H 1.5m (5ft) S 2m (6ft).
Aspect: sun
Hardiness: ✿✿ Zone: 9 (some borderline)

ABELIOPHYLLUM

A genus of just one species, that is grown for its masses of fragrant flowers borne on bare branches during late winter and early spring. A good alternative to forsythia, they can be grown in the border or trained against a wall or fence. To fully appreciate the almond-scented flowers, plant close to an entrance or path.

Cultivation Abeliophyllum will grow in well-drained garden soil that is reasonably fertile and in full sun.

Pruning No routine pruning is necessary. Neglected plants can be rejuvenated by cutting back one stem in three to near ground level after flowering, starting with the oldest stems.

Propagation Take softwood cuttings during early summer, semi-ripe cuttings in late summer or hardwood cuttings in mid-autumn.

Abeliophyllum distichum White forsythia

A much underrated, forsythia-like shrub that bears masses of fragrant, star-shaped, pink-tinged white flowers on bare branches during late winter and early spring. H 1.5m (5ft) S 1.5m (5ft).
Named varieties: 'Roseum Group', pale pink flowers on dark stems. H 1.5m (5ft) S 1.5m (5ft).
Aspect: sun
Hardiness: ✿✿✿ Zone: 9+

ABUTILON

A genus of about 150 species of graceful shrubs, many with spectacular, lantern-like flowers. Most are tender, but a few can be grown against a warm, sheltered wall or fence in mild areas, in a container on the patio or in the conservatory in colder areas.

Cultivation In the garden they will grow in well-drained garden soil that is reasonably fertile and in full sun. Indoors, grow in a soil-based compost (soil mix). Water freely during the spring and summer and sparingly at other times. Feed every fortnight during the growing season.

Pruning In the garden, prune out frosted shoots in early spring or mid-spring. Indoors, prune back established plants by half in mid-spring to restrict their size.

Propagation Take softwood cuttings in late spring or semi-ripe cuttings from early summer to late summer. They can also be raised from seed in mid-spring.

Abutilon 'Kentish Belle' Chinese lantern

This is a lax and graceful evergreen shrub with toothed, three- or five-lobed green leaves and delightful, long, pendent, bell-shaped flowers with pale yellow petals and burnt-orange base that are borne from late spring to mid-autumn. H 2.5m (8ft) S 2.5m (8ft).
Aspect: sun
Hardiness: ✿✿ Zone: 9+

Abelia x grandiflora 'Gold Spot'

Abutilon x suntense

Abutilon x suntense 'Geoffrey Gorer'

Abutilon megapotamicum
Brazilian bell-flower, trailing abutilon

This is a graceful, frost-hardy evergreen shrub with slender stems that carry red and yellow lantern-like flowers from late spring to mid-autumn. The toothed, three-lobed bright green leaves form an attractive backdrop at other times. H 2m (6ft) S 2m (6ft).

Named varieties: 'Variegatum' (variegated trailing abutilon), wonderful yellow-blotched leaves on self-layering branches means that it can be grown as deep ground cover in mild areas, but it also makes an attractive shrub if trained against a warm, sheltered wall or fence in cooler areas. H 2m (6ft) S 2m (6ft).
Aspect: sun
Hardiness: ✿✿ Zone: 9+

ACER
Maple

This genus of about 150 species of deciduous trees and shrubs contain many that are grown for their ornamental bark and foliage, as well as brilliant autumnal tints. Only the shrubs are covered here.

The 'palmatum' group have distinctively lobed leaves and attractive bark, while the 'dissectum' group are generally more compact and have leaves that are much more deeply cut. Both are slow growing and make superb garden specimens — creating spectacular seasonal focal points in spring, summer and autumn. They also make excellent specimens in containers.
Cultivation In the garden, grow in well-drained garden soil that doesn't dry out in summer and is reasonably fertile. Acers will grow in sun or partial shade, where they are sheltered from cold winds and late frosts that can scorch the emerging leaves. In containers, grow in a soil-based compost (soil mix). Feed every fortnight throughout the growing season and water as necessary.
Pruning No routine pruning is necessary. Neglected plants can have any wayward branches removed to balance the overall shape of the canopy.
Propagation Can be raised from seed in mid-autumn, but results are variable. Named varieties must be grafted in early spring or budded in late summer on to seedling stock of the same species.

Acer palmatum 'Atropurpureum' (syn. *A. palmatum* f. *atropurpureum*)
Japanese maple

This is a graceful and slow-growing maple that makes an excellent specimen for a small garden or for growing in a large container. The plant's attractive palm-like, deeply lobed, dark purple leaves look spectacular through all of the summer before turning brilliant shades of red in autumn. H 8m (26ft) S 8m (26ft).
Aspect: semi-shade
Hardiness: ✿✿✿ Zone: 4+

Acer palmatum 'Bloodgood'
Japanese maple

This is one of the best purple-leaved varieties. It has attractive deeply lobed, palm-like leaves that are sumptuous all summer long, turning brilliant red in autumn. This is an ideal specimen or accent plant for a partially shaded spot. The autumn hues are particularly long lasting, making it the perfect choice for a seasonal display. When its leaves fall, dark purple twigs and stems add winter interest. Can be grown in a container. H 5.5m (18ft) S 5.5m (18ft).
Aspect: semi-shade
Hardiness: ✿✿✿ Zone: 5+

Acer palmatum var. *dissectum* 'Atropurpureum' (syn. *A. palmatum* var. *dissectum* 'Atropurpureum Group')
Japanese maple

Ideal for growing in a container or as a specimen plant on the patio, this compact Japanese maple has a neat dome-like habit and particularly fine, deeply cut, red-purple, ferny foliage. In autumn the leaves turn dramatic fiery shades. Protect from cold winds and late frosts. Its delicate foliage can burn in full sun. H 2m (6ft) S 3m (10ft).
Aspect: semi-shade
Hardiness: ✿✿✿ Zone: 4+

Acer palmatum 'Garnet'
Japanese maple

A popular form of Japanese maple with a mound-like habit and dark purple, finely cut leaves. It makes an excellent specimen or focal point in a small garden that gets some sun. In autumn the leaves turn brilliant red before falling to reveal a tracery of fine twigs that provide winter interest. Protect from cold winds and late frosts, which can burn the delicate foliage. H 5.5m (18ft) S 5.5m (18ft).
Aspect: sun to semi-shade
Hardiness: ✿✿✿ Zone: 4+

Acer palmatum 'Orange Dream'
Japanese maple

A wonderful new variety that forms an attractive specimen for a

Acer palmatum 'Sango-kaku'

Acer palmatum 'Osakazuki'

Acer palmatum var. dissectum 'Crimson Queen'

small garden. The foliage emerges golden-yellow with pink edges in spring, slowly taking on a greenish hue in summer before transforming into a brilliant orange in the autumn. This plant is a good choice for a large container as its growth rate will be restricted. H 6m (20ft) S 1.5m (5ft).
Aspect: semi-shade
Hardiness: ❀❀❀ Zone: 5

Acer palmatum 'Osakazuki'
Japanese maple
Startling red autumn colour makes this slow-growing Japanese maple a dramatic addition to any garden. The large, palm-shaped leaves are rich green at other times and set off the hanging brilliant red fruits in summer. H 6m (20ft) S 6m (20ft).
Aspect: sun to semi-shade
Hardiness: ❀❀❀ Zone: 4+

Acer palmatum 'Sango-kaku' (syn. A. palmatum 'Senkaki')
Japanese maple, coral-bark maple
Perhaps the best maple for year-round interest, it is an ideal choice for small gardens. The brilliant coral-red young shoots dramatically set off the emerging palm-shaped, orange-yellow leaves in spring. The leaves gradually turn green in summer, before taking on fabulous shades of yellow in autumn. The leaves then fall to reveal the beautifully coloured stems that can be seen throughout the winter. Stem coloration is less pronounced on

mature specimens. H 6m (20ft) S 5.5m (18ft).
Aspect: semi-shade
Hardiness: ❀❀❀ Zone: 4+

ALOYSIA
A genus of about 35 species of deciduous or evergreen flowering shrubs, only one of which is commonly cultivated for its distinctive lemon-scented foliage that is widely used for culinary purposes. Plant it in a convenient location in full sun, such as next to a path or outside the kitchen door, where you can harvest the leaves for adding to dishes, making lemon tea or pot-pourri.
Cultivation In the garden, grow in well-drained, poor, dry soil in full sun – the base of a sunny wall is ideal. Indoors, grow in a soil-based compost (soil mix). Water freely during the spring and summer, sparingly at other times.

Aloysia triphylla

Pruning In mild areas where the plant can form a permanent framework of branches, prune in mid-spring to keep within bounds. Elsewhere, cut back in autumn and protect roots with a layer of dry leaves or bark chippings held in place with wire netting.
Propagation Take softwood cuttings in mid-summer.

Aloysia triphylla (syn. A. citriodora, Lippia citriodora)
Lemon verbena
An upright, deciduous shrub with narrow, lemon-scented leaves, that is covered in clusters of pale lilac flowers from mid-summer to late summer. Tolerates poor, dry soils. H 3m (10ft) S 3m (10ft).
Aspect: sun
Hardiness: ❀❀ Zone: 5+

AMELANCHIER
Juneberry, snowy mespilus
A genus of over 25 species of deciduous multi-stemmed trees and shrubs that offer pretty spring flowers, attractive felted leaves that turn dramatic shades in autumn, accompanied by juicy fruit that are loved by birds. They make ideal specimens or seasonal focal points for use at the back of a mixed border in full sun or partial shade.
Cultivation Amelanchier will grow in any neutral to acid garden soil provided that it is reasonably fertile and positioned in full sun or partial shade.
Pruning No routine pruning is necessary. Neglected plants can

have wayward branches removed to open the canopy and maintain the overall balance.
Propagation Layer suckers in early spring and separate when well rooted in mid-autumn. Take softwood cuttings during mid-spring or semi-ripe cuttings in mid-summer. Sow seed as soon as ripe in summer.

Amelanchier x grandiflora 'Ballerina'
This compact and free-flowering deciduous shrub produces clouds of white, star-shaped flowers from early spring to mid-spring. Emerging bronze-tinted, the foliage matures to dark green before turning brilliant shades of red and orange during autumn. Sweet and juicy dark red fruits are produced in early summer. H 6m (20ft) S 8m (26ft).
Aspect: sun or semi-shade
Hardiness: ❀❀❀ Zone: 4+

Amelanchier lamarckii
A spectacular shrub in spring and autumn, that is covered in a profusion of star-shaped, white flowers during early spring and mid-spring accompanied by bronze-tinted emerging leaves. By summer the leaves mature to dark green and then transform into a beacon of orange and red in autumn. Sweet and juicy dark red fruits are produced in early summer. H 10m (33ft) S 12m (40ft).
Aspect: sun or semi-shade
Hardiness: ❀❀❀ Zone: 4+

Amelanchier lamarckii

Aucuba japonica

Azara dentata

AUCUBA

A genus of three species of evergreen shrubs that offer robust, glossy foliage that is incredibly tough. Able to grow almost anywhere, including dry shade and wind tunnels found between buildings. Their tolerance of dry soil and urban pollution means they are widely used by landscapers in towns and cities. Their ability to cope with salt-laden air makes them ideal filler or hedging shrubs in coastal gardens. On female plants, bright red autumn berries are sometimes produced.

Cultivation Plant in almost any soil (except waterlogged soil), in sun or shade. To enhance berry production, plant one male to every five female plants. In containers, grow in a soil-based compost. Feed every fortnight throughout the growing season and water as necessary.

Pruning Prune in mid-spring to maintain the size and shape you require. Leave hedges until mid-summer or late summer. Use secateurs (pruners) so that you can avoid damaging any foliage that remains on the plant after trimming.

Propagation Take semi-ripe cuttings in late summer or hardwood cuttings in early autumn. Sow seed in early autumn or mid-autumn.

Aucuba japonica
Japanese laurel

Tough as old boots, this easy-to-please evergreen shrub is perfect for heavily shaded areas and wind tunnels found between buildings where little else will grow. However, its neat, domed habit and densely packed lustrous, dark green leaves means it is a bit on the boring side. On female plants, bright red autumn berries follow insignificant late spring flowers. H 3m (10ft) S 3m (10ft).

Named varieties: 'Crotonifolia' is the best spotted laurel with leathery, yellow-speckled, dark green leaves. Although female, it rarely produces fruit. H 3m (10ft) S 3m (10ft). 'Picturata' (spotted laurel) is the male variety, with yellow-splashed, dark green leaves that are yellow-speckled at the margins. H 3m (10ft) S 3m (10ft). 'Rozannie' is very compact, with glossy dark green leaves and large, bright red berries. H 1m (3ft) S 1m (3ft). 'Variegata' (spotted laurel) has yellow-speckled, dark green leaves and bright red berries. H 3m (10ft) S 3m (10ft).
Aspect: sun or deep shade
Hardiness: ✽✽✽ Zone: 4+

Azalea — see Rhododendron

AZARA

A genus of about 10 species of evergreen trees and shrubs, only one of which is widely grown. Frost-hardy, it should be given a sheltered position against a sunny wall or fence or among other hardier shrubs in the garden. In colder areas, try growing in a tub on the patio and move it into a cool greenhouse where the fragrant flowers can be best appreciated.

Cultivation Grow in any moist garden soil that is reasonably fertile, in full sun or partial shade.

Pruning No routine pruning is necessary unless it is grown as a wall shrub, where selected shoots should be trained in a fan shape and subsequent side shoots thinned as necessary to maintain the overall shape.

Propagation Take semi-ripe cuttings in mid-summer.

Azara dentata

Unusual early summer-flowering evergreen shrub with serrated, glossy green leaves. It produces masses of fragrant, golden-yellow spidery flowers during early summer. H 3m (10ft) S 3m (10ft).
Aspect: sun or semi-shade
Hardiness: ✽✽ Zone: 5+

BALLOTA

Ballota comprises a genus of over 30 species of shrubs and also perennials but only one of the shrubs is featured here. This borderline hardy shrub has evergreen foliage covered in woolly hairs that give it a grey sheen. It is an ideal choice for a gravel or Mediterranean garden where it will appreciate the good drainage and full sun. Grow in a container on a sunny patio elsewhere.

Cultivation In the garden, grow in well-drained, poor, dry soil in full sun — the base of a sunny wall is an ideal spot for this plant. In containers, grow in a soil-based compost. Feed monthly throughout the growing season and water as necessary.

Pruning To promote a neat habit, established plants should be cut back by about half each mid-spring.

Propagation Take softwood cuttings in mid-spring or semi-ripe cuttings in late summer.

Ballota acetabulosa

A compact, aromatic, evergreen, drought-tolerant shrub that is generally pest- and disease-resistant. This grey-stemmed, evergreen shrub has felty, sage-green, heart-shaped leaves and silvery shoot tips. A bonus of pretty purple-pink flowers are produced in whorls during mid-summer and late summer. H 60cm (24in) S 75cm (30in).
Aspect: sun
Hardiness: ✽✽ Zone: 5+

Ballotta acetabulosa

Banksia coccinea

BANKSIA

Named after the botanist Sir Joseph Banks, who discovered this genus at Botany Bay, the plant is now known to contain about 70 species of evergreen shrubs and trees. The one featured here is grown for its dramatic dome-like flower-spikes produced from late spring and into summer. Ideal for cutting for use in indoor flower arrangements.

Cultivation Grow in neutral to acid, well-drained, poor, dry soil in full sun. In frost-prone areas, grow under glass in containers filled with a half-and-half mixture of ericaceous compost and a soil-based compost (soil mix). Feed every fortnight in the growing season and water as necessary.

Pruning Deadhead plants after flowering.

Propagation Raise from seed in mid-spring.

Banksia coccinea
Scarlet banksia
Wonderful spikes of bright orange-red flowers are produced in late spring and early summer from the tips of an open, upright shrub. The serrated, heart-shaped, dark green leaves have a felty covering underneath and make an excellent foil for the conspicuous flowers that appear from late spring to mid-summer. Can also be cut to use in flower arrangements. H 5m (16ft) S 3m (10ft).
Aspect: sun
Hardiness: ❀ Zone: 9+

BERBERIS
Barberry
A genus of over 450 species of evergreen or deciduous shrubs. Most are hardy, easy to grow and have vicious thorns and autumn berries. Deciduous species are also grown for their yellow-orange flowers and dramatic autumn colours, while the evergreen species have year-round, dense, glossy foliage, with some species offering eye-catching, spring flowers, too. They can be grown as border fillers and some make excellent hedging plants.

Cultivation They will grow in almost any well-drained garden soil that is reasonably fertile in full sun or partial shade. Deciduous varieties are best planted in a sunny position to get the best of their autumn colour and berries.

Pruning No routine pruning necessary, but you can trim lightly after flowering to maintain the overall shape.

Propagation Can be raised from seed in late autumn, but the results can be variable. Take softwood cuttings from evergreen varieties in mid-summer or semi-ripe cuttings of deciduous varieties in early autumn.

Berberis darwinii
An upright, evergreen shrub with prickly, holly-like leaves, which produces a profusion of pendent burnt-orange coloured flowers during mid-spring and late spring, followed in autumn by purple

fruit with a bluish bloom. It is a useful filler for the shrub border or for growing as an informal flowering hedge where its prickly stems will provide a deterrent against intruders. H 3m (10ft) S 3m (10ft).
Aspect: sun or semi-shade
Hardiness: ❀❀❀ Zones: 7–8

Berberis julianae
This upright-growing, evergreen berberis has glossy, dark green leaves that turn red in autumn. A bonus of yellow flowers is produced during late spring, followed by black fruit with a bluish bloom. Although not as ornamental as some berberis, its dense growth and upright habit means it makes an excellent screen or hedge where its spiny leaves will provide an intruder deterrent to intruders. H 3m (10ft) S 1.2m (4ft).
Aspect: sun or semi-shade
Hardiness: ❀❀❀ Zones: 7–8

Berberis linearifolia 'Orange King'
This is an upright, carefree, evergreen shrub with viciously spiny, glossy, dark green leaves. Profuse burnt-orange coloured flowers are produced in clusters along stiffly arching stems during mid-spring, followed by rounded, blackish fruits. This vigorous evergreen makes an informal flowering hedge, as viciously thorny leaves provide a deterrent against intruders.

Berberis aristata

H 2.7m (9ft) S 2.7m (9ft).
Aspect: sun or semi-shade
Hardiness: ❀❀❀ Zones: 7–8

Berberis x *stenophylla* (syn. *B. darwinii* x *B. empetrifolia*)
The spiny, dark green leaves of this vigorous, evergreen barberry are the perfect foil for its dark yellow, double flowers, which are produced in arching clusters during mid-spring and late spring. A bonus of rounded, black fruits are produced in autumn. Easy to grow, it makes an excellent screen or hedge, where its spine-tipped leaves will provide a deterrent against intruders. H 3m (10ft) S 5m (16ft).
Named varieties: 'Claret Cascade', red shoots with bronze-green foliage, dark yellow flowers and

Berberis thunbergii f. *atropurpurea*

Other berberis plants to look out for:

Berberis thunbergii f. *atropurpurea*, purple leaves turn brilliant red in autumn; red-flushed pale yellow flowers are followed by glossy red fruit. H 1m (3ft) S 2.5m (8ft).

Berberis thunbergii 'Golden Ring', yellow-edged purple leaves turn brilliant red in autumn; red-flushed pale yellow flowers are followed by glossy red fruit. H 1m (3ft) S 2.5m (8ft).

Berberis thunbergii 'Red Chief', purple leaves turn fiery orange and red in autumn; purple stems provide winter interest. H 1.5m (5ft) S 1.5m (5ft).

Berberis thunbergii 'Red Pillar', purple leaves turn fiery orange and red in autumn; red-flushed pale yellow flowers. H 1.5m (5ft) S 1.5m (5ft).

Berberis thunbergii 'Rose Glow', pink-mottled, reddish-purple leaves turn fiery orange and red in autumn; red-flushed pale yellow flowers are followed by glossy red fruit. H 1m (3ft) S 2.5m (8ft).

black fruits. H 1.2m (4ft) S 1.2m (4ft). 'Corallina Compacta', very compact and slow growing with red-flushed yellow flowers that open from red buds. H 30cm (12in) S 30cm (12in). 'Crawley Gem', compact and very free flowering. Its orange blooms open from red buds. H 60cm (24in) S 60cm (24in). 'Irwinii', compact with spiky leaves and orange flowers. H 1.5m (5ft) S 1.5m (5ft). 'Lemon Queen' (syn. *B.* x *stenophylla* 'Cornish Cream', *B.* x *stenophylla* 'Cream Showers'), dark green leaves, creamy-white flowers and black fruits. H 3m (10ft) S 5m (16ft).
Aspect: sun or semi-shade
Hardiness: ❀❀❀ Zones: 7–8

Berberis thunbergii 'Atropurpurea Nana' (syn. *B. thunbergii* 'Crimson Pygmy', *B. thunbergii* 'Little Favourite')
Grown for its dark purple leaves, which turn a brilliant red in autumn, this compact deciduous shrub also bears pale yellow flowers with reddish highlights during mid-spring and late spring, followed by glossy red fruit in autumn. It is a useful filler for the front of a shrub border in sun or partial shade or for growing as a low, informal flowering hedge. It also makes a excellent foliage plant for containers. H 60cm (24in) S 75cm (30in).
Aspect: sun or semi-shade
Hardiness: ❀❀❀ Zones: 7–8

Berberis thunbergii 'Aurea'
Brilliant acid-yellow spring foliage is the main feature of this deciduous berberis with a neat rounded habit. The foliage colour deepens as the season progresses, eventually turning orange-red in autumn. Pale yellow flowers pass almost unnoticed during mid-spring and late spring, followed by more conspicuous glossy red fruit in autumn. An excellent choice for illuminating a shady corner. Avoid planting in full sun as it can scorch the foliage. H 1.5m (5ft) S 2m (6ft).
Aspect: semi-shade
Hardiness: ❀❀❀ Zones: 7–8

Berberis thunbergii 'Bagatelle'
Compact and easy to grow, this dwarf deciduous berberis has dark purple leaves that turn a brilliant red in autumn. It is ideal at the front of a border in sun or partial shade. The pale yellow flowers with reddish highlights are produced during mid-spring and late spring and are followed by glossy red fruit in autumn. H 30cm (12in) S 40cm (16in).
Aspect: sun or semi-shade
Hardiness: ❀❀❀ Zones: 7–8

Berberis thunbergii 'Dart's Red Lady'
This compact deciduous berberis has plum-red foliage that turns brilliant shades of red in autumn. The foliage is a perfect foil for the red-flushed, pale yellow flowers that are produced during mid-spring and late spring, followed by glossy red fruit in autumn. It is a useful specimen for a shrub border in sun or partial shade. H 1m (3ft) S 2.7m (9ft).
Aspect: sun or semi-shade
Hardiness: ❀❀❀ Zones: 7–8

Berberis thunbergii 'Harlequin'
An unusual deciduous berberis that has beetroot-red foliage marbled with pink and white, which turns pale crimson in the autumn. A bonus of pale yellow flowers with reddish highlights are produced during mid-spring and late spring, followed by glossy, red fruit in autumn. This compact, variegated

Berberis jamesiana

shrub makes a useful specimen for a shrub border in sun or partial shade. Lightly prune each winter to get the best foliage coloration. H 1.5m (5ft) S 2m (6ft).
Aspect: sun or semi-shade
Hardiness: ❀❀❀ Zones: 7–8

Berberis thunbergii 'Helmond Pillar'
A columnar, deciduous shrub with plum-purple leaves that take on brilliant shades of red in autumn. A bonus of red-tinged, pale yellow flowers are produced during mid-spring and late spring. This upright berberis makes a useful focal point or specimen for a shrub border in sun or partial shade, where it will add vertical interest to the planting scheme. H 150cm (5ft) S 60cm (2ft).
Aspect: sun or semi-shade
Hardiness: ❀❀❀ Zones: 7–8

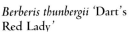

Berberis 'Georgii'

Berberis valdiviana

Brachyglottis compacta 'Sunshine'

Brugmansia suaveolens

BRACHYGLOTTIS

A genus of about 30 species, including several evergreen shrubs. The one featured here has felty grey leaves that show off its brilliant yellow, daisy-like flowers during early summer. This sun-loving shrub is also tolerant of salt-laden air, so is an ideal choice for coastal gardens.

Cultivation It will grow in almost any well-drained garden soil that is reasonably fertile in full sun. It makes a suitable addition to a gravel or 'dry' garden, where it will appreciate the open site and well-drained soil.

Pruning No routine pruning is necessary, but you can trim it lightly after flowering to maintain overall shape.

Propagation Take semi-ripe cuttings in mid-summer.

Brachyglottis compacta 'Sunshine' (syn. *Senecio* 'Sunshine')

A popular evergreen, grey-leaved shrub that bears bright yellow, daisy-like flowers on wiry stems during early summer and mid-summer. The attractive felty leaves emerge silvery-white and mature to a darker green as the hairs are shed. H 1m (3ft) S 2m (6ft).
Aspect: sun
Hardiness: ✽✽ Zone: 9

BRUGMANSIA
Angels' trumpet

A genus of five species that includes the vigorous shrub featured here, which produces conspicuous, night-scented trumpets. Ideal for adding an exotic touch to a sheltered patio. Bear in mind that all parts of the plant are highly toxic if eaten, so it is not suitable if young children are around.

Cultivation In the garden, moisture-retentive, well-drained garden soil that is reasonably fertile suits this plant. It also prefers full sun. In containers, grow in a soil-based compost (soil mix). Feed every month throughout the growing season and water as necessary. The plant should be moved to a warm spot under cover when the temperature falls below 7°C, and watered sparingly throughout the winter.

Pruning No routine pruning is necessary, but you can trim lightly after flowering to maintain its overall shape. Neglected plants can be rejuvenated by cutting back one stem in three to near ground level after flowering, starting with the oldest stems.

Propagation Take semi-ripe cuttings in late summer or sow seed in mid-spring.

Brugmansia suaveolens

This night-scented tender shrub bears stunning, 30cm-(12in-) long, trumpet-shaped, white, yellow or pink flowers from early summer to early autumn, which appear against leathery, wavy-edged, mid-green leaves. H 5m (16ft) S 3m (10ft).
Aspect: sun
Hardiness: tender Zone: 10

BUDDLEJA

Over 100 species are in this genus, which includes the popular deciduous shrubs featured here. They are grown for their profusion of flowers, usually produced in terminal spikes, which are loved by butterflies and other beneficial insects. Buddlejas are also quick growing and easy to please and so are an ideal choice for a new garden.

Cultivation Grow in any well-drained, dry soil in full sun.

Pruning For best flowering displays, most should be cut back hard in early spring to encourage new, vigorous and free-flowering shoots from the base during early spring. The exceptions are *B. alternifolia* and *B. globosa*, which, once established, should have their flowered shoots cut back to a healthy shoot or a bud lower down in order to maintain a compact shape and encourage new flowering shoots. This should be done directly after flowering.

Propagation Take semi-ripe cuttings in late summer or hardwood cuttings during late autumn.

Buddleja alternifolia

An open, deciduous shrub with stiffly arching branches that are covered in dense clusters of very fragrant, lilac flowers during early summer. The gracefully arching branches look particularly effective when the shrub is grown as a standard to make a striking seasonal focal point in a sunny border. Train a single stem to 1.5m (5ft), then pinch out the growing tip. Progressively remove sideshoots from the base to create attractive weeping heads on a clear stem. The leaves also turn butter-yellow in autumn. H 4m (13ft) S 4m (13ft).
Aspect: sun
Hardiness: ✽✽✽ Zones: 7–8

Buddleja alternifolia

Buddleja davidii 'Black Night'

Buddleja davidii 'Black Knight'
Butterfly bush

A dramatic, deciduous shrub that bears dense terminal spikes of fragrant, dark purple flowers from mid-summer to early autumn that are highly attractive to butterflies and other beneficial insects. The leaves also turn butter-yellow in autumn. H 3m (10ft) S 5m (16ft).

Aspect: sun

Hardiness: ❋❋❋ Zones: 7–8

Buddleja davidii 'Harlequin'
Variegated butterfly bush

Many gardeners would say that this is probably the best variegated version of this popular deciduous summer-flowering shrub. The lance-shaped, grey-green leaves are edged with yellow, maturing to cream, and provide added interest before the flowers appear. The dense spikes of fragrant, reddish-purple flowers are produced at the end of shoots in succession from mid-summer to early autumn and are a magnet for butterflies and other beneficial insects. H 3m (10ft) S 5m (16ft).

Aspect: sun

Hardiness: ❋❋❋ Zones: 7–8

Buddleja davidii 'Nanho Blue'
(syn. *B. davidii* 'Nanho Petite Indigo')
Butterfly bush

Slender, densely packed spikes of lilac-blue flowers are produced on the tips of gracefully arching branches on this deciduous shrub from mid-summer to early autumn. The fragrant flower spikes, up to 15cm (6in) long, are loved by butterflies and other beneficial insects. The leaves also turn butter-yellow in autumn. H 3m (10ft) S 5m (16ft).

Aspect: sun

Hardiness: ❋❋❋ Zones: 7–8

Buddleja davidii 'Pink Delight'
Butterfly bush

This splendid deciduous shrub bears densely packed, fragrant flower-spikes up to 30cm (12in) long at the end of arching shoots in succession from mid-summer to early autumn. Each flower-spike is made up of thousands of tiny orange-eyed, bright pink flowers that are a magnet for butterflies and other beneficial insects. The leaves are butter-yellow in autumn. H 3m (10ft) S 5m (16ft).

Aspect: sun

Hardiness: ❋❋❋ Zones: 7–8

Buddleja davidii 'White Profusion'
Butterfly bush

The best white form of the popular butterfly bush, this produces densely packed, fragrant terminal flower-spikes up to 40cm (15in) long in succession from mid-summer to early autumn. Each flower-spike is made up of thousands of tiny yellow-eyed, pure white flowers that become smothered in butterflies and other beneficial insects. The leaves also turn butter-yellow in autumn. For best displays, deadhead fading flower-spikes as they turn brown. H 3m (10ft) S 5m (16ft).

Aspect: sun

Hardiness: ❋❋❋ Zones: 7–8

Buddleja globosa
Orange ball tree

This is an unusual, semi-evergreen early summer-flowering shrub that bears ball-shaped clusters of fragrant, dark-orange and yellow flowers at the end of stiff stems from late spring to early summer. Although the plant is frost hardy (to −5°C/23°F), it prefers to be grown in the shelter of a warm wall or fence, where the deeply veined, dark green leaves are often retained over winter in mild areas. More protection will be required for this shrub in very cold areas. H 5m (16ft) S 5m (16ft).

Aspect: sun

Hardiness: ❋❋ Zone: 9+

Buddleja davidii 'Nanho Blue'

Buddleja 'Lochinch'
Butterfly bush

This is a popular compact form of the butterfly bush that bears densely packed spikes of honey-scented flowers on arching stems in succession from mid-summer to early autumn. Each flower-spike is made up of thousands of tiny orange-eyed, lavender-blue flowers that are loved by butterflies and other beneficial insects. The fresh-cut flowers are popular in floral arrangements. The downy, grey-green leaves turn butter-yellow in autumn. For best displays, deadhead the fading flower-spikes to encourage further flowering. H 2.5m (8ft) S 3m (10ft).

Aspect: sun

Hardiness: ❋❋❋ Zones: 7–8

Buddleja davidii 'Dartmoor'

BUPLEURUM

A genus of over 100 species that includes the open, evergreen, summer-flowering shrub featured here. This useful filler for the mixed or shrub border can cope well with salt-laden air, and so makes a good choice for seaside gardens, where it can be used as an informal screen, too.

Cultivation Grow in any well-drained soil in full sun. Protect in exposed gardens, especially while it is getting established. In cold gardens it is only borderline hardy.

Pruning No routine pruning is necessary, but you can trim lightly after flowering to maintain its overall shape. Neglected plants can be rejuvenated by cutting back one stem in three to near ground level after flowering, starting with the oldest stems.

Propagation Take softwood cuttings in early summer or sow seed in mid-spring.

Bupleurum fruticosum
Shrubby hare's ear

A dense and spreading evergreen shrub with dark green leaves that are silvery on the underside. Greenish-yellow ball-shaped clusters of star-shaped flowers are produced at the end of new growth from mid-summer to early autumn, followed by brown seedheads that provide winter interest. H 2m (6ft) S 2.5m (8ft).
Aspect: sun
Hardiness: ❀❀❀ Zones: 7–8

Bupleurum fruticosum

Buxus sempervirens 'Suffruticosa'

BUXUS
Box

This genus of about 70 species includes the low-growing, hardy, evergreen shrubs featured here. These slow- and dense-growing shrubs are useful for adding structure to any size of garden. Left to their own devices in borders, they will form rounded shrubs that add a sense of permanence to the planting scheme, or can be clipped into a neat hedge or border edging. Alternatively, grow in containers and trim regularly to add a year-round sense of formality to shady patios, paths and entrances. Some can also be trained and trimmed into intricate topiary shapes.

Cultivation In the garden, grow in any well-drained soil that is reasonably fertile in partial shade. Trim hedges and topiary into shape during late summer or early autumn. In containers, grow in a soil-based compost. Water as necessary.

Pruning Trim before new growth appears in early spring. Clip intricately shaped plants in mid-summer to maintain the neat outline.

Propagation Take semi-ripe cuttings in late summer.

Buxus sempervirens

A slow-growing, bushy, evergreen shrub with densely packed, lustrous, dark green leaves. Its rate of growth and dense, compact habit make it ideal for clipping into a formal, low-growing hedge or shaping into topiary.

H 5m (16ft) S 5m (16ft).
Named varieties: 'Elegantissima', compact, flame-shaped evergreen with densely packed tiny, white-margined, dark green leaves. Ideal for illuminating shady corners or adding light to other parts of the garden. Regular clipping may cause it to revert to green.
H 1.5m (5ft) S 1.5m (5ft).
'Suffruticosa' is a very slow-growing, dwarf, evergreen with densely packed, tiny, lustrous, dark green leaves. It makes an excellent very low-growing cloud-like hedge if left unclipped. It also responds well to regular trimming and so is the best choice for clipping into a low, formal edging for beds and borders, or for framing seasonal planting schemes. It is also an ideal choice for growing in containers and for shaping into topiary. H 1m (3ft) S 1.5m (5ft).
Aspect: semi-shade
Hardiness: ❀❀❀ Zones: 7–8

CALLICARPA
Beauty berry

A large genus of over 140 species that includes the deciduous shrub featured here. Sought after by flower arrangers, the bare branches of this bushy, upright shrub are laden with eye-catching, violet berries that light up the autumn and winter garden if left by the birds.

Cultivation Grow in any well-drained soil that's reasonably fertile in sun or partial shade.

Pruning No routine pruning is necessary. Neglected plants can have awkwardly placed branches removed to maintain the overall balance of the canopy.

Propagation Take softwood cuttings in late spring or semi-ripe cuttings during mid-summer.

Callicarpa bodinieri var. giraldii 'Profusion'
Beauty bush

Aptly named, the beauty bush is a sight to behold when the garden becomes dormant. This upright, deciduous shrub bears astonishingly vibrant violet, bead-like berries during mid-autumn that last well after the autumn leaves have fallen. A bonus of small pink flowers are produced in July (mid-summer) and the dark green leaves emerge bronze tinted and turn yellow in autumn. H 3m (10ft) S 2.5m (8ft).
Aspect: sun or semi-shade
Hardiness: ❀❀❀ Zones: 7–8

CALLISTEMON

A genus of over 25 species that includes exotic-looking, half-hardy or frost-hardy evergreens that make excellent seasonal specimens for a sunny, sheltered spot on the patio. In frost-prone areas, grow in a large container and move into the protection of a greenhouse or conservatory over winter.

Cultivation In the garden, grow in any well-drained soil in sun that is sheltered from cold and winds – the base of a sunny wall is ideal. In containers, grow in a soil-based compost. Water as necessary.

Callicarpa bodinieri var. *giraldii* 'Profusion'

Callistemon citrinus

Pruning No routine pruning is necessary. Neglected plants can have old branches removed after flowering to encourage new shoots from the base.
Propagation Take semi-ripe cuttings during late summer or sow seeds in early spring.

Callistemon citrinus 'Splendens' Crimson bottlebrush

Striking crimson, bottlebrush-shaped flower-spikes are produced at the tips of stiffly arching branches throughout early summer and mid-summer. The downy, pink-tinged young shoots mature to dark green and produce a distinctive lemon fragrance when lightly crushed. H 4m (13ft) S 3m (10ft).
Aspect: sun
Hardiness: ✽ Zone: 10

Callistemon rigidus Stiff bottlebrush

A bit hardier and more compact than other species, this plant bears distinctive, rich red flower-spikes up to 15cm (6in) long at the tips of arching branches from early summer to late summer. H 1m (3ft) S 2.5m (8ft).
Aspect: sun
Hardiness: ✽ Zone: 10

CALLUNA
Ling, Scots heather

A genus of just one species of hardy, evergreen shrubs with colourful summer flowers, some of which offer autumn foliage tints, too. There are literally hundreds of named varieties, the best of which are featured here. All Scots heathers make excellent ground cover plants for open, sunny areas with acid soil. Many make useful permanent container plants, while others are used for cut-flower arrangements.
Cultivation In the garden, grow in any well-drained, but moisture-retentive acid soil in full sun. Add plenty of organic matter (but not alkaline mushroom compost) to the soil before planting. In containers, grow in an ericaceous soil mix on a sunny patio. Keep well watered.
Pruning Trim off flowering stems as they fade. Encourage bushy growth by trimming lightly before new growth appears in spring.
Propagation Take semi-ripe cuttings in mid-summer or layer side-shoots in early spring.

Calluna vulgaris 'Blazeaway'

Year-round colour is provided by the superb golden foliage that turns dark red in winter. A bonus of lilac flower-spikes are produced continuously from mid-summer to early autumn. Its neat habit and year-round display means it is a good choice for a permanent container. H 35cm (14in) S 60cm (24in).
Aspect: sun
Hardiness: ✽✽✽ Zones: 7–8

Calluna vulgaris 'Dark Star'

This compact evergreen produces dense spikes of semi-double, crimson flowers amid a neat mound of dark green leaves from mid-summer to mid-autumn. H 20cm (8in) S 35cm (14in).
Aspect: sun
Hardiness: ✽✽✽ Zones: 7–8

Calluna vulgaris 'H. E. Beale' (syn. *C. vulgaris* 'Pink Beale')

This old favourite produces slim spikes of double, shell-pink flowers from late summer to late autumn above a mound of dark green leaves. The long, tapering flower-spikes are ideal for cutting. H 30cm (12in) S 60cm (24in).
Aspect: sun
Hardiness: ✽✽✽ Zones: 7–8

Calluna vulgaris 'Silver Queen'

This is a wonderful, vigorous and spreading silver-leaved Scots heather with silky foliage that lasts throughout the year. An added bonus of lavender-pink flowers are produced on short spikes from late summer to early autumn. H 40cm (16in) S 55cm (22in).
Aspect: sun
Hardiness: ✽✽✽ Zones: 7–8

Calluna vulgaris 'Wickwar Flame'

You can use this colourful heather to add much-needed winter interest to the middle of sunny beds and borders. Its open mounds of golden foliage turn bright red in winter, with the bonus of upright, mauve flower-spikes from mid-summer to late summer. H 50cm (20in) S 65cm (26in).
Aspect: sun
Hardiness: ✽✽✽ Zones: 7–8

Calluna vulgaris 'Wickwar Flame'

Camellia japonica 'Elegans'

CAMELLIA

This is a very large genus of over 250 species that includes many evergreen shrubs with beautiful, flamboyant blooms during the spring that stand out against the dark, glossy foliage. Generally slow growing and long lived, they make excellent border fillers, while some compact varieties are also suitable for growing in large containers.

Cultivation In the garden, grow in any well-drained acid soil in dappled shade, but in colder areas provide shelter and plant in a position that gets afternoon sun. Add plenty of organic matter (but not alkaline mushroom compost/ soil mix) before planting. In pots, grow in ericaceous compost and keep well watered. Wherever the camellia is planted, bear in mind that the flowers are susceptible to damage by a frost that is followed by a rapid thaw, so avoid positioning in east-facing areas that get early morning sun in spring.

Pruning Deadhead after flowering. Prune straggly branches of established plants to maintain the overall shape during late winter or early spring.

Propagation Layer low branches in early spring or take semi-ripe cuttings in late summer.

Camellia japonica 'Adolphe Audusson'

A compact evergreen shrub that bears masses of large, semi-double, bright red flowers intermittently from early spring

to late spring against a backdrop of glossy, dark green foliage. Reliable and free-flowering, it offers great garden value. H 5m (16ft) S 4m (13ft).
Aspect: semi-shade
Hardiness: ❀❀❀ Zones: 7–8

Camellia japonica 'Elegans' (syn. *C. japonica* 'Chandleri Elegans')

Superb, sugar-pink, anemone-like flowers are produced during mid-spring and late spring against a backdrop of lustrous, wavy-edged, dark green leaves. H 3.5m (12ft) S 3m (10ft).
Aspect: semi-shade
Hardiness: ❀❀❀ Zones: 7–8

Camellia japonica 'Nobilissima'

This is one of the earliest flowering camellias, bearing peony-shaped, yellow-centred, white flowers from mid-winter to early spring against a backdrop of glossy, dark green leaves. This tough evergreen shrub will survive

cold and windy conditions and so is an ideal choice for colder areas. H 5m (16ft) S 3.5m (12ft).
Aspect: semi-shade
Hardiness: ❀❀❀ Zones: 7–8

Camellia x williamsii 'Anticipation'

This is a handsome evergreen camellia that is deservedly popular for its large, peony-like, bright red flowers during late winter and early spring. Its narrow habit makes it an ideal container camellia or for use as an informal flowering hedge. Fast growing. H 4m (13ft) S 2m (6ft).
Aspect: semi-shade
Hardiness: ❀❀❀ Zones: 7–8

Camellia x williamsii 'Debbie'

An excellent camellia that bears dark rose-pink, peony-shaped flowers during mid-spring and late spring that are reputed to have good weather resistance. This free-flowering, vigorous evergreen has a dense mound of

Camellia x *williamsii* 'Anticipation'

Camellia x *williamsii* 'Debbie'

Other good cultivars to look out for:

Camellia 'Leonard Messel', large, semi-double peony-flowered variety with clear-pink blooms from early spring to May. H 4m (13ft) S 3m (10ft).

Camellia japonica 'Hagoromo', early flowering, semi-double, pale-pink flowers borne throughout late winter and early spring. H 5m (15ft) S 4m (13ft).

Camellia japonica 'Mikenjaku', early flowering, semi-double, rosy-red and white-marbled weather-resistant flowers are borne during late winter to early spring. H 4m (13ft) S 4.5m (14ft).

Camellia japonica 'Lady Vansittart', unusual holly-like leaves and semi-double, pink-striped, white flowers, which are borne from late winter to mid-spring. H 4m (13ft) S 3.5m (11ft).

Camellia x *williamsii* 'Jury's Yellow', anemone-flowered variety that bears yellow-centred white flowers from late winter to mid-spring. H 5m (15ft) S 3m (10ft).

Camellia x *williamsii* 'Mary Phoebe Taylor', this is a large, peony-flowered variety with semi-double, clear-pink flowers borne from late winter and early spring. H 4m (13ft) S 2m (6ft).

Camellia sasanqua 'Narumigata', scented, single, pink-tinged white flowers are borne from mid-autumn to early winter. H 6m (20ft) S 3m (10ft).

Camellia x *williamsii* 'E.G. Waterhouse', an upright camellia that bears double, sugar-pink flowers from late winter to mid-spring. H 5m (15ft) S 3m (10ft).

Camellia x williamsii 'Donation'

glossy, bright green foliage and tends to drop its blooms as they fade, so it always looks attractive. H 3m (10ft) S 2m (6ft).
Aspect: semi-shade
Hardiness: ✿✿✿ Zones: 7–8

Camellia x williamsii 'Donation'
A very long-flowering evergreen camellia, it produces its large, semi-double, sugar-pink flowers from late winter to late spring against lustrous, bright green leaves. Its compact, yet upright shape makes it an ideal choice for growing in a large container filled with ericaceous compost. H 5m (16ft) S 2.5m (8ft).
Aspect: semi-shade
Hardiness: ✿✿✿ Zones: 7–8

Camellia x williamsii 'J. C. Williams'
Beautiful single, rose-pink flowers are produced in early spring and mid-spring on open evergreen branches that can be trained effectively against a semi-shaded wall or fence. This free-flowering, fast-growing evergreen covered in lustrous, bright green foliage tends to drop its blooms as they fade and so always looks attractive. H 5m (16ft) S 3m (10ft).
Aspect: semi-shade
Hardiness: ✿✿✿ Zones: 7–8

CARPENTERIA
A genus of just one species of frost-hardy shrubs with beautiful, scented summer flowers. This upright, spreading evergreen is ideal for growing in the middle of a border in mild areas, but needs a sheltered wall or fence if grown elsewhere. *Carpenteria* can also be trained to grow effectively as a fan-shaped wall shrub.
Cultivation Grow this shrub in any well-drained, but moisture-retentive, soil in a sheltered spot in full sun.
Pruning Established plants can have one stem in three removed after flowering in late summer, starting with the oldest, to promote better flowering and a more compact shape.

Carpenteria californica

Propagation Take softwood cuttings from new growth or semi-ripe cuttings in mid-summer, or sow seed in mid-spring.

Carpenteria californica
Brilliant white and fragrant anemone-like flowers, each with a pronounced central boss of yellow stamens, are produced in succession throughout early summer and mid-summer against a backdrop of lustrous, dark green leaves. H 2m (6ft) S 2m (6ft).
Named varieties: 'Ladhams' Variety' has brilliant white flowers up to 8cm (3in) across. H 2m (6ft) S 2m (6ft).
Aspect: sun
Hardiness: ✿✿ Zone: 9+

CARYOPTERIS
A genus of over five species, including deciduous shrubs with aromatic foliage and late-summer flowers. The misty profusion of fragrant blooms are a magnet to bees and butterflies and provide much-needed colour to the late summer display. Ideal for growing alongside other shrubs or in a mixed border.
Cultivation Grow in any well-drained soil that is reasonably fertile and situate in full sun. In very cold areas, grow by a south-facing wall or fence.

Caryopteris x clandonensis

Pruning Once established, prune the shrub by cutting back to 5cm (2in) of the ground in early spring. This will help promote more vigorous flowering.
Propagation Take softwood cuttings from new growth in mid-summer or semi-ripe cuttings in late summer, or sow seed in early autumn.

Caryopteris x clandonensis Bluebeard
This is a mound-forming shrub that has grey-green, lance-shaped, aromatic leaves covered in silvery hairs on the underside. The leaves form the perfect foil for the whorls of purplish-blue flowers that are borne throughout late summer and early autumn and which are a valuable source of nectar for butterflies and other useful insects.
Named varieties: 'First Choice', a new variety bearing dark blue buds that open to reveal a haze of rich, cobalt-blue flowers. H 1m (3ft) S 1m (3ft). 'Heavenly Blue', upright deciduous variety with dark blue flowers. H 1m (3ft) S 1m (3ft). 'Worcester Gold' (golden bluebeard), glowing yellow, aromatic foliage and dense clusters of lavender-blue flowers. The fragrant flowers act almost as a magnet to beneficial insects such as bees and butterflies. H 1m (3ft) S 1m (3ft).
Aspect: sun
Hardiness: ✿✿✿ Zones: 7–8

Ceanothus 'Concha'

CEANOTHUS

This genus of over 50 species includes both deciduous and evergreen shrubs that are covered in masses of blue flowers in either late spring or late summer. Quick growing, they make effective border fillers, or can be trained against walls and fences in colder areas, where they will help to extend the flowering season. The deciduous varieties tend to be hardier than the evergreen.

Cultivation Grow in any well-drained soil that is reasonably fertile in full sun, but sheltered from cold winds. In very cold areas, grow in the protection of a south-facing wall or fence.

Pruning Once the plant has become established, prune deciduous varieties in early spring by cutting back the previous year's growth to an outward-facing side shoot within a few centimetres of the base. Evergreen varieties should be pruned only lightly after flowering. Do not cut back into old wood as it is reluctant to resprout.

Propagation Take semi-ripe cuttings from deciduous varieties in early autumn, or take stem cuttings from evergreen varieties in mid-summer.

Ceanothus arboreus
'Trewithen Blue'
Blueblossom

This is a large, vigorous evergreen shrub with notched, dark green leaves that is smothered in fragrant, rich blue flowers from late spring to early summer. It is

less hardy than some other varieties and so is not a good choice for colder regions. H 6m (20ft) S 8m (26ft).
Aspect: sun
Hardiness: ✿✿ Zone: 9+

Ceanothus 'Autumnal Blue'
California lilac

A useful evergreen filler shrub with apple-green glossy leaves, and clouds of bright blue flowers borne from late summer to mid-autumn. Although it is hardier than other forms, it still needs protection in colder areas. H 3m (10ft) S 3m (10ft).
Aspect: sun
Hardiness: ✿✿✿ Zones: 7–8

Ceanothus 'Burkwoodii'
California lilac

Clouds of sky-blue flowers provide a dramatic seasonal accent to sunny beds and borders from late summer to early autumn above a compact evergreen shrub with bright green glossy leaves. H 1.5m (5ft) S 2m (6ft).
Aspect: sun
Hardiness: ✿✿ Zone: 9+

Ceanothus 'Concha'
California lilac

This dense, evergreen shrub with lustrous dark green foliage transforms into a dazzling mound of dark blue flowers during late spring and early summer. The flowers emerge dramatically from purple buds borne in dense clusters along arching stems to smother the entire shrub in a cloak of colour.

H 3m (10ft) S 3m (10ft).
Aspect: sun
Hardiness: ✿✿ Zone: 9+

Ceanothus 'Italian Skies'
California lilac

This is a relatively new variety with a spreading habit that is covered in dense clusters of brilliant blue flowers during late spring to early summer above glossy evergreen foliage. It is less hardy than some other varieties and so is not a good choice for colder regions. H 1.5m (5ft) S 3m (10ft).
Aspect: sun
Hardiness: ✿✿ Zone: 9+

Ceanothus 'Puget Blue'
Santa Barbara ceanothus

A vigorous spreading, evergreen shrub that is covered in masses of dark blue flowers from mid-spring to early summer above heavily veined, dark green leaves. Protect from cold winds as the leaves are easily scorched. H 3m (10ft) S 3m (10ft).
Aspect: sun
Hardiness: ✿✿ Zone: 9+

Ceanothus thyrsiflorus var. repens
(syn. C. repens)
Creeping blueblossom

A steadfast, mound-forming, evergreen shrub that is excellent for covering sunny banks in mild areas where its profusion of pale blue flowers can be seen at their best during late spring and early summer. Although it is hardier

Ceanothus thyrsiflorus 'Millerton Point'

Ceanothus 'Julia Phelps'

than other forms, it still needs protection in colder areas. H 1m (3ft) S 2.5m (8ft).
Aspect: sun
Hardiness: ✿✿ Zone: 9+

CERATOSTIGMA

A genus of eight species, including both deciduous and semi-evergreen shrubs with vivid late-summer flowers and brilliant autumn foliage colours. These spreading shrubs are perfect for a sunny, sheltered site positioned in a prominent position in the garden where they can be appreciated most.

Cultivation In the garden, grow in a moisture-retentive, but well-drained soil in full sun. Add plenty of organic matter to the soil before planting. When grown in containers, use a soil-based

Ceratostigma griffithii

compost (soil mix) and site on a sunny patio. Keep well watered.
Pruning In early spring, cut back straggly stems to a plump bud or side shoot near to ground level.
Propagation Take semi-ripe cuttings in mid-summer.

Ceratostigma griffithii

Excellent for autumn colour, this small, rounded semi-evergreen with purple-edged green leaves turns brilliant red in autumn and lasts well into winter. From late summer to mid-autumn the shrub is transformed by terminal clusters of large, purple-blue flowers. An ideal choice for the front of a sunny, sheltered border. H 1m (3ft) S 1.5m (5ft).
Aspect: sun
Hardiness: ✿✿ Zone: 9+

Ceratostigma willmottianum
Hardy plumbago

A spreading deciduous shrub that bears terminal clusters of pale blue flowers from late summer to mid-autumn over a mound of purple-edged, dark green leaves. The attractive foliage then turns brilliant fiery shades in autumn. H 1m (3ft) S 1.5m (5ft).
Named varieties: 'Desert Skies' (golden plumbago, syn. *C. willmottianum* 'Palmgold'), a new variety with brilliant yellow foliage that forms a dramatic foil for the cobalt-blue flowers

produced throughout late summer and early autumn. Slightly less hardy than the other varieties, so grow as a container plant in colder areas. H 1m (3ft) S 1.5m (5ft). 'Forest Blue' (Chinese plumbago), vivid blue flowers are produced in clusters over a mound of purple-edged, dark green leaves that turn flaming shades of red and orange in autumn. H 1m (3ft) S 1.5m (5ft).
Aspect: sun
Hardiness: ✿✿✿ Zones: 7–8

CHAENOMELES
Flowering quince

A genus of just three species that includes the deciduous, spring-flowering shrubs featured here. The yellow-tinged green fruit that follow the flowers are edible when cooked, and the flowering stems are valued in early spring and autumn by flower arrangers. The neat habit of these shrubs makes them particularly useful in the border or trained against a wall or fence. They are also ideal for growing as an informal flowering hedge in sun or shade, where their thorny branches form an impenetrable thicket.
Cultivation Grow in any well-drained soil that is reasonably fertile in full sun or dappled shade. Flowering and fruiting is reduced if planted in full shade.

Chaenomeles x superba 'Crimson and Gold'

Pruning In the border, no routine pruning is necessary. Informal hedges can be pruned after flowering to keep within bounds. You can also prune established shrubs grown against a wall or fence to enhance the overall display. Cut back all new stems to just after the main cluster of flower buds in early early spring, then prune again after flowering in late spring by cutting back the shoots to two or three buds from the main framework.
Propagation Take softwood cuttings in early summer or layer shoots in early autumn.

Chaenomeles speciosa 'Geisha Girl'

Apricot-pink and yellow double flowers add subtle charm to this compact, deciduous shrub from early spring to late spring, followed by aromatic, yellow-tinged green fruit. The twiggy, thorn-covered branches form a thicket, covered in lustrous, oval, dark green leaves. H 2m (6ft) S 1.2m (4ft).
Aspect: sun or semi-shade
Hardiness: ✿✿✿ Zones: 7–8

Chaenomeles speciosa 'Moerloosei' (syn. *C. speciosa* 'Apple Blossom')

Many gardeners consider this plant to be one of the most outstanding cultivars of this popular species. Beautiful large, white, apple blossom-like flowers that are delicately flushed with

pink cover the twiggy branches of this vigorous flowering quince and appear from early spring to late spring. H 2.5m (8ft) S 5m (16ft).
Aspect: sun or semi-shade
Hardiness: ✿✿✿ Zones: 7–8

Chaenomeles speciosa 'Nivalis'

Brilliant, snow-white flowers smother the twiggy, spine-covered stems of this vigorous flowering quince from early spring to late spring. H 2.5m (8ft) S 5m (16ft).
Aspect: sun or semi-shade
Hardiness: ✿✿✿ Zones: 7–8

Chaenomeles x superba 'Crimson and Gold'

Compact and easy to grow, this popular variety bears striking crimson flowers with contrasting golden anthers along twiggy, spine-covered branches from early spring to late spring. The aromatic, yellow-tinged, green fruit that follow are edible when cooked. H 1m (3ft) S 2m (6ft).
Aspect: sun or semi-shade
Hardiness: ✿✿✿ Zones: 7–8

Chaenomeles x superba 'Nicoline'

Striking scarlet flowers are produced in profusion along twiggy, thorn-covered stems from early spring to late spring. The branches form a thicket, covered in lustrous, oval, dark green leaves. H 1.5m (5ft) S 2m (6ft).
Aspect: sun or semi-shade
Hardiness: ✿✿✿ Zones: 7–8

Chaenomeles speciosa 'Geisha Girl'

Chamaedorea elegans

Chamaerops humilis

CHIMONANTHUS

A genus of about five species that includes both deciduous and evergreen shrubs. The deciduous shrubs featured here are grown for their waxy-looking, fragrant yellow flowers that are borne on bare branches from late winter to early spring, when the garden needs them most. They make unassuming plants for the rest of the year and are most effective when planted in sun close to a path or entrance. The winter stems can be cut when in bud, so the superb sweetly scented flowers can be enjoyed inside over the Christmas period.

Cultivation Grow in any well-drained soil that is reasonably fertile in full sun.

Pruning Once established, prune out one stem in three, starting with the oldest, to encourage a continuous supply of young flowering stems. This should be done directly after flowering.

Propagation Take softwood cuttings in mid-summer. Layer lower stems in late summer.

Chimonanthus praecox
Wintersweet

A vigorous deciduous shrub that bears waxy-looking, fragrant, sulphur-yellow flowers, often with a contrastingly tinted throat, on branches from early winter to late winter. H 4m (13ft) S 3m (10ft).

Named varieties: 'Grandiflorus', large, slightly scented, dark yellow flowers, each with a purple-stained throat. H 4m (13ft) S 3m (10ft). var. *luteus* (syn. *C. praecox* 'Concolor'), waxy-looking, fragrant, clear-yellow flowers that open widely on bare stems from mid-winter to early spring. H 4m (13ft) S 3m (10ft).
Aspect: sun
Hardiness: ❁❁❁ Zones: 7–8

CHOISYA

A popular genus of over five species, including several compact, aromatic evergreen shrubs that produce star-like, white, flowers with a scent that is reminiscent of orange blossoms during late spring and again in late summer. The evergreen foliage is attractive all year round and provides the

Chimonanthus praecox

perfect foil for other flowers, too. It makes a good border filler and can be grown as a permanent container plant, and moved into a prominent position, such as the patio, while in flower.

Cultivation In the garden, grow in any well-drained soil that is reasonably fertile in full sun or dappled shade. In containers, grow in a soil-based compost on a sunny patio. Keep well watered. In colder gardens, plant in a sheltered spot, as cold winds can damage the foliage. Also, protect the less hardy yellow-leaved varieties in winter.

Pruning No routine pruning is required. Remove frost-damaged shoots in spring. Rejuvenate by cutting one stem in three to the ground, starting with the oldest.

Propagation Take semi-ripe cuttings in early summer or mid-autumn.

CHAMAEDOREA

This large genus of over 100 species includes the parlour palm, which is a tender plant often grown as a house plant in frost-prone areas. Very small plants can be used successfully as temporary additions in bottle gardens, where they thrive in humid conditions.

Cultivation In areas where the temperature does not drop below 15°C (60°F), the tender parlour palm can be grown outside in neutral to acid, well-drained soil in shade. Elsewhere, it is best grown as a house plant, in a peat-based compost (soil mix), and placed in a well-lit spot on a tray of moist gravel to increase humidity around the leaves. Feed every fortnight with a balanced fertilizer and water as necessary during the growing season. Water sparingly in winter.

Pruning No routine pruning is necessary, but remove damaged leaves as soon as they are noticed.

Propagation Sow seed in mid-spring.

Chamaedorea elegans (syn. *Neanthe bella*)
Parlour palm

This popular house plant has a suckering habit and produces upright bamboo-like stems and arching, leathery, dark green, divided fronds. Tiny yellow flowers appear on mature plants during the growing season, followed by small black berries. H 2m (6ft) S 1m (3ft).
Aspect: semi-shade to full shade
Hardiness: tender Zone: 10

CHAMAEROPS

A genus of just one species of suckering, half-hardy, bushy, palms that can be grown outside in full sun in mild areas to help create a tropical atmosphere. However, in frost-prone areas, grow in a large pot on the patio and move to a frost-free spot during the winter months. They also make handsome and easy-to-grow house plants.

Cultivation In frost-free areas this half-hardy fan palm can be grown outside in neutral to acid, well-drained soil in full sun. If grown as a house plant, use soil-based compost and stand the pot in a well-lit spot. Feed every fortnight with a balanced fertilizer and water as necessary during the growing season. Water sparingly during the winter months.

Pruning No routine pruning is necessary but remove damaged leaves as soon as they are noticed.

Propagation Sow seed in mid-spring. Separate and pot up rooted suckers in late spring.

Chamaerops humilis
Dwarf fan palm

This plant has spiky, glossy, fan-shaped, grey-green leaves that grow up to 1m (3ft) in length and are produced from suckering palm-like stems. On mature specimens of this plant, insignificant yellow flowers are produced in dense spikes throughout the growing season. H 2m (6ft) S 1m (3ft).
Aspect: sun
Hardiness: ❁ Zone: 10

Choisya ternata

Choisya ternata 'Sundance'

Cistus x cyprius

Cistus x pulverulentus 'Sunset'

Named varieties: 'Aztec Pearl', starry, white flowers that open from pink-tinged buds. H 2.5m (8ft) S 2.5m (8ft). 'Goldfingers', a new introduction that forms a compact shrub with bold yellow foliage and sweetly scented white flowers during mid-spring and late spring. H 1.5m (5ft) S 1.5m (5ft). 'Sundance', a compact evergreen shrub with bright yellow, glossy young leaves that mature to yellow-green, especially when grown in deep shade. A bonus of pretty white flowers are sometimes produced during mid-spring and late spring. H 2.5m (8ft) S 2.5m (8ft).

Neither of the yellow-leaved forms are as hardy as the green-leaved varieties, and can also suffer from scorch if positioned in strong sunlight.

Choisya ternata
Mexican orange blossom
This is a compact evergreen shrub that bears masses of fragrant, starry white flowers in succession during mid-spring and late spring, often with a second flush from late summer to early autumn. The bright green, glossy leaves provide the perfect foil for the sweet and spicy-smelling flowers that give off a lovely aroma when lightly crushed.

H 2.5m (8ft) S 2.5m (8ft).
Aspect: sun and semi-shade
Hardiness: ✿✿✿ Zones: 7–8

CISTUS
Rock rose, sun rose
This genus of 20 species includes many compact evergreen shrubs with spectacular papery summer flowers that thrive in well-drained sun-baked sites. They are an ideal choice for a prominent dry border or bank in sun, or can be grown in a large container on the patio.
Cultivation In the garden, grow in any well-drained soil in full sun. In containers, grow in a soil-based compost (soil mix). Water as necessary.
Pruning Trim the shrub as the flowers fade, cutting back new growth by about two-thirds. Remove frost-damaged shoots in spring.
Propagation Take semi-ripe cuttings in early autumn.

Cistus x corbariensis (syn. C. x hybridus)
This is a bushy, evergreen shrub with delicate-looking, papery, white flowers that open from bright red buds during early summer and mid-summer, each with a central boss of yellow stamens. The wavy-edged, dark green leaves make it an attractive

foil for other flowers at other times. H 1m (3ft) S 1.5m (5ft).
Aspect: sun
Hardiness: ✿✿ Zone: 9+

Cistus x pulverulentus 'Sunset' (syn. C. crispus 'Sunset')
This is a free-flowering variety that is covered in a succession of rose-pink blooms during early summer and mid-summer, each with a distinctive central boss of yellow stamens. The dense and spreading habit of this shrub makes it a useful ground cover plant. It tolerates salt-laden air. H 60cm (24in) S 90cm (36in).
Aspect: sun
Hardiness: ✿✿ Zone: 9+

Cistus 'Silver Pink' syn. C. 'Grayswood Pink'
Masses of delicate-looking, papery, silvery-pink flowers are produced on 'Silver Pink'. These gradually fade to white towards the middle of the petals, with each flower having a distinctive central boss of yellow stamens. The flowers are produced in succession throughout early summer and mid-summer on this compact, evergreen shrub that has narrow, dark green leaves, which have a grey underneath. H 75cm (30in) S 90cm (36in).
Aspect: sun
Hardiness: ✿✿ Zone: 9+

Other good cultivars to look out for:

Cistus x *aguilarii* 'Maculatus', yellow-centred white flowers with burgundy markings at the base of each petal during early summer and mid-summer H 1.2m (4ft) S 1.2m (4ft).

Cistus x *argenteus* 'Peggy Sammons', pale pinkish-purple, flowers are borne in early summer and mid-summer above grey-green, downy leaves, H 1m (3ft) S 1m (3ft).

Cistus x *dansereaui* 'Decumbens', white flowers with faint yellow and crimson marks at the base

of each petal are produced during early summer and mid-summer. H 60cm (24in) S 90cm (36in).

Cistus 'Grayswood Pink', pale pink flowers that fade towards the centre are borne in early summer and mid-summer above wavy-edged, grey-green leaves. H 1m (3ft) S 1m (3ft).

Cistus x *skanbergii*, yellow-centred, pale pink flowers are produced in early summer and mid-summer above wavy-edged, grey-green leaves. H 75cm (30in) S 90cm (36in).

Clerodendrum trichotomum
var. fargesii

CLERODENDRUM

A huge genus of over 400 species, including the deciduous shrub featured here, that bears white, star-like late-summer flowers, followed by striking bright blue berries in autumn. It makes a perfect filler for a shrub or mixed border next to an access point, where its unusual berries can be viewed at close quarters.
Cultivation Grow in well-drained, moisture-retentive soil that is reasonably fertile in full sun.
Pruning No routine pruning is required. Remove frost-damaged shoots in spring.
Propagation Take root cuttings in early winter. Remove rooted suckers in spring.

Clerodendrum trichotomum var. *fargesii*
An upright, deciduous shrub that is covered in striking turquoise-blue berries, surrounded by a contrasting, star-shaped, maroon calyx during mid-autumn and late autumn. The fruit follow pretty, pink-budded, scented, white, star-shaped flowers that are borne from late summer to early autumn. H 6m (20ft) S 6m (20ft).
Aspect: sun
Hardiness: ✿✿✿ Zones: 7–8

CLETHRA

This genus of over 60 species includes the deciduous summer-flowering shrubs featured here. They are useful, upright-growing shrubs for a shady border or for

under-planting deciduous trees in a woodland garden with acid soil.
Cultivation Grow in any acidic well-drained, moisture-retentive soil that is reasonably fertile in dappled shade.
Pruning No routine pruning is required. Neglected shrubs can be rejuvenated in spring by cutting out one stem in three back to a side shoot lower down, starting with the oldest.
Propagation Take softwood cuttings from new shoots in mid-summer.

Clethra alnifolia
Sweet pepper bush
A delightful deciduous shrub that bears candle-like spikes of fragrant, bell-shaped white flowers throughout late summer and early autumn above the oval green foliage. H 2.5m (8ft) S 2.5m (8ft). Named varieties: 'Paniculata', H 10cm (4in) white flower spikes. H 2.5m (8ft) S 2.5m (8ft). 'Pink Spire', large pink flower-spikes. H 2.5m (8ft) S 2.5m (8ft). 'Rosea', large deep pink flower-spikes. H 2.5m (8ft) S 2.5m (8ft).
Aspect: semi-shade
Hardiness: ✿✿✿ Zones: 7–8

COLUTEA
Bladder senna
A genus of some 25 species, including the deciduous, summer-flowering shrubs featured here, that are loved by children – who take great pleasure in popping their bloated seed-pods that

Clethera areorea

Colutea arborescens

follow. An unusual novelty shrub for a sunny spot.
Cultivation Grow in any well-drained soil that is reasonably fertile in full sun.
Pruning No routine pruning is required. Neglected shrubs can be rejuvenated in spring by cutting out one stem in three back to a side shoot lower down, starting with the oldest.
Propagation Take softwood cuttings from new shoots in mid-summer. Sow seed in late winter or early spring.

Colutea arborescens
A vigorous, rounded, deciduous shrub that bears 12cm- (4in-) long racemes of bright yellow flowers from early summer to early autumn above finely divided pale green foliage. Green seed-pods follow that become bloated and translucent as they mature. H 3m (10ft) S 3m (10ft).
Aspect: sun
Hardiness: ✿✿✿ Zones: 7–8

Colutea x media 'Copper Beauty'
A bushy deciduous shrub with finely divided, grey-green leaves that set off the 10cm- (4in-)

long strings of attractive copper-red flowers from early summer to early autumn. Greenish-brown seed-pods (up to 8cm/3in long) follow that become bloated and turn increasingly copper-tinged and translucent as they mature. H 3m (10ft) S 3m (10ft).
Aspect: sun
Hardiness: ✿✿✿ Zones: 7–8

CONVOLVULUS

A huge genus of over 250 species, including the popular compact silver-leaved, evergreen, early summer flowering shrub featured here. A superb shrub for a hot, sunny rockery, bank or border edge with well-drained soil. Can be grown in a pot on the patio.
Cultivation Needs well-drained, reasonably fertile soil in full sun. If grown in containers, use a soil-based compost (soil mix). Water as necessary.
Pruning Trim as the flowers fade, cutting back new growth by about two-thirds. Remove frost-damaged shoots in spring.
Propagation Take softwood cuttings in late spring or early summer, or semi-ripe cuttings in early autumn.

Convolvulus cneorum

Convolvulus cneorum

Clusters of open, white, trumpet-shaped flowers, each with pinkish veins and a pale yellow centre, are produced in succession throughout late spring and early summer and intermittently thereafter. Silvery foliage looks good at other times. H 60cm (24in) S 90cm (36in).
Aspect: sun
Hardiness: ❀❀ Zone: 9+

CORDYLINE

A genus of around 15 species, including these palm-like shrubs that are grown for their delightfully elegant plumes of arching, lance-shaped, evergreen leaves produced in fountain-like clumps at ground level while the plants are young. These useful evergreens make eye-catching focal points, where they add a tropical touch to borders and in containers on the patio.
Cultivation In the garden, grow in any well-drained soil that is reasonably fertile in full sun or dappled shade. In containers, grow in a soil-based compost (soil mix). Water as necessary. Give winter protection in frost-prone areas.
Pruning No routine pruning is required. Remove dying or damaged leaves to tidy its appearance in spring.
Propagation Remove rooted suckers in spring.

Cordyline australis (syn. *Dracaena australis*)
New Zealand cabbage palm

This elegant plant forms a plume of arching, lance-shaped, evergreen leaves at ground level when young, eventually growing into a palm-like tree. Give winter protection in frost-prone areas. H 10m (33ft) S 4m (13ft).

Cordyline australis 'Red Star'

Named varieties: 'Atropurpurea', broad, strap-shaped leaves flushed with purple from the base. H 10m (33ft) S 4m (13ft). 'Purple Tower', broad, deep-purple, lance-shaped leaves. H 10m (33ft) S 4m (13ft). 'Purpurea Group', broad, plum-purple, lance-shaped leaves. H 10m (33ft) S 4m (13ft). 'Red Star', spiky fountain of bronze-purple, narrow, strap-like leaves. H 6m (20ft) S 7m (23ft). 'Torbay Dazzler', green leaves strikingly edged and striped with cream. H 10m (33ft) S 4m (13ft).
Aspect: sun
Hardiness: ❀ Zone: 10

CORNUS
Dogwood

Some 45 species make up this genus, including many useful garden shrubs offering a variety of features, including early summer flowers, attractive foliage, autumn tints and colourful winter stems. As they are very easy to grow, they offer great garden value – making them an ideal choice for the first-time gardener.
Cultivation Grow flowering dogwoods in any neutral to acid moisture-retentive, well-drained soil that is reasonably fertile in full sun or dappled shade. Most other varieties can be grown in any moist garden soil, but autumn colour and winter stems are best in full sun.
Pruning Flowering dogwoods require no routine pruning. Dogwoods grown for their decorative stems should be cut back to within a few centimetres of ground level in late winter or early spring every other year. Dogwoods with variegated foliage should have one stem in three removed each year, starting with the oldest.
Propagation Layer low shoots on all types of dogwood in mid-spring. Take hardwood cuttings from thicket-forming dogwoods in late autumn.

Cornus alba 'Aurea'
Red-barked dogwood

Superb golden-yellow leaves and stunning red new stems are the main features of this valuable garden shrub. The leaves also provide autumn colour and there is the bonus of small cream-coloured flowers during late spring and early summer, followed by bluish fruits. The leaf coloration is best in full sun. H 3m (10ft) S 3m (10ft).
Aspect: sun or semi-shade
Hardiness: ❀❀❀ Zones: 7–8

Cornus alba 'Kesselringii'

Grown for its dramatic, near-black, purple-brown winter stems and colourful autumn tints, this unusual dogwood looks particularly striking when planted in sun alongside yellow- or red-stemmed varieties, where it will help to transform the winter garden. Clusters of tiny, creamy-white flowers also appear during late spring and early summer. H 3m (10ft) S 3m (10ft).
Aspect: sun or semi-shade
Hardiness: ❀❀❀ Zones: 7–8

Cornus alba 'Sibirica'
Red-barked dogwood

Brilliant red winter stems make this red-barked dogwood ideal for growing alongside water features, where it will provide much-needed winter interest. Its dark green leaves take on reddish hues in autumn before falling to reveal the stem display. Clusters of tiny, creamy-white flowers also appear during late spring and early summer. H 3m (10ft) S 3m (10ft).
Aspect: sun or semi-shade
Hardiness: ❀❀❀ Zones: 7–8

Cornus alba 'Sibirica'

Cornus kousa

Cornus alba 'Spaethii'
Red-barked dogwood

The yellow-edged, bright green leaves on this plant look good all summer, after which they then take on striking autumn leaf tints before falling to reveal bright red stems that add much-needed interest throughout the winter. Clusters of tiny, creamy-white flowers also appear during late spring and early summer. H 3m (10ft) S 3m (10ft).
Aspect: sun to semi-shade
Hardiness: ❀❀❀ Zones: 7–8

Cornus 'Eddie's White Wonder'
Flowering dogwood

Striking white, petal-like bracts surround each insignificant purplish-green flower during late spring. Great value in a small garden, the green leaves of this bushy dogwood also turn brilliant fiery shades in autumn. Grows and flowers best in full sun, although it will tolerate dappled shade. H 6m (20ft) S 5m (16ft).
Aspect: sun to semi-shade
Hardiness: ❀❀❀ Zones: 7–8

Cornus florida
Flowering dogwood

A conical, deciduous shrub that produces insignificant yellow-tipped green flowers during late spring, surrounded by eye-catching white or pink bracts. The puckered green leaves look attractive during the summer and take on reddish-purple hues in autumn. Ideal for gardens with neutral to acid soil, but unsuitable for gardens with chalky soil. H 6m (20ft) S 8m (26ft).
Named varieties: 'Cherokee Chief', deepest pink bracts, red-purple autumn tints. H 6m (20ft) S 8m (26ft). 'Rainbow', compact shrub with white or pink bracts and yellow-edged green leaves turning red-purple in autumn with bright red margins. H 3m (10ft) S 2.5m (8ft). 'Rubra', dark pink bracts, red-purple autumn tints. H 6m (20ft) S 8m (26ft).
Aspect: sun to semi-shade
Hardiness: ❀❀❀ Zones: 7–8

Cornus kousa var. *chinensis*
Chinese dogwood

The conspicuous, creamy-white flower bracts fade to white before turning red-pink, surrounding insignificant green flowers during early summer, that are followed by strawberry-like fleshy fruit. This conical, deciduous shrub with dark green leaves takes on crimson-purple tints in autumn. The best leaf colour is achieved when grown in neutral to acid soil. H 7m (23ft) S 5m (16ft).
Aspect: sun to semi-shade
Hardiness: ❀❀❀ Zones: 7–8

Cornus sanguinea 'Midwinter Fire'

A relatively new variety, this shrub has glowing red-tipped orange and yellow winter stems that shine out in the garden. Clusters of tiny, creamy-white flowers also appear in early summer against green leaves that take on orange-yellow hues in autumn. Spherical bluish fruits are also produced. H 3m (10ft) S 2.5m (8ft).
Aspect: sun to semi-shade
Hardiness: ❀❀❀ Zones: 7–8

Cornus stolonifera 'Flaviramea'

Rich yellow stems provide winter interest and look striking planted in sun beside red-stemmed varieties. The dark green leaves take on reddish tints in autumn, before falling to reveal the eye-catching winter stems. Clusters of tiny, creamy-white flowers also appear during late spring and early summer. H 75cm (30in) S 150cm (60in).
Aspect: sun to semi-shade
Hardiness: ❀❀❀ Zones: 7–8

CORONILLA

This genus of about 20 species includes the following very long-flowering evergreen shrubs, with pretty, scented, yellow flowers that are borne from late winter until late summer. This shrub is ideal for planting in a container on the patio, where the flowers and foliage can be appreciated at close quarters.
Cultivation Grow in any well-drained soil that is reasonably fertile in full sun. Shelter from cold winds.
Pruning No routine pruning is required. Neglected shrubs can be rejuvenated by removing one stem in three each year in spring, starting with the oldest.
Propagation Take semi-ripe cuttings in mid-summer or late summer.

Coronilla valentia subsp. *glauca*
(syn. *C.* 'Glauca')

This is an exceptionally long-flowering, rounded, bushy, evergreen shrub with dense evergreen growth and blue-green leaves. The scented, clear yellow pea-like flowers are produced throughout late winter and early spring and then intermittently all summer until a further flush in late summer and early autumn. H 80cm (33in) S 80cm (33in).
Named varieties: 'Citrina', pale yellow flowers. H 80cm (33in) S 80cm (33in).
Aspect: sun
Hardiness: ❀❀ Zone: 9

Coronilla valentina subsp. *glauca*

Corylus avellana 'Contorta'

CORYLUS

A genus of over ten species that includes native, deciduous trees and upright shrubs that can be grown as specimens or as an easy-to-grow hedge. Ornamental varieties offer attractive features including colourful spring catkins, good-looking foliage, autumn tints and winter stems. Ideal for growing in a sunny border or in a large permanent container on the patio.

Cultivation In the garden, grow in any well-drained soil that is reasonably fertile in full sun or dappled shade. In containers, grow in a soil-based compost (soil mix). Water as necessary.

Pruning No routine pruning is required for most types. Hazels grown for their colourful foliage should have one stem in three removed each year, starting with the oldest. Do this after flowering in early spring.

Propagation Layer low stems in mid-spring. Remove rooted suckers in early autumn.

Corylus avellana 'Contorta'
Corkscrew hazel, Harry Lauder's walking stick

The amazingly contorted bare stems carry golden catkins throughout late winter and early spring. The unusual stems of this slow-growing shrub are valued by flower arrangers. Will provide year-round interest in a large container. H 5m (16ft) S 5m (16ft).
Aspect: sun or semi-shade
Hardiness: ✿✿✿ Zones: 7–8

Corylus maxima 'Purpurea'

Glossy, dark purple, heart-shaped leaves cover this upright, deciduous shrub, which makes a superb specimen for a sunny garden. Reddish-purple catkins are produced during late winter and early spring and are followed by edible nuts ripening in late summer. This shrub makes a useful border filler. H 6m (20ft) S 5m (16ft).
Aspect: sun
Hardiness: ✿✿✿ Zones: 7–8

COTINUS
Smoke bush

A genus of two species, including the bushy deciduous shrubs featured here. Their airy plumes of flowers create a smoke-like illusion over the shrub during the summer, giving rise to its common name. Brilliant autumn foliage is the main ornamental feature of this plant. Grow in full sun for the most dramatic foliage effects.

Cultivation Grow in any moisture-retentive, well-drained soil that is reasonably fertile in full sun or dappled shade. Grow in full sun for the dramatic foliage effects.

Pruning Cotinus grown for their colourful foliage and smoke-like flowers should have one stem in

Cotinus obovatus

three removed each year, starting with the oldest. Do this in early spring.

Propagation Layer low stems in mid-spring. Remove rooted suckers in early autumn.

Cotinus coggygria 'Flame' (syn. *C.* 'Flame')
Smoke bush

The plumes of pale pink flowers that appear on 'Flame' gradually darken during mid-summer and late summer. Later, the foliage spectacularly turns fiery shades of red and orange during the autumn months. H 6m (20ft)

Cotinus coggygria 'Royal Purple'

S 5m (16ft).
Aspect: sun or semi-shade
Hardiness: ✿✿✿ Zones: 7–8

Cotinus coggygria 'Golden Spirit'

A relatively new and compact variety with golden-yellow leaves, that take on eye-catching pink, orange and red coloration in autumn. Plumes of green flowers appear during mid-summer and late summer. H 2m (6ft) S 2m (6ft).
Aspect: sun or semi-shade
Hardiness: ✿✿✿ Zones: 7–8

Cotinus 'Grace'
Smoke bush

The purple-tinged foliage of 'Grace' transforms in mid-summer and late summer when it is covered by airy plumes of pale pink flowers that darken with age. Stunning autumn colour appears as it turns a glowing shade of red. H 6m (20ft) S 5m (16ft).
Aspect: sun or semi-shade
Hardiness: ✿✿✿ Zones: 7–8

Cotinus coggygria 'Royal Purple'

This purple-leaved, bushy, deciduous shrub makes an impressive specimen in any size garden as it responds particularly well to hard pruning each spring. Airy plumes of pale pink flowers that darken with age are produced during mid-summer and late summer. The rich, red-purple leaves then turn brilliant scarlet in autumn. H 6m (20ft) S 5m (16ft).
Aspect: sun or semi-shade
Hardiness: ✿✿✿ Zones: 7–8

Cotoneaster conspicuus 'Red Alert'

COTONEASTER

A large genus of over 200 species, including the deciduous, semi-evergreen and evergreen ornamental shrubs featured here. Larger varieties make useful border fillers, while low-growing types can be used to cover the ground or trained as a wall shrub. You can even train cascading varieties into unusual and attractive standards.

Cultivation Grow in any reasonably fertile, well-drained soil in full sun or dappled shade.

Pruning No routine pruning is required. Restrict the size of evergreen shrubs by trimming back to a new shoot lower down in mid-spring. Deciduous varieties can be kept within bounds by having one stem in three removed each year in late winter, starting with the oldest.

Propagation Take semi-ripe cuttings during mid-summer or hardwood cuttings in late autumn.

Cotoneaster dammeri

A prostrate evergreen that spreads vigorously, carpeting the ground with twiggy shoots covered in lustrous, dark green leaves. Dainty white flowers, borne during early summer, are followed by glossy, bright red berries in early autumn. It is a superb ground-cover shrub that will grow in most conditions, including the dry soil found at the base of evergreen hedges. H 20cm (8in) S 2m (6ft).
Aspect: sun or semi-shade
Hardiness: ❀❀❀ Zones: 7–8

Cotoneaster frigidus 'Cornubia'

An upright, evergreen shrub that is often trained as a single-stemmed tree, which makes an attractive specimen for a sunny spot. The dark green leaves provide the perfect backdrop for the dainty clusters of white flowers during early summer. Spherical bright red berries follow as the leaves become bronze-tinted for the winter. H 10m (33ft) S 10m (33ft).
Aspect: sun or semi-shade
Hardiness: ❀❀❀ Zones: 7–8

Cotoneaster horizontalis

This is a popular ground-cover deciduous shrub that has dainty pink-tinted white flowers that appear during the early summer and are followed by spherical, bright red berries in autumn. The twiggy branches are produced in an attractive herringbone pattern that make it easy to train over flat surfaces and provide winter interest. H 1m (3ft) S 1.5m (5ft).
Aspect: sun or semi-shade
Hardiness: ❀❀❀ Zones: 7–8

Cotoneaster 'Hybridus Pendulus'

A low-growing evergreen that bears dainty, small white flowers during early summer, followed by glossy, bright red berries in autumn. It can also be grown into a spectacular specimen when grown as a standard. Tolerant of a wide range of conditions. H 2m (6ft) S 2m (6ft).
Aspect: sun or semi-shade
Hardiness: ❀❀❀ Zones: 7–8

Cotoneaster salicifolius 'Gnom' (syn. C. 'Gnom', C. 'Gnome')

A prostrate, compact evergreen shrub with twiggy branches that are covered in dark green leaves. Dainty white flowers in early summer are followed by a limited number of rounded, glossy, bright red fruit. Excellent ground cover. H 30cm (1ft) S 2m (6ft).
Aspect: sun or semi-shade
Hardiness: ❀❀❀ Zones: 7–8

Cotoneaster x suecius 'Coral Beauty'

A low-growing evergreen with lustrous dark green leaves that bears dainty white flowers from late spring to early summer. It makes excellent ground cover for sun or semi-shade. Long-lasting glossy, bright-orange berries provide much-needed colour in early autumn and last until mid-winter or late winter. H 1m (3ft) S 2m (6ft).
Aspect: sun or semi-shade
Hardiness: ❀❀❀ Zones: 7–8

CYTISUS
Broom

A genus of over 50 species, including the busy deciduous summer-flowering shrubs featured here. They are a good choice for adding colour to a sunny border next to a wall, as they thrive in poor soils.

Cultivation Grow in any well-drained soil that is reasonably fertile in full sun. Shelter less hardy varieties from cold winds.

Pruning Pineapple broom requires no routine pruning. Keep most other brooms compact and free-flowering by cutting back new growth by about half directly after flowering. Do not prune back into the previous year's wood since this is unlikely to re-shoot.

Propagation Take semi-ripe cuttings in mid-summer. Sow seed in late winter.

Cytisus battandieri (syn. Argyrocytisus battandieri) Pineapple broom

Eyecatching, pineapple-scented, golden, cone-shaped flower-spikes are produced during mid-summer and late summer at the tips of silvery-grey shoots on this vigorous, deciduous shrub. Makes an ideal specimen in a sunny, but sheltered site next to a path or entrance, where its fruity scent can be appreciated. H 4m (13ft) S 4m (13ft).
Aspect: sun
Hardiness: ❀❀ Zone: 9

Cytisus 'Boskoop Ruby'

A compact deciduous shrub with arching stems that are covered in ruby-red, pea-like flowers throughout late spring and early summer. Downy green seed-pods follow. H 1.2m (4ft) S 1.2m (4ft).
Aspect: sun
Hardiness: ❀❀❀ Zones: 7–8

Cytisus multiflorus (syn. C. x praecox 'Albus', C. albus) Portuguese broom, white Spanish broom

Pure white, pea-like flowers are produced in masses along

Cytisus battandieri

Cytisus 'Boskoop Ruby'

elegantly arching stems from mid-spring to late spring on this upright, spreading, deciduous shrub. Reliable, early-flowering variety. H 1.2m (4ft) S 1.5m (5ft).
Aspect: sun
Hardiness: ❋❋❋ Zones: 7–8

Cytisus x praecox 'Allgold'
This is another popular variety that carries a profusion of rich-yellow, pea-like flowers along arching stems throughout mid-spring and late spring on a compact deciduous shrub. 'Allgold' is one of the earliest-flowering varieties. H 1.2m (4ft) S 1.5m (5ft).
Aspect: sun
Hardiness: ❋❋❋ Zones: 7–8

Cytisus x praecox 'Warminster'
Warminster broom
Creamy-yellow, pea-like flowers with an acid scent are produced in profusion along arching stems during mid-spring and late spring on this compact deciduous shrub. Easy to grow and early flowering. H 1.2m (4ft) S 1.5m (5ft).
Aspect: sun
Hardiness: ❋❋❋ Zones: 7–8

DABOECIA
A genus of just two species of hardy, evergreen shrubs with an exceptionally long flowering period, from early summer to mid-autumn. They look their best when planted in bold drifts and make excellent ground cover plants. They can also be grown in containers.

Cultivation In the garden, grow in open, sunny areas with well-drained acid soil. However, they will tolerate dappled shade and neutral soil. In containers, grow in ericaceous compost (soil mix), feed monthly and water regularly to keep the compost moist.
Pruning Trim off flowering stems as they fade, using shears. Encourage bushy growth by trimming lightly before new growth appears in spring.
Propagation Take semi-ripe cuttings in mid-summer, or layer side shoots in early spring.

Daboecia cantabrica f. alba
Loose spikes of urn-shaped white flowers are produced from June (early summer) to October (mid-autumn) above glossy, dark green leaves that are silvery underneath. H 45cm (18in) S 75cm (30in).
Aspect: sun or semi-shade
Hardiness: ❋❋❋ Zones: 7–8

Daboecia cantabrica 'Atropurpurea'
The open spikes of dark purple urn-shaped flowers on this stunning shrub are produced from early summer to mid-autumn above glossy, dark green leaves that are silvery underneath. H 45cm (18in) S 75cm (30in).
Aspect: sun or semi-shade
Hardiness: ❋❋❋ Zones: 7–8

Daboecia cantabrica 'Bicolor'
This is an unusual plant that produces white, pink and dark red

Daboecia cantabrica f. alba

Daboecia cantabrica 'Atropurpurea'

urn-shaped flowers in loose spikes from early summer to mid-autumn. H 45cm (18in) S 75cm (30in).
Aspect: sun or semi-shade
Hardiness: ❋❋❋ Zone: 7–8

DAPHNE
This is a genus of 50 species, including upright-growing, evergreen and deciduous shrubs, that bear very fragrant flowers in winter and early spring. They are best grown in a sheltered corner in sun, next to a path or entrance, where their intoxicating fragrance can be best appreciated.
Cultivation This shrub can be grown in any moisture-retentive, well-drained garden soil provided it is reasonably fertile and it is positioned in full sun or partial shade. The less hardy varieties should be protected from cold winds in winter. This is a plant set in its ways, so avoid moving these plants, as they do not re-establish easily.
Pruning No routine pruning is necessary.
Propagation Sow seed in early autumn. Take semi-ripe cuttings in mid-summer.

Daphne bholua 'Jacqueline Postill'
This is an upright evergreen shrub that bears clusters of strongly fragrant rose-pink flowers during mid-winter and late winter above glossy, strap-shaped, dark green leaves. H 4m (13ft) S 1.5m (5ft).
Aspect: sun or semi-shade
Hardiness: ❋❋ Zone: 9

Daphne mezereum
Mezereon
Fragrant rose-pink flowers appear on bare branches during late winter and early spring. The upright habit of this deciduous shrub makes it a good choice for late winter interest. H 1.2m (4ft) S 1m (3ft).
Aspect: sun or semi-shade
Hardiness: ❋❋❋ Zones: 7–8

Daphne odora 'Aureomarginata' (syn. D. odora 'Marginata')
The attractive, evergreen, yellow-edged, glossy, dark green foliage provides interest during the winter. A bonus of fragrant, rose-pink flowers are produced from early winter to early spring. H 1.5m (5ft) S 1.5m (5ft).
Aspect: sun or semi-shade
Hardiness: ❋❋ Zone: 9

Daphne bholua 'Jacqueline Postill'

DESFONTAINIA

A genus of just one species of densely growing evergreen shrubs with eye-catching, tubular summer flowers. If you can provide the right growing conditions, it makes a useful and unusual border filler in all but the coldest areas, ideally at the base of a sheltered wall or fence.

Cultivation Grow in any moisture-retentive, humus-rich, acid or neutral soil in dappled shade. Provide a sheltered position where it is protected from drying and cold winds.

Pruning No routine pruning is necessary. Any frost-damaged growth should be removed in spring.

Propagation Take semi-ripe cuttings in mid-summer. Remove rooted suckers in early autumn.

Desfontainia spinosa

A bushy evergreen, with holly-like, glossy, dark green leaves. From mid-summer to mid-autumn it bears pendent tubular scarlet flowers with yellow-tipped petals. H 2m (6ft) S 2m (6ft).
Aspect: sun or semi-shade
Hardiness: ❀❀ Zone: 9

DEUTZIA

This genus of about 60 species includes the bushy deciduous shrubs featured here, grown for their early summer flowers that are borne in abundance. Plant in a shrubbery or in a mixed border to provide late spring and early summer colour. A good choice for small gardens.

Cultivation Grow in any moisture-

Deutzia x elegantissima

retentive, well-drained garden soil that is reasonably fertile and in full sun or dappled shade.

Pruning To encourage good displays year after year, cut back one stem in three to near ground level after flowering, starting with the oldest stems.

Propagation Take hardwood cuttings in mid-autumn.

Deutzia x elegantissima 'Rosealind'

Dark, pink-flushed, white star-like flowers are produced in clusters during late spring and early summer on this compact, rounded shrub. H 1.2m (4ft) S 1.5m (5ft).
Aspect: sun or semi-shade
Hardiness: ❀❀❀ Zones: 7–8

Deutzia gracilis

Fragrant, snow-white, star-like flowers are produced from late spring to early summer on

upright stems clothed in light green leaves. H 1m (3ft) S 1m (3ft).
Aspect: sun or semi-shade
Hardiness: ❀❀❀ Zones: 7–8

Deutzia x hybrida 'Mont Rose'

This elegant, upright shrub bears clusters of star-like, rose-pink flowers with yellow anthers during early summer. H 1.2m (4ft) S 1.2m (4ft).
Aspect: sun or semi-shade
Hardiness: ❀❀❀ Zones: 7–8

DIERVILLA
Bush honeysuckle

A genus of three species that includes the following deciduous shrub with colourful summer flowers and attractive autumn tints – a good choice for a shrubbery or mixed border, or for stabilizing soil on sunny banks.

Cultivation Grow in any well-drained garden soil that is

Diervilla x splendens

reasonably fertile and in full sun or dappled shade.

Pruning Maintain a compact shape by cutting back one stem in three to near ground level after flowering, starting with the oldest stems.

Propagation Take semi-ripe cuttings in mid-summer. Remove rooted suckers in early autumn.

Diervilla x splendens

Vibrant sulphur-yellow flowers are produced in clusters at the end of shoots from early summer to late summer on this thicket-forming deciduous shrub. The mid-green leaves take on purple tints in autumn. H 1m (3ft) S 1.5m (5ft).
Aspect: sun or semi-shade
Hardiness: ❀❀❀ Zones: 7–8

DRIMYS

This is a genus of 30 species that includes the upright, evergreen

Desfontainia spinosa

Drimys winteri

Elaeagnus x ebbingei 'Limelight'

shrub with late spring and early summer flowers featured here. It is ideal for a shrubbery or situated in the dappled shade of a woodland edge.

Cultivation Grow in any moisture-retentive, well-drained garden soil that is reasonably fertile and in full sun or dappled shade. In colder regions, grow in a sheltered position where it is protected from cold winds.

Pruning No routine pruning is necessary. Any frost-damaged growth should be removed in spring.

Propagation Take semi-ripe cuttings in late summer. Layer lower stems in early spring.

Drimys winteri
Winter's bark

This shrub produces delightful jasmine-scented, creamy-white flowers from mid-spring to early summer and lance-shaped, leathery, dark green leaves. H 15m (50ft) S 10m (33ft).
Aspect: sun or semi-shade
Hardiness: ❀❀ Zone: 9

ELAEAGNUS

A genus of about 45 species, including the following brightly coloured variegated evergreens, that provide permanent interest throughout the year. They make ideal border fillers, where they will help give lacklustre displays an uplift. They are all easy to grow and tolerate cold winds and salt-laden air – making them ideal for providing shelter and screens in coastal gardens. Their tolerance of dry soil and urban pollution means they are widely used by landscapers in towns and cities. Their handsome foliage is also popular with flower arrangers.

Cultivation They will grow in well-drained garden soil that is reasonably fertile and in full sun or dappled shade. However, leaf coloration will be best in full sun.

Pruning No routine pruning is necessary. Neglected plants can be rejuvenated by cutting back one stem in three to near ground level after flowering, starting with the oldest stems. Trim hedges in early summer and early autumn. Remove any reverted plain green shoots as soon as they are noticed.

Propagation Take hardwood cuttings during late winter.

Elaeagnus x *ebbingei* 'Gilt Edge'

The lustrous, golden-edged, dark green leaves make this a noticeable shrub in winter. Insignificant slightly scented white flowers appear in mid-autumn. H 4m (13ft) S 4m (13ft).
Aspect: sun or semi-shade
Hardiness: ❀❀❀ Zones: 7–8

Elaeagnus x *ebbingei* 'Limelight'

Silvery when they emerge, the attractive lime-green and yellow-splashed dark green, leathery leaves are loved by flower arrangers. Insignificant, slightly scented, creamy-white flowers are also produced in mid-autumn. This really tough evergreen will tolerate dry soil too. H 3m (10ft) S 3m (10ft).
Aspect: sun or semi-shade
Hardiness: ❀❀❀ Zones: 7–8

Elaeagnus pungens 'Maculata'

Leathery dark green leaves are boldly marked with bright yellow in the centre and have a slightly frosted shine. Insignificant, slightly scented white flowers are also produced in mid-autumn, followed by brown fruit that ripen to red. H 4m (13ft) S 5m (16ft).
Aspect: sun or semi-shade
Hardiness: ❀❀❀ Zones: 7–8

ENKIANTHUS

This comprises a genus of about ten species, including the deciduous shrubs featured here, that offer early summer flowers and good autumn leaf tints. They are ideal for dappled shade, such as in a woodland-edge planting scheme. A useful and unusual border addition that is easy to grow if you can provide the right growing conditions.

Cultivation Grow in any well-drained neutral to acid soil in full sun or dappled shade. In colder areas, shelter from winds. Add plenty of organic matter (but not alkaline mushroom compost/soil mix) to the soil before planting.

Pruning No routine pruning is necessary. Any frost-damaged growth should be removed in spring.

Propagation Sow seed in early winter. Layer suitable stems in early autumn.

Enkianthus campanulatus

Spreading deciduous shrub that bears clusters of bell-shaped, pink-edged, pale yellow flowers during late spring and early summer. The toothed, matt-green leaves provide an attractive backdrop and take on vivid shades of orange and red in autumn. H 5m (16ft) S 5m (16ft).
Aspect: sun or semi-shade
Hardiness: ❀❀❀ Zones: 7–8

Enkianthus cernuus f. *rubens*

A bushy, deciduous shrub that is covered in pretty clusters of bell-shaped, red flowers during late spring and early summer. The leaves emerge bright green and turn plum-purple in summer, then take on blood-red hues in autumn. Protect in cold gardens. H 2.5m (8ft) S 2.5m (8ft).
Aspect: sun or semi-shade
Hardiness: ❀❀ Zone: 9

Enkianthus chinensis

ERICA

A huge genus of over 700 species of hardy evergreen shrubs with colourful winter flowers, some varieties of which offer autumn and winter foliage tints as well. There are literally thousands of named varieties. All winter-flowering heathers make excellent ground cover plants for open, sunny areas with acid soil. Some are tolerant of neutral or even slightly alkaline soil, as well as dappled shade. Many make useful permanent container plants.
Cultivation In the garden, grow in any well-drained, but moisture-retentive, acid soil in full sun. Add plenty of organic matter (but not alkaline mushroom compost/soil mix) before planting. In pots, grow in ericaceous compost on a sunny patio. Keep watered.
Pruning Trim flowering stems as they fade. Prune those grown for their colourful foliage in spring.
Propagation Take semi-ripe cuttings in mid-summer or layer side shoots in early spring.

Erica carnea 'Ann Sparkes'
Winter heath
Deep pink clusters of urn-shaped flowers that mature to blood-red as they age are produced from mid-winter to mid-spring. The burnished-gold foliage is bronze-tipped in spring. Tolerates slightly alkaline soils and dappled shade. H 25cm (10in) S 45cm (18in).
Aspect: sun or semi-shade
Hardiness: ❀❀❀ Zones: 7–8

Erica carnea 'Challenger'
Winter heath
Masses of urn-shaped flowers provide a splash of magenta from mid-winter to mid-spring above a mound of dark green foliage. Tolerates slightly alkaline soils and dappled shade. H 15cm (6in) S 45cm (18in).
Aspect: sun or semi-shade
Hardiness: ❀❀❀ Zones: 7–8

Erica carnea 'December Red'
Winter heath
Lilac-pink, urn-shaped flowers are produced in clusters from mid-winter to mid-spring above a mound of dark green foliage. Tolerates slightly alkaline soils and dappled shade. H 15cm (6in)
S 45cm (18in).
Aspect: sun or semi-shade
Hardiness: ❀❀❀ Zones: 7–8

Erica carnea 'Foxhollow'
Winter heath
Urn-shaped lilac flowers appear from mid-winter to mid-spring above mounds of yellow foliage that is bronze-tipped in spring, darkening to orange in winter. Tolerates slightly alkaline soils and dappled shade. H 15cm (6in) S 45cm (18in).
Aspect: sun or semi-shade
Hardiness: ❀❀❀ Zones: 7–8

Erica carnea 'King George'
Winter heath
Clusters of dark pink, urn-shaped flowers that darken as they mature are produced from early winter to early spring. Tolerates slightly alkaline soils and dappled shade. H 15cm (6in) S 25cm (10in).
Aspect: sun or semi-shade
Hardiness: ❀❀❀ Zones: 7–8

Erica carnea 'Myretoun Ruby'
Winter heath
Large, urn-shaped, ruby-red flowers that mature to crimson are produced from mid-winter to late spring above a mound of dark green foliage. Tolerates slightly alkaline soils and dappled shade. H 15cm (6in) S 45cm (18in).
Aspect: sun or semi-shade
Hardiness: ❀❀❀ Zones: 7–8

Erica carnea 'Pink Spangles'
Winter heath
Clusters of urn-shaped shell-pink flowers are produced from mid-

Erica x veitchii 'Exeter'

winter to mid-spring above a mound of dark green foliage. Tolerates slightly alkaline soils and dappled shade. H 15cm (6in) S 45cm (18in).
Aspect: sun or semi-shade
Hardiness: ❀❀❀ Zones: 7–8

Erica carnea 'Springwood White'
Winter heath
Long spikes of urn-shaped white flowers are produced from mid-winter to mid-spring above a mound of dark green foliage. Tolerates slightly alkaline soils and dappled shade. H 15cm (6in) S 45cm (18in).
Aspect: sun or semi-shade
Hardiness: ❀❀❀ Zones: 7–8

Erica cinerea f. alba 'Pink Ice'
Bell heather
Mini rosy-pink, bell-shaped flowers are produced in masses

Erica x darleyensis 'Darley Dale'

from early summer to early autumn above a mound of dark green foliage that is bronze-tinted in spring and again during winter. H 20cm (8in) S 35cm (14in).
Aspect: sun
Hardiness: ❀❀❀ Zones: 7–8

Erica x darleyensis 'Darley Dale'
Clusters of urn-shaped, shell-pink flowers that darken with age are produced from mid-winter to mid-spring above a mound of green foliage that is cream-tipped in spring. H 15cm (6in) S 55cm (22in).
Aspect: sun
Hardiness: ❀❀❀ Zones: 7–8

Erica x darleyensis 'Furzey'
Urn-shaped, lilac-pink flowers are produced in clusters from early winter to late spring above a mound of lance-shaped green leaves that are pink-tipped in spring. H 35cm (14in) S 60cm (24in).
Aspect: sun
Hardiness: ❀❀❀ Zones: 7–8

ESCALLONIA

This genus of over 50 species includes several useful bushy evergreen shrubs with pretty summer flowers that shine out against a backdrop of glossy, dark green leaves. They make excellent border fillers but can be used to make an informal flowering hedge. They tolerate salt-laden air and so are ideal for providing shelter and screens in mild coastal gardens.
Cultivation Grow in well-drained garden soil that is reasonably

Escallonia

Eucryphia x nymansensis 'Nymansay'

fertile and in full sun. Choose a sheltered position for the less hardy varieties.
Pruning Cut back wayward shoots in spring to maintain a balanced shape. Trim flowered shoots after flowering to keep shrub compact. Trim hedges after flowering, if necessary, to keep in shape.
Propagation Take softwood cuttings in late spring or semi-ripe cuttings during mid-summer or late summer.

Escallonia 'Apple Blossom'
Masses of pretty, pale pink flowers are produced from early summer to late summer over a compact mound of glossy, dark green foliage. Good for growing as an informal, flowering hedge, but not on exposed sites. H 2.5m (8ft) S 2.5m (8ft).
Aspect: sun
Hardiness: ❀❀ Zones: 9

Escallonia 'Donard Seedling'
An open form of escallonia that produces arching shoots covered in blossom-like, pink-tinted white flowers from early summer to late summer. Very hardy, it is ideal for growing as an informal, flowering hedge even in cold areas. H 2.5m (8ft) S 2.5m (8ft).
Aspect: sun
Hardiness: ❀❀❀ Zones: 7–8

Escallonia 'Iveyi'
A vigorous, upright, evergreen shrub that is covered in clusters of fragrant, white flowers from mid-summer to early autumn. The glossy, dark green leaves

become bronze-tinted in winter. H 3m (10ft) S 3m (10ft).
Aspect: sun
Hardiness: ❀❀❀ Zones: 7–8

Escallonia rubra 'Crimson Spire'
Masses of tubular flowers provide a splash of pale crimson from early summer to late summer against a backdrop of glossy, dark green foliage. Good for growing as an informal, flowering hedge. H 2.5m (8ft) S 2.5m (8ft).
Aspect: sun
Hardiness: ❀❀ Zone: 9

EUCRYPHIA
A genus of about five species, including the following evergreen shrubs, grown for their late summer flowers. Rated among the most attractive summer-flowering shrubs, these shrubs are an ideal choice for planting in a sheltered woodland garden with acid soil, where there is plenty of room to spread, but they are borderline hardy in colder areas.
Cultivation Grow in any well-drained but moisture-retentive, acid to neutral soil in dappled shade. Add plenty of organic matter (but not alkaline mushroom compost) to the soil before planting to ensure that it gets a good start. Make sure the planting site is sheltered from cold winds.
Pruning No routine pruning is necessary. Any frost-damaged growth should be removed in spring.
Propagation Take semi-ripe cuttings in mid-summer or late summer.

Eucryphia x intermedia 'Rostrevor'
A large, evergreen, upright shrub that is covered in splendid white-scented, cup-shaped flowers up to 5cm (2in) across throughout late summer and early autumn. H 10m (33ft) S 3m (10ft).
Aspect: semi-shade
Hardiness: ❀❀❀ Zones: 7–8

Eucryphia x nymansensis 'Nymansay'
Very large, upright-growing, evergreen shrub with toothed, leathery foliage that is smothered in large, showy, white cup-shaped flowers throughout late summer and early autumn. H 15m (50ft) S 5m (16ft).
Aspect: semi-shade
Hardiness: ❀❀❀ Zones: 7–8

EUONYMUS
Spindle tree
This comprises a large genus of about 175 species that includes the useful and varied garden shrubs featured here. The evergreen varieties provide striking variegated foliage and make excellent ground cover and mid-border fillers anywhere in the garden, as well as attractive low hedges in mild areas. Some varieties will also make good wall shrubs, where they will produce aerial roots that are self-supporting. Deciduous euonymus

provide intense autumn colour and attractive berries.
Cultivation Grow in any well-drained soil that is reasonably fertile, in full sun or dappled shade. Make sure the planting site for evergreens is sheltered from cold winds.
Pruning No routine pruning is necessary. Any damaged growth should be removed in spring. Remove any plain green reverted shoots from variegated varieties. Rejuvenate neglected plants by cutting back one stem in three to near ground level after flowering, starting with the oldest stems. Evergreen hedges can be trimmed lightly in mid-spring to maintain a neat shape.
Propagation Take semi-ripe cuttings mid-summer or late summer or hardwood cuttings in mid-winter.

Euonymus europaeus 'Red Cascade'
The dark green leaves of this deciduous European native transform themselves into wonderfully vivid fiery shades during the autumn. Insignificant flowers produced during late spring and early summer are followed by eye-catching rosy-pink berries that last into the winter. Although it will grow in dappled shade, plant in full sun for the best

Euonymus europaeus 'Red Cascade'

Euonymus alatus

Euonymus fortunei 'Emerald 'n' Gold'

autumn colours. H 3m (10ft)
S 2.5m (8ft).
Aspect: sun or semi-shade
Hardiness: ❀❀❀ Zones: 7–8

Euonymus fortunei 'Emerald Gaiety'
The white-edged, bright evergreen
foliage on this compact, bushy
shrub provides useful winter
interest when there is little else
happening in the garden.
Insignificant clusters of tiny green
flowers are produced during late
spring and early summer.
'Emerald Gaiety' makes a useful
ground cover and low hedging
plant and does well in sun or
shade. It is a good plant for
training against a wall or fence.
H 1m (3ft) S 1.5m (5ft).
Aspect: sun or shade
Hardiness: ❀❀❀ Zones: 7–8

Euonymus fortunei 'Emerald 'n' Gold'
A bushy, variegated evergreen with
glossy, yellow-edged, bright green
leaves that become pink-tinged in
winter. Insignificant clusters of
tiny green flowers are produced
during late spring and early
summer. It is a useful ground
cover and low hedging plant in
sun or light shade. H 60cm
(24in) S 90cm (36in).
Aspect: sun or semi-shade
Hardiness: ❀❀❀ Zones: 7–8

Euonymus fortunei 'Silver Queen'
A low-growing, compact, busy
evergreen with dark green leaves
that have creamy-yellow or
creamy-white margins that are
pink-tinged in winter. Clusters of
insignificant, tiny green flowers

appear in late spring and early
summer, followed by orange fruits.
A good choice for training against
a wall or fence in sun or light
shade. H 3m (10ft) S 2m (6ft).
Aspect: sun or semi-shade
Hardiness: ❀❀❀ Zones: 7–8

Euonymus fortunei 'Sunspot'
A compact, bushy, evergreen shrub
with glossy foliage splashed with
gold and held on bright yellow
stems. Excellent for winter colour.
H 1m (3ft) S 1.5m (5ft).
Aspect: sun or semi-shade
Hardiness: ❀❀❀ Zones: 7–8

EXOCHORDA
Pearl bush
A genus of four species, including
the graceful, deciduous shrub
featured here, that is smothered
with pretty blooms during late
spring. Its lax habit makes it an
ideal choice for a mixed border,
but all look good covering banks
or growing as a wall shrub.
Cultivation Grow in any moisture-
retentive, well-drained soil that is
reasonably fertile in full sun or
dappled shade. Shelter evergreens
from cold winds.
Pruning Cut back one stem in
three to near ground level after
flowering, starting with the oldest
stems, to keep flowering profuse.
Propagation Take softwood
cuttings in mid-spring.

Exochorda x macrantha 'The Bride'
Elegant arching branches are
covered in brilliant white flowers
during mid-spring and late spring.

The delicate, bluish-green foliage
makes a good foil for adjacent
flowering plants at other times
and then takes on yellow and
orange shades in autumn. H 2m
(6ft) S 3m (10ft).
Aspect: sun or semi-shade
Hardiness: ❀❀❀ Zones: 7–8

X FATSHEDERA
This bi-generic cross between a
bushy evergreen shrub (*Fatsia*) and
ivy (*Hedera*) is grown mainly for
its handsome foliage. Can be
grown as a shrub, trained up a
wall or fence or left to sprawl as
deep ground cover under
deciduous trees. It is an excellent
choice for town or coastal gardens
since it can tolerate shade, urban
pollution and salt-laden winds.
Cultivation Grow in any moisture-
retentive well-drained garden soil
that is reasonably fertile and in
full sun or dappled shade. Grow
at the base of a sunny wall in
colder areas.
Pruning No routine pruning is
necessary. Remove wayward or
crossing shoots if necessary
during early spring.
Propagation Take semi-ripe
cuttings in mid-summer.

x fatshedera lizei
An open, branching shrub with
glossy, evergreen, ivy-like leaves
that are leathery to the touch. A
bonus of creamy-white flowers are
sometimes produced during in
mid-autumn and late autumn.
H 1.2m (4ft) S 3m (10ft).
Named varieties: 'Variegata', frost-
hardy form with white-edged

Exochorda x *macrantha* 'The Bride'

leaves. H 1.2m (4ft) S 3m (10ft).
Aspect: sun or semi-shade
Hardiness: ❀❀❀ Zones: 7–8

FATSIA

A genus of two species, including the popular evergreen shrub featured here. They make excellent focal points when positioned in a sheltered area of the garden, where they will help to create a tropical atmosphere. They can also be grown as a permanent specimen in a large container. This shrub is an excellent choice for town or costal gardens as it can tolerate shade, urban pollution and salt-laden winds.
Cultivation In the garden, grow in any moisture-retentive, well-drained soil that is reasonably fertile in full sun or dappled shade where it is sheltered from cold winds. If planted in a container, grow in a soil-based compost (soil mix). Feed every fortnight throughout the growing season and water as necessary.
Pruning No routine pruning is required. Keep plants compact by cutting back one stem in three to near ground level in mid-spring, starting with the oldest stems.
Propagation Can be air layered in mid-spring. Take softwood cuttings in early summer.

Fatsia japonica
A tropical-looking shrub with large, glossy, leathery, palmate leaves that help to reflect light into lacklustre corners. A bonus of creamy-white flowers is produced in ball-shaped flower-

Fatsia japonica

heads in early autumn and mid-autumn, followed by rounded black fruit. H 4m (13ft) S 4m (13ft). Named varieties: 'Variegata', half-hardy variegated form with bright green leaves that are cream-splashed at the margins. Ideal for brightening up dark corners. H 4m (13ft) S 4m (13ft).
Aspect: sun or semi-shade
Hardiness: ❀❀❀ Zones: 7–8

FORSYTHIA

A genus of over five species, including the following popular and spring-flowering shrubs that can be used as back-of-the-border fillers, focal points or trimmed as a deciduous flowering hedge. They can even be trained into wall shrubs, arches and standards.
Cultivation Grow in any moisture-retentive, well-drained soil that is reasonably fertile in full sun or dappled shade.
Pruning Keep plants compact and flowering well by cutting back one stem in three to near ground level during early spring, starting with the oldest stems. Prune hedges and other ornamental forms lightly after flowering in mid-spring.
Propagation Take softwood cuttings in early summer or hardwood cuttings in late autumn.

Forsythia 'Beatrix Farrand'
Masses of 3cm- (1¼in-) wide orange-yellow blooms are produced on arching, bare stems during early spring and mid-spring. Sharply toothed leaves

Forsythia

provide a plain green backdrop during the growing season. Very good for training against a wall. H 2m (6ft) S 2m (6ft).
Aspect: sun or semi-shade
Hardiness: ❀❀❀ Zones: 7–8

Forsythia x intermedia 'Lynwood'
Masses of delicate, golden-yellow flowers are produced on bare stems during mid-spring and late spring. A dense crop of lobed, mid-green leaves follows. H 3m (10ft) S 2m (6ft).
Aspect: sun or semi-shade
Hardiness: ❀❀❀ Zones: 7–8

Forsythia x intermedia 'Spring Glory'
Pale yellow flowers smother the branches of this deciduous shrub during early spring and mid-spring before the lance-shaped leaves emerge. An excellent choice for growing as a flowering hedge. H 2m (6ft) S 3m (10ft).
Aspect: sun or semi-shade
Hardiness: ❀❀❀ Zones: 7–8

Forsythia x intermedia 'Week End'
Masses of rich yellow flowers are produced on bare stems during early spring and mid-spring as the leaf buds break. H 3m (10ft) S 3m (10ft).
Aspect: sun or semi-shade
Hardiness: ❀❀❀ Zones: 7–8

FOTHERGILLA

A genus of just two species, including the deciduous shrubs featured here, grown for their brilliant autumn colour. A bonus

of sweetly scented flowers are borne from mid-spring before the leaves emerge. They make good border fillers and seasonal specimens where suitable growing conditions can be provided. A good choice for a woodland-edge planting on acid soil.
Cultivation Grow in any moisture-retentive but well-drained acid soil in full sun or partial shade. Add plenty of organic matter (but not alkaline mushroom compost/soil mix) to the soil before planting. Flowering and foliage displays are best in full sun.
Pruning No routine pruning is required.
Propagation Layer low branches in early autumn.

Fothergilla gardenii
Witch alder
Upright deciduous shrub with coarsely toothed green leaves that turn brilliant crimson in autumn. Sweetly scented clusters of white flowers are produced on bare stems during mid-spring and late spring. H 1m (3ft) S 1m (3ft).
Aspect: sun or semi-shade
Hardiness: ❀❀❀ Zones: 7–8

Fothergilla major (syn. Fothergilla monticola)
Glossy, dark green leaves turn fiery shades of orange, yellow and red in autumn. Clusters of sweetly scented white flowers are produced on bare stems during mid-spring and late spring. H 2.5m (8ft) S 2m (6ft).
Aspect: sun or semi-shade
Hardiness: ❀❀❀ Zones: 7–8

Fothergilla 'Huntsman'

Fremontodendron 'California Glory'

Fuchsia

Garrya elliptica

FREMONTODENDRON

A genus of just two species, including the long-flowering evergreen shrub featured here that is ideal for training against a sunny wall in mild areas but can also be grown as a free-standing shrub at the back of a sheltered border. It is mainly grown for its spectacular, waxy-looking flowers and handsome foliage.

Cultivation Grow in any well-drained neutral to alkaline soil in full sun that is sheltered from cold winds.

Pruning No routine pruning is required. Remove frost damaged and awkwardly positioned stems in spring.

Propagation Sow seed in early spring.

Fremontodendron 'California Glory'

Eye-catching, saucer-shaped, butter-yellow and waxy-looking flowers are produced in succession from late spring to mid-autumn against a backdrop of leathery, lobed dark green leaves. H 6m (20ft) S 4m (13ft).
Aspect: sun
Hardiness: ✽✽ Zone: 9

FUCHSIA

A large genus of over 100 species, including the hardy types featured here that are grown for their superb summer flowers. In mild areas they can be treated as deciduous shrubs, making useful fillers in mixed borders and shrubberies, or even an unusual informal flowering hedge.

Cultivation Grow in any well-drained soil in full sun or dappled shade protected from cold winds. In colder areas, protect crowns with an insulating layer of leaves or similar material over the winter months.

Pruning In frost-free areas no routine pruning is required. They are more or less evergreen and grown with a permanent woody framework to make good border fillers or an informal long-flowering hedge. Remove any dead or damaged wood each spring. Hedges can be kept in shape by tipping back the new shoots in early spring or mid-spring to maintain dense growth. In colder areas, hardy fuchsias are treated more like herbaceous plants – the top cut back in early spring before new growth starts.

Propagation Take softwood cuttings from mid-spring to early autumn.

Fuchsia 'Mrs Popple'

Scarlet and purple single pendant flowers are produced from early summer to mid-autumn against a foil of dark green leaves. Borderline hardy. H 1.2m (4ft) S 1.2m (4ft).
Aspect: sun or semi-shade
Hardiness: ✽✽✽ Zones: 7–8

Fuchsia 'Pumila'

Scarlet and violet-blue single flowers are produced in succession from early summer to mid-autumn on this dwarf shrub. Borderline hardy. H 50cm (20in) S 50cm (20in).

Aspect: sun or semi-shade
Hardiness: ✽✽✽ Zones: 7–8

Fuchsia 'Riccartonii'

Red and dark purple single flowers are produced in succession from early summer to mid-autumn over bronze-tinted dark green leaves. Borderline hardy, it makes an excellent hedge in frost-free areas. H 3m (10ft) S 2m (6ft).
Aspect: sun or semi-shade
Hardiness: ✽✽✽ Zones: 7–8

GARRYA

This genus of over 10 species includes the tough, upright-growing, evergreen shrubs featured here, grown for their late-winter catkin-like flower tassels. They make an excellent choice for growing against a south- or west-facing wall or fence where they will provide valuable winter interest as well as an attractive foil for other plants throughout the year. This shrub makes a useful plant for town and coastal gardens as they tolerate both pollution and salt-laden air.

Cultivation Grow in well-drained , moderately fertile soil in full sun or dappled shade. In colder areas, protect from icy winds.

Pruning Keep plants in shape by cutting back one stem in three to near ground level in mid-spring, starting with the oldest stems.

Propagation Take semi-ripe cuttings in mid-summer, or hardwood cuttings in early autumn.

Garrya elliptica

A useful wall shrub with leathery, lustrous, wavy-edged evergreen leaves, that is decorated with elegant grey-green catkins tassels from early winter to late winter. H 4m (13ft) S 4m (13ft).
Named varieties: 'James Roof', dramatic silvery catkins up to 20cm long. H 4m (12ft) S 4m (13ft).
Aspect: sun or semi-shade
Hardiness: ✽✽✽ Zones: 7–8

GAULTHERIA

This is a large genus of 170 species, including the low-growing evergreen shrubs that are featured here The plants are mainly grown for their red berries and attractive winter tints. To ensure fruit production, it will be necessary to grow both male and female plants.

Cultivation Grow in a moisture-retentive, well-drained neutral to acid soil in full sun or dappled shade that is moderately fertile.

Pruning No routine pruning is required. Remove any dead or damaged stems each mid-spring.

Propagation Take semi-ripe cuttings in mid-summer or layer shoots in mid-spring.

Gaultheria mucronata 'Mulberry Wine'

Urn-shaped, pinkish-white flowers are produced during late spring and early summer, followed by aromatic, magenta fruit in early autumn that darken to purple. H 1.2m (4ft) S 1.2m (4ft).
Aspect: sun or semi-shade
Hardiness: ✽✽✽ Zones: 7–8

Gaultheria procumbens

Gaultheria mucronata 'Wintertime'

Aromatic, snow-white fruit in early autumn follow pink-flushed, urn-shaped white flowers that were produced during late spring and early summer. H 1.2m (4ft) S 1.2m (4ft).
Aspect: sun or semi-shade
Hardiness: ✿✿✿ Zones: 7–8

Gaultheria procumbens

Urn-shaped flowers in shades of white and pink are produced during late spring and early summer, followed by aromatic scarlet fruit in early autumn. The green leaves take on red and purple tints in winter. They are useful ground cover plants between acid-loving trees and shrubs. H 15cm (6in) S 1m (3ft).
Aspect: sun or semi-shade
Hardiness: ✿✿✿ Zones: 7–8

GENISTA

A genus of over 90 species, including the late-spring and early summer flowering spiny deciduous shrubs. They make excellent border specimens for providing a seasonal splash of colour and can be used to make informal flowering hedges in mild areas. Lower-growing forms also make useful ground cover on sunny banks or can be used to soften the edges of raised beds and rockeries.
Cultivation Grow in a well-drained poor soil in full sun.
Pruning No routine pruning is required. Keep plants bushy by

pinching out shoot tips after flowering.
Propagation Sow seeds in early autumn. Take semi-ripe cuttings in mid-summer.

Genista hispanica
Spanish gorse

Golden-yellow flowers produced in clusters on spiny stems in late spring and early summer stand out against the mound of green leaves. Its prickles make it an excellent impenetrable hedging plant in mild areas. Borderline hardy. H 75cm (30in) S 1.5m (5ft).
Aspect: sun
Hardiness: ✿✿✿ Zones: 7–8

Genista lydia

The prickly, arching, grey-green leaves of this spreading shrub are festooned in golden-yellow flowers throughout late spring and early summer. H 60cm (24in) S 1m (3ft).
Aspect: sun
Hardiness: ✿✿✿ Zones: 7–8

Genista pilosa 'Vancouver Gold'

A spreading, mound-forming shrub that is covered in masses of golden-yellow flowers produced during late spring and early summer. H 45cm (18in) S 1m (3ft).
Aspect: sun
Hardiness: ✿✿✿ Zones: 7–8

Genista tinctoria 'Royal Gold'
Dyer's greenwood

An extremely long-flowering, upright-growing deciduous shrub that bears golden-yellow flowers

Grevillea 'Robyn Gordon'

intermittently from late spring to late summer. H 1m (3ft) S 1m (3ft).
Aspect: sun
Hardiness: ✿✿✿ Zones: 7–8

GREVILLEA

A large genus of over 250 species, including the evergreen shrubs featured here, that are grown for their exotic-looking early summer flowers. If you have the right growing conditions, they make useful and unusual border fillers.
Cultivation In the garden, grow in any well-drained neutral to acid soil that is moderately fertile in full sun. Provide protection in frost-prone areas. Use ericaceous compost if grown in pots. Feed fortnightly in the growing season.
Pruning No routine pruning is required. Remove any dead or damaged stems each mid-spring.
Propagation Take semi-ripe cuttings in mid-summer.

Grevillea juniperina f. sulphurea

A rounded evergreen shrub with upright, branching stems that carry spiky yellow flowers from late spring to mid-summer. Although the plant is frost hardy, but it will need a sheltered site and winter protection in colder gardens. H 1m (3ft) S 1.8m (6ft).
Aspect: sun
Hardiness: ✿✿ Zone: 9

Grevillea 'Robyn Gordon'

This is a spreading evergreen shrub with upright branches that bear dark pink petal-less flowers produced intermittently all year round, but mainly during early summer. In frost-free areas, grow in a sunny, sheltered spot. Elsewhere, grow in a pot and move it inside during the winter. H 1m (3ft) S 1.8m (6ft).
Aspect: sun
Hardiness: ✿ Zones: 7–8

Genista lydia

HAMAMELIS
Witch hazel

This genus of about five species, including the hardy deciduous shrubs featured here, are grown for their fragrant, spidery winter flowers that look spectacular in the garden when illuminated by the low winter sun. Ideal for a sunny shrub border or woodland-edge planting.

Cultivation Grow in a moisture-retentive, well-drained, neutral to acid soil that is reasonably fertile in full sun or dappled shade.

Pruning No routine pruning is necessary. Neglected plants can have wayward branches removed to balance the overall shape of the canopy after flowering in early spring.

Propagation Difficult to propagate. Sow seeds when ripe in mid-autumn; graft named varieties in late winter.

Hamamelis x intermedia 'Arnold Promise'

This vase-shaped deciduous shrub bears clusters of large, sweetly scented, spidery golden flowers from early winter to late winter. The green leaves turn into brilliant autumnal colours in shades of rich yellow. H 4m (13ft) S 4m (13ft).
Aspect: sun or semi-shade
Hardiness: ✹✹✹ Zones: 7–8

Hamamelis x intermedia 'Diane'

Clusters of sweetly scented, spidery, dark copper-red flowers are produced on bare stems from early winter to late winter. The

Hamamelis mollis 'Pallida'

green leaves turn fiery shades of orange, red and yellow in autumn. H 4m (13ft) S 4m (13ft).
Aspect: sun or semi-shade
Hardiness: ✹✹✹ Zones: 7–8

Hamamelis x intermedia 'Jelena'

Large, fragrant, coppery-red or orange flowers are produced in clusters on bare stems from early winter to mid-winter. The green leaves transform into attractive autumnal colours with shades of rich orange and red. H 4m (13ft) S 4m (13ft).
Aspect: sun or semi-shade
Hardiness: ✹✹✹ Zones: 7–8

Hamamelis x intermedia 'Moonlight'

Clusters of sweetly scented, spidery, pale yellow flowers are produced on bare stems from early winter to late winter. Green leaves turn yellow in autumn.

H 4m (13ft) S 4m (13ft).
Aspect: sun or semi-shade
Hardiness: ✹✹✹ Zones: 7–8

Hamamelis x intermedia 'Pallida' (syn. *H. mollis* 'Pallida')

Bare branches from early winter to late winter carry clusters of large, sweetly scented, sulphur-yellow flowers. The green leaves transform into autumn colours with shades of rich orange and red. H 4m (13ft) S 4m (13ft).
Aspect: sun or semi-shade
Hardiness: ✹✹✹ Zones: 7–8

Hamamelis mollis

Clusters of sweetly scented, spidery, golden flowers are produced on bare stems from early winter to late winter. The slightly hairy mid-green leaves turn bright yellow in autumn. H 4m (13ft) S 4m (13ft).
Aspect: sun or semi-shade
Hardiness: ✹✹✹ Zones: 7–8

HEBE

A genus of around 100 species, including the evergreen shrubs featured here, that are grown for their colourful flowers and attractive foliage. Most are long flowering and make good filler shrubs for a border in sun or dappled shade. They are tolerant of pollution and salt-laden air, and so make a good choice for town and coastal gardens. Some also make excellent low hedges or edging in milder areas.

Cultivation Grow in a moisture-retentive, well-drained neutral to

slightly alkaline soil that is poor to reasonably fertile in full sun or dappled shade, but sheltered from cold winds and freezing temperatures. Borderline hardy, they need winter protection in colder areas.

Pruning No routine pruning is required. Straggly shoots on larger varieties can be pruned right back in mid-spring. Remove all-green reverted shoots from variegated varieties as soon as they are noticed. Trim hedges lightly after flowering to keep the plants dense and compact.

Propagation Take softwood cuttings in late spring or semi-ripe cuttings in early autumn.

Hebe cupressoides 'Boughton Dome'

An unusual hebe that looks more like a conifer, with its grey-green, scale-like evergreen leaves. Slow growing and hardy, it is an ideal choice for troughs and rock gardens. Small blue flowers in late spring are seldom produced.
H 30cm (12in) S 60cm (24in).
Aspect: sun or semi-shade
Hardiness: ✹✹✹ Zones: 7–8

Hebe 'Great Orme'

Slender spikes of bright pink flowers that fade to white are produced from mid-summer to mid-autumn above a mound of lustrous, evergreen leaves on this rounded shrub. Useful foil and gap filler. H 1.2m (4ft) S 1.2m (4ft).
Aspect: sun or semi-shade
Hardiness: ✹✹ Zones: 7–8

Hebe 'Marjorie'

A compact, rounded, evergreen shrub that bears long spikes of mauve flowers that gradually fade to white from mid-summer to early autumn. A useful foil and gap filler and for flower arranging. H 1.2m (4ft) S 1.5m (5ft).
Aspect: sun or semi-shade
Hardiness: ✹✹ Zones: 9

Hebe 'Midsummer Beauty'

The bright evergreen leaves emerge purple-tinged on this rounded shrub that produces dark lilac flower-spikes that fade to white from mid-summer to early

Hebe 'Great Orme'

Hebe pinguifolia 'Pagei'

autumn on purplish-brown stems. H 2m (6ft) S 1.5m (5ft).
Aspect: sun or semi-shade
Hardiness: ❀❀ Zone: 9

Hebe ochracea 'James Stirling'
The golden conifer-like foliage of this compact evergreen adds colour to the winter garden. Clusters of white flowers on arching stems are produced in early summer. H 45cm (18in) S 60cm (24in).
Aspect: sun or semi-shade
Hardiness: ❀❀❀ Zones: 7–8

Hebe pinguifolia 'Pagei'
A low-growing, compact but spreading evergreen that bears masses of snow-white flowers on purple stems throughout late spring and early summer above fleshy blue-green leaves. Good for edging beds and borders. H 30cm (12in) S 90cm (36in).
Aspect: sun or semi-shade
Hardiness: ❀❀❀ Zones: 7–8

Hebe rakaiensis
A neat, rounded shrub that bears clusters of large white flowers during early summer and mid-summer above glossy evergreen leaves. Its neat habit makes it a good choice for Japanese-style gardens. H 1m (3ft) S 1.2m (4ft).
Aspect: sun or semi-shade
Hardiness: ❀❀❀ Zones: 7–8

Hebe 'Red Edge'
A low-growing, spreading evergreen that bears lilac-blue flowers that fade to white throughout early summer and mid-summer. The grey-green leaves of young plants have attractive red margins and veining. Good for edging beds and borders. H 45cm (18in) S 60cm (24in).
Aspect: sun or semi-shade
Hardiness: ❀❀ Zone: 9

Hebe 'Rosie'
Its compact mound of evergreen foliage is decorated with pink flower-spikes from late spring to early autumn. H 60cm (24in) S 60cm (24in).
Aspect: sun or semi-shade
Hardiness: ❀❀ Zone: 9

HELIANTHEMUM
Rock rose, sun rose
A genus of over 100 species that includes the short-lived, spreading, evergreen shrubs featured here, grown for their early summer flowers. These low-growing shrubs are ideal for edging a sunny border and can be used in pots and for cascading over the edge of a raised bed. However, they tend to lose vigour as they age so are best replaced when they reach this stage.
Cultivation Grow in a well-drained neutral to slightly alkaline soil that is reasonably fertile in full sun.
Pruning Cut back hard after flowering to encourage a fresh mound of foliage and a second flush of flowers in late summer.
Propagation Take semi-ripe cuttings in early summer or mid-summer.

Helianthemum 'Ben Fhada'
A low-growing, spreading shrub that is covered in golden-yellow, cup-shaped flowers with orange centres from late spring to mid-summer. H 30cm (12in) S 30cm (12in).
Aspect: sun
Hardiness: ❀❀❀ Zone: 7–8

Helianthemum 'Ben Heckla'
Cup-shaped, brick-red flowers with orange centres are produced *en masse* from late spring to mid-summer above a spreading mound of grey-green leaves. H 30cm (12in) S 30cm (12in).
Aspect: sun
Hardiness: ❀❀❀ Zones: 7–8

Helianthemum 'Ben Hope'
A spreading shrub that bears bright red flowers with orange centres in succession from late spring to mid-summer over downy, silvery-green leaves. H 30cm (12in) S 30cm (12in).
Aspect: sun
Hardiness: ❀❀❀ Zones: 7–8

Helianthemum 'Chocolate Blotch'
Cup-shaped, pale orange flowers with chocolate-brown centres appear in succession from late spring to mid-summer above a spreading mound of grey-green leaves. H 30cm (12in) S 30cm (12in).
Aspect: sun
Hardiness: ❀❀❀ Zones: 7–8

Helianthemum 'Henfield Brilliant'
Bright-red, cup-shaped flowers are

Helianthemum 'Wisley Pink'

produced from late spring to mid-summer above a spreading mound of grey-green leaves. H 30cm (12in) S 30cm (12in).
Aspect: sun
Hardiness: ❀❀❀ Zones: 7–8

Helianthemum 'Wisley Pink'
Clear rose flowers are produced from late spring to mid-summer above a spreading mound of grey-green leaves. H 30cm (12in) S 45cm (18in).
Aspect: sun
Hardiness: ❀❀❀ Zones: 7–8

Helianthemum 'Wisley Primrose'
Primrose-yellow flowers with golden-yellow centres are produced from late spring to mid-summer above a spreading mound of grey-green leaves. H 30cm (12in) S 45cm (18in).
Aspect: sun
Hardiness: ❀❀❀ Zones: 7–8

Helianthemum

Hibiscus rosa-sinensis 'The President'

HIBISCUS

This large genus of over 200 species includes the exotic-looking shrubs featured here, grown for their eyecatching, colourful, trumpet-shaped, late-summer flowers. Useful for creating a tropical feel to a sunny corner or patio.

Cultivation In the garden, grow in a moisture-retentive, well-drained neutral to slightly alkaline soil that is reasonably fertile in full sun. In containers, use a soil-based compost (soil mix), water regularly and feed monthly during the growing season. Water as necessary during winter months.

Pruning No routine pruning is necessary. Remove any frost-damaged growth during spring.

Propagation Take semi-ripe cuttings in mid-summer.

Hibiscus rosa-sinensis 'The President'
Chinese hibiscus
Huge, red, ruffled-edged flowers with darker eyes across (up to 18cm/7in), are produced from mid-summer to early autumn. It is tender, so grow in a heated greenhouse or conservatory in cold areas (minimum temperature 10°C/ 50°F). H 3m (10ft) S 2m (6ft).
Aspect: sun
Hardiness: tender Zones: 9–10

Hibiscus syriacus 'Blue Bird'
(syn. *H. syriacus* 'Oiseau Bleu')
Violet-blue, trumpet-shaped flowers with a maroon eye (up to 8cm/3in across) are produced in succession from late summer to mid-autumn against lobed, dark green leaves. H 3m (10ft) S 2m (6ft).
Aspect: sun
Hardiness: ❀❀❀ Zones: 7–8

Hibiscus syriacus 'Woodbridge'
Large, deep pink, trumpet-shaped flowers with a maroon eye (up to 10cm/4in across) are produced in succession from late summer to mid-autumn against lobed, dark green leaves. H 3m (10ft) S 2m (6ft).
Aspect: sun
Hardiness: ❀❀❀ Zones: 7–8

HYDRANGEA

A genus of about 80 species, including the summer-flowering deciduous shrubs featured here, that are also grown for their autumn tints and winter seed-heads. Hydrangeas make useful border fillers where their late-summer displays can be appreciated.

Cultivation Grow in a moisture-retentive, well-drained reasonably fertile soil in full sun or dappled shade. Add plenty of organic matter to the soil before planting and mulch annually so that plants do not run short of moisture during the summer months. On shallow, chalky soils, some varieties show signs of chlorosis.

Pruning No pruning is necessary. Remove dead flower-heads in early spring. Remove any frost-damaged growth in spring.

Propagation Take softwood cuttings of deciduous varieties in early summer or mid-summer or hardwood cuttings in late autumn. Take semi-ripe cuttings of evergreen varieties in late summer.

Hydrangea arborescens 'Annabelle' Sevenbark
Large heads of creamy-white flowers are produced from mid-summer to early autumn. Pointed, dark green leaves. H 2.5m (8ft) S 2.5m (8ft).
Aspect: sun or semi-shade
Hardiness: ❀❀❀ Zones: 7–8

Hydrangea macrophylla 'Blue Wave'
From mid-summer to late summer flattened heads of dark blue to mauve flowers (lilac-pink on chalky soils) are produced above a mound of coarsely toothed, lustrous, dark green leaves on this lacecap hydrangea. H 2m (6ft) S 2.5m (8ft).
Aspect: sun or semi-shade
Hardiness: ❀❀❀ Zones: 7–8

Hydrangea macrophylla 'Mariesii'
A rounded, lacecap hydrangea with coarsely toothed, glossy, dark green leaves that is covered in flattened heads of pale-blue flowers (rose-pink on chalky soils) from mid-summer to late summer. H 1.2m (4ft) S 1.2m (4ft).
Aspect: sun or semi-shade
Hardiness: ❀❀❀ Zones: 7–8

Hydrangea macrophylla 'Veitchii'
This is a lacecap hydrangea that bears large, somewhat flattened, heads of blue, pink and white flowers that darken to red with age from mid-summer to late summer. It is an ideal plant for a shady site. H 1.2m (4ft) S 1.2m (4ft).
Aspect: sun or semi-shade
Hardiness: ❀❀❀ Zones: 7–8

Hydrangea paniculata 'Floribunda'
This upright shrub has toothed, dark green leaves with white flower-heads that become pinkish in late summer and early autumn H 4m (13ft) S 2.5m (8ft).
Aspect: sun or semi-shade
Hardiness: ❀❀❀ Zones: 7–8

Hydrangea paniculata 'Tardiva'
A later bloomer, the 23cm- (9in-) white-coloured panicles begin to turn blush pink in autumn as the leaves begin to turn in mid-autumn. The dark green foliage is hairy to the touch. This can grow into a big plant if not pruned to remain contained. H 4m (13ft) S 2.5m (8ft).
Aspect: semi-shade
Hardiness: ❀❀❀ Zones: 7–8

Hydrangea quercifolia
White flowers that fade to pink are produced in conical clusters from mid-summer to early autumn. The foliage turns shades of bronze-purple in autumn. H 2m (6ft) S 2.5m (8ft).
Named varieties: 'Snow Queen', brilliant white conical flower clusters that fade to pink with age. H 2m (6ft) S 2m (6ft).
Aspect: sun or semi-shade
Hardiness: ❀❀❀ Zones: 7–8

Hydrangea serrata 'Bluebird'
(syn. *H.* 'Acuminata')
A lacecap hydrangea that bears flattened heads of blue flowers (they appear as pink when grown on alkaline soil) from early summer to early autumn. It makes a compact mound of pointed green leaves that dramatically turn shades of red in autumn. Surprisingly resistant to drought. H 1.2m (4ft) S 1.2m (4ft).
Aspect: sun or semi-shade
Hardiness: ❀❀❀ Zones: 7–8

Hydrangea arborescens 'Annabelle'

Hydrangea paniculata 'Tardiva'

Hydrangea villosa (syn. *H. aspera* Villosa Group)

Flattened heads of dark blue flowers are produced throughout late summer and early autumn against lance-shaped dark-green leaves on this upright shrub. H 3m (10ft) S 3m (10ft).
Aspect: sun or semi-shade
Hardiness: ❀❀❀ Zones: 7–8

HYPERICUM
St John's wort

This huge genus of more than 400 species contains the long-flowering shrubs featured here. Tough and easy to grow, they are ideal for covering dry banks and shady corners where little else will grow. In fertile soil they can be invasive.
Cultivation Grow in a well-drained soil that is reasonably fertile in full sun or dappled shade.
Pruning Keep plants in good shape by cutting back one stem in three to near ground level in mid-spring, starting with the oldest stems. Cut *Hypericum calycinum* right back to ground level each spring.
Propagation Take semi-ripe cuttings in early summer or mid-summer.

Hypericum 'Hidcote'

A semi-evergreen bushy shrub with pointed leaves that are decorated by large, cup-shaped, golden-yellow flowers produced in succession from mid-summer to early autumn. H 1.2m (4ft) S 1.5m (5ft).
Aspect: sun or semi-shade
Hardiness: ❀❀❀ Zone: 7–8

Hypericum calycinum
Rose of Sharon

A dwarf, vigorously spreading evergreen shrub with lance-shaped leaves that is covered in saucer-shaped bright yellow flowers, which are produced in succession from early summer to early autumn. Can be invasive, but makes excellent ground cover in shade. H 1.2m (4ft) S 3m (10ft).
Aspect: sun to shade
Hardiness: ❀❀❀ Zones: 7–8

Hypericum x moserianum 'Tricolor' (syn. *H.* 'Variegatum')

An attractive flowering shrub with green-and-white variegated foliage and distinct red margins. Grow only in shady areas as strong sunlight can scorch the foliage. Cup-shaped yellow flowers are produced from early summer to early autumn. H 30cm (12in) S 60cm (24in).
Aspect: semi-shade
Hardiness: ❀❀❀ Zones: 7–9

ILEX
Holly

This huge genus of over 400 species, including the large shrubs featured here, are grown for their handsome, evergreen foliage and colourful berries that appear in the winter, and greatly help in keeping the wildlife fed. These shrubs are very useful for using as specimens as they take well to being trimmed to form dense, slow-growing hedges or more eyecatching topiary.

Hypericum 'Hidcote'

Cultivation Grow in a moisture-retentive, well-drained soil that is reasonably fertile in full sun or dappled shade. Grow variegated varieties in sun for the best leaf coloration. Make sure you get a female variety if you want berries.
Pruning No routine pruning is necessary. All-green shoots on variegated varieties should be removed as soon as they are noticed. Trim hedges and topiary in late spring.
Propagation Take semi-ripe cuttings in late summer or early autumn.

Ilex x altaclerensis 'Golden King' (female form)

This compact evergreen carries a small crop of red autumn berries that stand out from the brilliant, yellow-edged, glossy, grey-green, spiny leaves. Good for hedging. H 6m (20ft) S 5m (16ft).
Aspect: sun or semi-shade
Hardiness: ❀❀❀ Zones: 7–8

Ilex aquifolium 'Argentea Marginata' (syn. *I. aquifolium* 'Argentea Variegata') (female form)

Thick and spiny, glossy, silver-edged, dark green leaves emerge pink-tinged. Brilliant red berries are produced *en masse* in autumn and last well into winter. This holly is a useful shrub for urban or coastal gardens as it copes well with pollution and salt-laden air. Good for hedging. H 14m (46ft) S 5m (16ft).
Aspect: sun or semi-shade
Hardiness: ❀❀❀ Zones 6–10

Ilex aquifolium 'Ferox Argentea' (male form)

A slow-growing upright shrub with cream-edged, leathery, dark green leaves that are covered with spines. No berries. H 8m (26ft) S 4m (13ft).
Aspect: sun or semi-shade
Hardiness: ❀❀❀ Zones: 7–8

Ilex aquifolium 'Golden Queen' (syn. *I. aquifolium* 'Aurea Regina') (male form)

A fruitless male variety of common English holly with spiny-edged dark green leaves that are decoratively splashed with gold. H 10m (33ft) S 6m (20ft).
Aspect: sun or semi-shade
Hardiness: ❀❀❀ Zones: 7–8

Ilex aquifolium 'J.C. van Tol' (female form)

The lustrous, dark green leaves on dark purple stems are almost prickle-free. Masses of bright red berries are produced from autumn and into winter. Good for hedging. H 6m (20ft) S 4m (13ft).
Aspect: sun or semi-shade
Hardiness: ❀❀❀ Zones: 7–8

Ilex aquifolium 'Silver Queen' (syn. *I. aquifolium* 'Silver King') (male form)

This slow-growing male variety of holly carries cream-edged, spiny, dark green leaves that emerge pink-tinged on purple stems. It does not produce berries. Good for a large pot. H 10m (33ft) S 4m (13ft).
Aspect: sun or semi-shade
Hardiness: ❀❀❀ Zones: 7–8

Ilex 'J. C. van Tol'

Indigofera amblyantha

Itea ilicifolia

INDIGOFERA

A huge genus of over 700 species, including the exotic deciduous shrubs featured here, valued for their sprays of pink, pea-like late-summer flowers. Excellent choice for growing as a wall shrub. It is very late coming into leaf and so is ideal for under-planting with spring-flowering bulbs and bedding or pairing it with an early flowering climber.

Cultivation Grow in a moisture-retentive, well-drained soil that is reasonably fertile in full sun.

Pruning No routine pruning is necessary. Frost-damaged growth should be removed in spring. If grown as a wall shrub, prune back new growth from the established framework by about two-thirds in mid-spring to late spring.

Propagation Take softwood cuttings in mid-spring or semi-ripe cuttings in mid-summer.

Indigofera amblyantha
Delicate-looking deciduous shrub with light green leaflets. Slender, arching flower-spikes of pea-like, shrimp-pink flowers are produced from mid-summer to early autumn. H 2m (6ft) S 2.5m (8ft).
Aspect: sun
Hardiness: ❋❋❋ Zones: 7–8

Indigofera heterantha (syn. I. gerardiana)
A spreading shrub with delicate-looking light green leaflets that provide a foil for the dense flower-spikes of pea-like,

purplish-pink flowers from early summer to early autumn. H 2.5m (8ft) S 2.5m (8ft).
Aspect: sun
Hardiness: ❋❋❋ Zones: 7–8

ITEA

A genus of some 10 species grown for its handsome foliage and dramatic catkin-like late-summer flowers. It is a useful shrub for growing against sheltered walls and fences. It can also be grown in a large, permanent container, but you will need to wrap up both the top-growth and the container during the winter in colder gardens.

Cultivation Grow in a moisture-retentive, well-drained soil that is reasonably fertile in full sun, but sheltered from cold winds.

Pruning No routine pruning is necessary. Any frost-damaged growth should be removed in spring.

Propagation Take semi-ripe cuttings in mid-summer.

Itea ilicifolia
This shrub has lustrous, dark green, holly-like leaves that provide the perfect backdrop for the 30cm- (12in-) long catkins of vanilla-scented, greenish-white flowers borne throughout late summer and early autumn. Although the shrub is frost hardy, it will require siting where it will get the protection of a sunny wall or fence in colder areas. H 5m (16ft) S 3m (10ft).
Aspect: sun
Hardiness: ❋❋ Zone: 9

JASMINUM
Jasmine

A large genus of over 200 species, including the useful wall shrubs featured here, grown for their often fragrant flowers. An excellent choice for providing winter colour near to a well-used entrance or path. It can be allowed to sprawl over banks, or be trained up walls and fences where space is limited.

Cultivation Grow in a well-drained soil that is reasonably fertile in full sun or dappled shade.

Pruning Keep established plants in good shape by cutting back one stem in three to near ground level in mid-spring, starting with the oldest stems.

Propagation Take semi-ripe cuttings in mid-summer. Layer suitable stems in early autumn.

Jasminum humile 'Revolutum' (syn. J. reevesii)
A semi-evergreen bushy, spreading shrub with bright green leaves that is exceptionally long-flowering, producing its pretty yellow fragrant flowers in succession from late spring to early autumn. H 2.5m (8ft)

S 3m (10ft).
Aspect: sun or semi-shade
Hardiness: ❋❋ Zone: 9

Jasminum nudiflorum
Winter jasmine
A popular deciduous shrub with bright green arching shoots that are decorated by unscented yellow trumpet flowers from late autumn to late winter before the dark green leaves emerge in spring. H 3m (10ft) S 3m (10ft).
Aspect: sun or semi-shade
Hardiness: ❋❋❋ Zones: 7–8

JUSTICIA

A huge genus of over 400 species, including the tender evergreen shrub featured here, they are grown for their exotic-looking, late-summer flowers. This is an ideal, flamboyant border shrub in mild gardens or can be grown as a conservatory or greenhouse exotic in colder areas.

Cultivation In the garden, grow in a moisture-retentive, well-drained garden soil that is reasonably fertile in dappled shade, but protected from cold winds. In containers, grow in a soil-based compost (soil mix). Feed every

Jasminum nudiflorum

Justicia carnea

month throughout the growing season and water as necessary. Move to a warm spot undercover when the temperature falls below 7°C (45°F) and water sparingly during the winter.
Pruning No routine pruning is required. Pinch out the growing tips of shoots to keep the shrub compact.
Propagation Take softwood cuttings in late spring or semi-ripe cuttings in mid-summer.

Justicia carnea (syn. *Jacobinia carnea*, *Justicia pohliana*) Flamingo plant

A stiffly branching evergreen shrub with leathery green leaves and flamboyant conical clusters of tubular, lipped, rose-pink flowers from mid-summer to early autumn. H 2m (6ft) S 1m (3ft).
Aspect: semi-shade
Hardiness: tender Zone: 10+

KALMIA

This genus contains around five species, including the evergreen shrubs featured here, grown for their bright pink early summer flowers. An excellent seasonal focal point and border filler if you can provide the right growing conditions. Elsewhere, they can be grown in larger, permanent containers.
Cultivation In the garden, grow in a moisture-retentive, well-drained acid soil in sun or dappled shade. In containers, grow in ericaceous compost (soil mix). Feed monthly during the growing season and water as and when necessary.

Pruning No routine pruning is required. Neglected shrubs can be smartened up and reduced in size by cutting back one stem in three to near ground level in mid-spring, starting with the oldest stems first.
Propagation Take softwood cuttings in late spring or semi-ripe cuttings in mid-summer. Suitable shoots can be layered in mid-spring.

Kalmia angustifolia f. *rubra*

This mound-forming, evergreen shrub has dark green leaves and is covered in clusters of dark rosy-red, saucer-shaped flowers that appear throughout early summer. H 60cm (24in) S 150cm (60in).
Aspect: sun or semi-shade
Hardiness: ❋❋❋ Zones: 7–8

Kalmia latifolia 'Ostbo Red'

Clusters of bright red buds open to reveal pale-pink saucer-shaped flowers from late spring to mid-summer on this mound-forming evergreen shrub with dark green leaves. H 3m (10ft) S 3m (10ft).
Aspect: sun or semi-shade
Hardiness: ❋❋❋ Zones: 7–8

KERRIA

A genus of just one species of deciduous suckering shrubs that bear golden-yellow late-spring flowers. Easy to grow, it is an ideal choice for the first-time gardener and is ideal for filling gaps at the back of a border.
Cultivation Grow in well-drained

Kalmia latifolia

soil that is reasonably fertile in sun or dappled shade.
Pruning You can encourage a continuous supply of flowering shoots by cutting back one stem in three to near ground level in early summer, starting with the oldest stems. Remove any all-green reverted shoots on variegated varieties as soon as they are noticed.
Propagation Take hardwood cuttings in late autumn. Rooted suckers can be separated in mid-spring.

Kerria japonica 'Golden Guinea'

Masses of large, single, golden-yellow flowers are produced in succession on graceful arching stems during early spring and mid-spring on this upright shrub. H 2m (6ft) S 2.5m (8ft).
Aspect: sun or semi-shade
Hardiness: ❋❋❋ Zones: 7–8

Kerria japonica 'Picta' (syn. *K. japonica* 'Variegata')

The sharply toothed cream-and-green variegated foliage on this compact and less invasive shrub is a good choice for the smaller garden. Single golden yellow flowers are produced during early spring and mid-spring. H 1m (3ft) S 1.5m (5ft).
Aspect: sun or semi-shade
Hardiness: ❋❋❋ Zones: 7–8

Kerria japonica 'Pleniflora'

Pompon-like, double, golden-yellow early spring flowers are produced in succession during

Kerria japonica 'Golden Guinea'

Kolkwitzia amabilis 'Pink Cloud'

early spring and mid-spring on graceful arching stems with sharply toothed green leaves. Good wall shrub. H 3m (10ft) S 3m (10ft).
Aspect: sun or semi-shade
Hardiness: ❋❋❋ Zones: 7–8

KOLKWITZIA

A genus of just one species of deciduous suckering shrubs that bear masses of bell-shaped pink early summer flowers. It is an undemanding shrub that provides a useful splash of late spring colour when planted in a sunny border. It can also be used as a filler shrub in a mixed border or planted to grow up against walls and fences.
Cultivation Grow in any well-drained soil that is reasonably fertile in sun.
Pruning Encourage a continuous supply of flowering shoots by cutting back one stem in three to near ground level in early summer, starting with the oldest stems first.
Propagation Take semi-ripe cuttings in late summer. Rooted suckers can be separated in mid-spring.

Kolkwitzia amabilis 'Pink Cloud'

Masses of dark pink flowers are produced on arching stems during late spring and early summer. They appear against a backdrop of pointed dark green leaves that turn yellow in autumn. H 4m (13ft) S 3m (10ft).
Aspect: sun
Hardiness: ❋❋❋ Zones: 7–8

Lantana camara

LANTANA

This genus of about 150 species includes the long-flowering evergreen shrub featured here that is loved by butterflies and other beneficial insects. Ideal for growing as a specimen or in a sunny border, or in a large container in a heated conservatory or greenhouse in cold areas.

Cultivation In the garden, grow in any moisture-retentive, well-drained garden soil that is reasonably fertile and in full sun. In containers, grow in a soil-based compost (soil mix). Feed every month throughout the growing season and water as necessary. Move to a warm spot under cover when the temperature falls below 10°C (50°F) and water sparingly during the winter.

Pruning No routine pruning is necessary. Any damaged growth should be removed in spring. In the conservatory or greenhouse, prune back new growth on established plants to 10cm (4in) of the permanent framework during late winter.

Propagation Take semi-ripe cuttings in mid-summer.

Lantana camara
The attractively wrinkled dark green leaves of this tender evergreen shrub provide the perfect foil for clusters of vibrant flowers borne from late spring to late autumn in different colours ranging from white to pink. H 2m (6ft) S 2m (6ft).
Named varieties: 'Fabiola', pink and yellow flowers. H 2m (6ft)

S 2m (6ft). 'Goldmine' (syn. 'Mine d'Or'), bright yellow flowers. H 2m (6ft) S 2m (6ft). 'Radiation', red and orange flowers. H 2m (6ft) S 2m (6ft). 'Snow White', pure white flowers. H 2m (6ft) S 2m (6ft).
Aspect: sun
Hardiness: tender Zone: 10

LAVANDULA
Lavender

A genus of over 20 species, including the popular long-flowering, mostly fragrant and nectar-rich evergreen shrubs with aromatic foliage featured here. Lavender makes a useful specimen plant on the patio or in pots. The more compact varieties also make excellent low hedges. In the border, plant in groups of three or five for impact, although larger varieties can be used as single specimens. The flowers can also be used to make pot pouris.

Cultivation In the garden, grow in any well-drained garden soil that is reasonably fertile and in full sun. In colder regions, grow less hardy varieties in a sheltered position, protected from cold winds and excessive wet. In containers, grow in a soil-based compost (soil mix). Feed monthly throughout the growing season and water as necessary.

Pruning Trim off any flowering stems as they fade. Encourage bushy growth by trimming lightly before the new growth appears in the spring. Be careful not to cut back into old wood. Trim hedges lightly during early spring or mid-

spring to maintain shape.
Propagation Take semi-ripe cuttings in early autumn.

Lavandula angustifolia
Very fragrant purple flowers are produced in dense spikes from mid-summer to early autumn above a mound of grey-green aromatic foliage. Excellent for hedging and pot pourri. H 1m (3ft) S 1.2m (4ft).
Named varieties: 'Hidcote', dark violet flowers. H 60cm (24in) S 75cm (30in). 'Hidcote Pink', pale pink flowers. H 60cm (24in) S 75cm (30in). 'Lady', mauve-blue flowers. H 25cm (10in) S 25cm (10in). 'Loddon Pink', soft pink flowers. H 45cm (18in) S 60cm (24in). 'Munstead', purplish-blue flowers. H 45cm (18in) S 60cm (24in). 'Nana Alba', white flowers. H 30cm (12in) S 30cm (12in). 'Rosea', rose-pink flowers. H 75cm (30in) S 75cm (30in). 'Royal Purple', bluish-purple flowers. H 75cm (30in) S 75cm (30in).
Aspect: sun
Hardiness: ❀❀❀ Zones: 7–8

Lavandula 'Fathead'
French lavender
A recent introduction with very broad, almost rounded, midnight-purple flower-heads from late spring to mid-summer each topped by plum-purple wing-like bracts. Borderline hardy. H 40cm (16in) S 40cm (16in).
Aspect: sun
Hardiness: ❀❀❀ Zones: 7–8

Lavandula stoechas

Lavandula 'Helmsdale'
French lavender
Plump spikes of fragrant dark purple flowers topped by purple wing-like bracts are produced from late spring to mid-summer above a compact mound of grey-green aromatic foliage. Borderline hardy. H 60cm (24in) S 60cm (24in).
Aspect: sun
Hardiness: ❀❀❀ Zones: 7–8

Lavandula x intermedia 'Grappenhall'
Slightly fragrant purplish-blue flowers appear on slender spikes from mid-summer to late summer above large grey-green, aromatic leaves. It is only frost hardy, so it is best grown in a container and moved indoors in cold areas. H 1m (3ft) S 1.5m (5ft).
Aspect: sun
Hardiness: ❀❀ Zones: 9

Lavandula x intermedia 'Grosso'
Dense spikes of fragrant, deep violet flowers on slender stems are produced *en masse* from mid-summer to early autumn above a mound of grey-green aromatic foliage. H 30cm (12in) S 40cm (16in).
Aspect: sun
Hardiness: ❀❀❀

Lavandula stoechas 'Kew Red'
French lavender
A recent introduction with plump, fragrant, cerise-pink flower-heads that are borne from early summer to late summer, topped by pale pink wing-like bracts. Borderline

Lavandula angustifolia

hardy. H 60cm (24in) S 60cm (24in).
Aspect: sun
Hardiness: ✿✿✿ Zones: 7–8

Lavandula stoechas 'Papillon'
French lavender

Tufted spikes of lavender-purple flowers, with long, wing-like bracts, are produced during early summer and mid-summer above a mound of grey-green aromatic foliage. Borderline hardy. H 60cm (24in) S 60cm (24in).
Aspect: sun
Hardiness: ✿✿✿ Zones: 7–8

Lavandula stoechas 'Rocky Road'
French lavender

A new variety that bears goblet-shaped purple flower-spikes topped by large, pale-violet, wing-like bracts from mid-summer to late summer above a mound of grey-green aromatic foliage. Borderline hardy. H 50cm (20in) S 50cm (20in).
Aspect: sun
Hardiness: ✿✿✿ Zones: 7–8

Lavandula stoechas 'Snowman'
French lavender

Slender spikes of white flowers, topped by snow-white wing-like bracts throughout early summer and mid-summer above a mound of grey-green aromatic foliage. Only frost hardy, so best grown in a pot and moved indoors in cold areas. H 60cm (24in) S 60cm (24in).
Aspect: sun
Hardiness: ✿✿ Zones: 7–8

LAVATERA

A genus of about 25 species, including the fast-growing, deciduous summer-flowering shrubs featured here, grown for their speed of growth and eye-catching, hibiscus-like, trumpet-shaped flowers. Quick to establish and flowering well, they are ideal for new borders. They also make useful gap fillers.
Cultivation Grow in any well-drained garden soil (preferably sandy) that is reasonably fertile and in full sun. In colder regions, protect from cold winds.
Pruning For best flowering, cut back all stems to within a few centimetres of ground level in

mid-spring. Remove reverted shoots with the wrong colour flowers.
Propagation Take semi-ripe cuttings in mid-summer. Take hardwood cuttings in late autumn.

Lavatera x clementii 'Barnsley'

Large white blooms, each with a red eye, are produced from early summer to early autumn. The blooms gracefully age to pale pink. H 2m (6ft) S 2m (6ft).
Aspect: sun
Hardiness: ✿✿✿ Zones: 7–8

Lavatera x clementii 'Burgundy Wine'

A succession of dark pink flowers that are attractively veined are produced from early summer to early autumn on this compact variety with dark foliage. H 1.5m (5ft) S 1.5m (5ft).
Aspect: sun
Hardiness: ✿✿✿ Zones: 7–8

Lavatera x clementii 'Kew Rose'

A succession of attractively veined, frilly, dark pink blooms appear from early summer to early autumn. H 2m (6ft) S 2m (6ft).
Aspect: sun
Hardiness: ✿✿✿ Zones: 7–8

Lavatera olbia 'Rosea' (syn. L. x clementii 'Rosea')

A succession of large dark pink blooms are produced from early summer to early autumn on this vigorous-growing variety. H 2m (6ft) S 2m (6ft).
Aspect: sun
Hardiness: ✿✿✿ Zones: 7–8

Lavatera

LEPTOSPERMUM

A genus of about 80 species, including the slightly tender, early summer flowering shrub featured here. It makes a good back-of-the-border seasonal focal point.
Cultivation In the garden, grow in any well-drained garden soil that is reasonably fertile and in full sun or dappled shade. In colder regions, grow in pots of soil-based compost. Feed monthly and water as necessary during the growing season. Before frosts, move under cover, stop feeding and water sparingly in winter.
Pruning No routine pruning is required.
Propagation Take semi-ripe cuttings in mid-summer.

Leptospermum scoparium 'Red Damask'

A compact shrub with arching stems and narrow, pointed, aromatic, green leaves. During late spring and early summer it is covered in masses of double, dark red flowers. H 3m (10ft) S 3m (10ft).
Aspect: sun or semi-shade
Hardiness: ✿ Zone: 10

LEUCOTHOE

A genus of about 50 species, including the versatile evergreen shrub featured here, that are grown for their eye-catching foliage and clusters of pretty, urn-shaped spring flowers. They are ideal for a shady shrub or mixed border that offers suitable growing conditions. It can also be used as a deep

Leptospernum

Leucothoe fontanesiana 'Rainbow'

groundcover plant between deciduous trees in a woodland-edge planting.
Cultivation Grow in any moisture-retentive, well-drained acid soil in deep or dappled shade. Add plenty of organic matter (but not alkaline mushroom compost/soil mix) to the soil before planting.
Pruning To get the best foliage displays and maintain a compact shape, cut back one stem in three to near ground level during mid-spring, starting with the oldest stems first.
Propagation Layer low branches in early spring or take semi-ripe cuttings in late summer.

Leucothoe fontanesiana 'Rainbow'

A spectacular shrub with glossy, lance-shaped, dark green variegated foliage splashed with cream and pink. A bonus of white, urn-shaped flowers are produced in clusters during mid-spring and late spring. H 1.5m (5ft) S 2m (6ft).
Aspect: semi-shade or deep shade
Hardiness: ✿✿✿ Zones: 7–8

Leucothoe fontanesiana 'Scarletta'

Although first emerging red-purple, the dark evergreen foliage turns bronze during the winter. A bonus of white, urn-shaped flowers are produced in clusters during early spring and mid-spring. H 150cm (60in) S 40cm (16in).
Aspect: semi-shade or deep shade
Hardiness: ✿✿✿

Leycesteria formosa

Ligustrum lucidum 'Tricolor'

LEYCESTERIA

A genus of about five species, including the fast-growing and suckering deciduous shrub featured here, that is grown for its unusual pendent, Chinese-lantern-shaped bracts, tipped with summer flowers, followed by autumn berries. A useful shrub for extending the season of interest in the garden and for filling a space at the back of a border.

Cultivation Grow in any well-drained garden soil that is reasonably fertile and site in full sun or dappled shade. In colder regions, these shrubs need to be protected from cold winds. In addition, you will need to cover the roots with a deep insulating mulch, which should be applied during the autumn.

Pruning For best flowering performance, cut back one stem in three to near ground level during mid-spring, starting with the oldest stems.

Propagation Take softwood cuttings in early summer or take hardwood cuttings in late autumn.

Leycesteria formosa
Himalayan honeysuckle

Long-lasting clusters of pendent, wine-coloured bracts, tipped with white flowers, are produced in succession from mid-summer to early autumn, followed by eye-catching purple berries. Borderline hardy. H 2m (6ft) S 2m (6ft).
Aspect: sun or semi-shade
Hardiness: ❀❀❀ Zones: 7–8

LIGUSTRUM
Privet

This genus of about 50 species includes the deciduous and evergreen shrubs featured here, grown for their foliage and dense growing habit. These shrubs are very useful back-of-the-border fillers and make very popular hedging plants.

Cultivation Grow in any well-drained garden soil that is reasonably fertile and in full sun or dappled shade. However, for best foliage coloration, grow in full sun.

Pruning No routine pruning is necessary. Clip occasionally to maintain the plant's shape or to keep it compact. Neglected or overgrown plants can be rejuvenated by cutting back all the stems to within 10cm (4in) of ground level. All-green reverted shoots on variegated varieties should be removed completely when they are noticed. Trim hedges into shape in late spring and early autumn.

Propagation Take semi-ripe cuttings in mid-summer or take hardwood cuttings in late autumn.

Ligustrum japonicam '**Rotundifolium**'

A compact and slow-growing evergreen with glossy, dark green, leathery leaves. Insignificant white flowers are produced in mid-summer and late summer. H 1.5m (5ft) S 1m (3ft).
Aspect: sun or semi-shade
Hardiness: ❀❀❀ Zones: 7–8

Ligustrum lucidum '**Excelsum Superbum**'

A variegated evergreen with cream-edged, bright green leaves. Insignificant white flowers are produced in late summer and early autumn. H 10m (33ft) S 10m (33ft).
Aspect: sun or semi-shade
Hardiness: ❀❀❀ Zones: 7–8

Ligustrum lucidum '**Tricolor**'

A variegated evergreen with white-edged, grey-green leaves that emerge pink-tinged. Insignificant white flowers are produced in late summer and early autumn. H 10m (33ft) S 10m (33ft).
Aspect: sun or semi-shade
Hardiness: ❀❀❀ Zones: 7–8

Ligustrum ovalifolium

The glossy, dark green, evergreen foliage of the oval leaf privet makes an excellent hedge in urban areas as it is particularly pollution-tolerant. Insignificant white flowers are produced in mid-summer and late summer, followed by shiny black berries. H 4m (13ft) S 4m (13ft).
Aspect: sun or semi-shade
Hardiness: ❀❀❀ Zones: 7–8

Ligustrum ovalifolium '**Aureum**' (syn. *L. ovalifolium* '**Aureomarginatum**') **Golden privet**

The yellow-margined, broad green leaves are retained all winter in all but the coldest of gardens. Makes a useful hedge in urban areas as it is particularly pollution-tolerant. Insignificant white flowers are produced in mid-summer and late summer, followed by shiny black berries. H 4m (13ft) S 4m (13ft).
Aspect: sun or semi-shade
Hardiness: ❀❀❀ Zones: 7–8

LONICERA

A varied genus of over 180 species, including the deciduous and evergreen shrubs featured here, grown for either its fragrant winter flowers or colourful evergreen leaves. Plant winter-flowering varieties with fragrant blooms next to much-used paths and sheltered entrances, where they will be appreciated most. Evergreen types make excellent border fillers or edging plants and can be trimmed into low hedges.

Cultivation Grow in any well-drained garden soil that is

Lonicera nitida 'Baggesen's Gold'

reasonably fertile and in full sun or dappled shade. For best foliage coloration, grow in full sun.
Pruning Flowering shrubby honeysuckles require no routine pruning. Neglected specimens can be rejuvenated by cutting back one stem in three to near ground level after flowering, starting with the oldest stems. Small-leaved, evergreen varieties need to be trimmed in mid-spring to maintain a compact shape.
Propagation Take semi-ripe cuttings in mid-summer or take hardwood cuttings in late autumn.

Lonicera fragrantissima
A bushy, semi-evergreen shrub that bears scented, creamy-white flowers on naked stems during mild spells in mid-winter and early spring. Plant next to an entrance or path to appreciate its fragrant winter flowers. H 2m (6ft) S 3m (10ft).
Aspect: sun or semi-shade
Hardiness: ❀❀❀ Zones: 7–8

Lonicera nitida 'Baggesen's Gold'
Arching shoots are covered in masses of tiny golden leaves on this fast-growing, bushy evergreen. Insignificant, creamy-white flowers are produced in mid-spring. Ideal for trimming into a low hedge or garden topiary. H 1.5m (5ft) S 1.5m (5ft).
Aspect: sun or semi-shade
Hardiness: ❀❀❀ Zones: 7–8

Lonicera pileata
A low-growing, spreading, dense, evergreen shrub with glossy, dark green leaves. It also makes an excellent ground cover plant in urban areas as it is very pollution-tolerant. Insignificant, creamy-white flowers are produced in late spring followed by purple berries. H 60cm (24in) S 250cm (96in).
Aspect: sun or semi-shade
Hardiness: ❀❀❀ Zones: 7–8

Lonicera x purpusii 'Winter Beauty'
The bare branches of this shrubby honeysuckle carry clusters of highly fragrant, creamy-white flowers from early winter to early spring. Plant next to an entrance

or path to appreciate its fragrant winter flowers. H 2m (6ft) S 2.5m (8ft).
Aspect: sun or semi-shade
Hardiness: ❀❀❀ Zones: 7–8

MAGNOLIA
A genus of about 125 species, including the spectacular early-flowering deciduous shrubs featured here, many of which are compact enough for the smallest of gardens. Although they are grown for their flamboyant floral displays in spring, many varieties look good at other times – offering handsome foliage, autumn tints and attractive winter buds. Grow as seasonal focal points anywhere in the garden, even in large, permanent containers.
Cultivation In the garden, grow in well-drained garden neutral to acid soil that doesn't dry out in summer and is reasonably fertile. Star magnolias can tolerate slightly alkaline soils. All will grow in sun or partial shade where they are sheltered from cold winds. In containers, grow in a soil-based compost. Feed every fortnight throughout the growing season and water as necessary.
Pruning No routine pruning necessary.
Propagation Layer low-growing shoots in mid-spring.

Magnolia 'Heaven Scent'
An upright, deciduous magnolia that bears scented, goblet-shaped, pale pink flowers with white inside from mid-spring to early

Magnolia stellata

summer. This later flowering variety avoids most frosts. H 10m (33ft) S 10m (33ft).
Aspect: sun or semi-shade
Hardiness: ❀❀❀ Zones: 7–8

Magnolia x loebneri 'Leonard Messel'
A large, deciduous shrub with mid-green leaves that bears deep pink buds that open during mid-spring to reveal pale pink, star-shaped flowers. H 8m (26ft) S 8m (26ft).
Aspect: sun or semi-shade
Hardiness: ❀❀❀ Zones: 7–8

Magnolia x soulangeana
A spreading deciduous shrub that has large dark green leaves bearing white to rose-pink flowers on branches during mid-spring and late spring as the leaves start to emerge. H 6m (20ft) S 6m (20ft).

Named varieties: 'Alba' (syn. *M. x soulangeana* 'Alba Superba'), large, fragrant, white flowers that are pink-flushed at the base. H 6m (20ft) S 6m (20ft). 'Lennei', dark pinkish-purple, goblet-shaped flowers. H 6m (20ft) S 6m (20ft).
Aspect: sun or semi-shade
Hardiness: ❀❀❀ Zones: 7–8

Magnolia stellata Star magnolia
Silky buds open on bare branches during early spring and mid-spring to reveal lightly scented, white, star-shaped flowers. A compact, bushy, deciduous shrub that is ideal for small gardens. H 3m (10ft) S 3m (10ft).
Named varieties: 'Rosea', rose-pink star-shaped flowers. H 3m (10ft) S 4m (13ft). 'Royal Star', pink-flushed buds open into white, star-shaped flowers. H 3m (10ft) S 4m (13ft). 'Waterlily', white, waterlily-like flowers. H 3m (10ft) S 4m (13ft).
Aspect: sun or semi-shade
Hardiness: ❀❀❀ Zones: 7–8

Magnolia 'Susan'
A bushy, upright shrub, 'Susan' produces beautiful dark red flowering buds that open from mid-spring to early summer to reveal slim, goblet-shaped, fragrant, purple blooms with slightly twisted petals. It makes a glorious deciduous magnolia for a small garden with acidic soil. H 4m (13ft) S 3m (10ft).
Aspect: sun or semi-shade
Hardiness: ❀❀❀ Zones: 7–8

Magnolia 'Susan'

Mahonia aquifolium 'Apollo'

MAHONIA

This genus of about 70 species includes the winter-flowering evergreen shrubs featured here. They make useful architectural specimens and border fillers to provide winter interest or can be pruned to form ground cover.

Cultivation Grow in any moisture-retentive, well-drained garden soil that is reasonably fertile. Position the shrub in full sun or dappled shade.

Pruning No routine pruning is required for this shrub. However, straggly plants can be renovated by pruning back hard in mid-spring. Plants grown for ground cover should be cut back hard in mid-spring.

Propagation Take semi-ripe cuttings in late summer.

Mahonia aquifolium 'Apollo'

A compact shrub that bears masses of large, fragrant, yellow flowers on densely packed spikes from late winter to mid-spring. The holly-like leaves are tinged red in winter. A good ground cover plant between deciduous trees in a woodland-edge planting. H 1m (3ft) S 1m (3ft).
Aspect: sun or semi-shade
Hardiness: ❊❊❊ Zones: 7–8

Mahonia japonica Bealei Group

Handsome whorls of blue-green, holly-like leaves provide year-round interest topped by upright sprays of fragrant, pale yellow flowers from early winter to early spring. H 2m (6ft) S 3m (10ft).
Aspect: sun or semi-shade
Hardiness: ❊❊❊ Zones: 7–8

Mahonia x media 'Buckland'

Long, arching, fragrant sprays of bright yellow flowers are produced from early winter to mid-spring above handsome evergreen holly-like leaves. H 5m (16ft) S 4m (13ft).
Aspect: sun or semi-shade
Hardiness: ❊❊❊ Zones: 7–8

Mahonia x media 'Charity'

Upright spreading sprays of fragrant lemon-yellow flowers are produced from late autumn to early spring, above whorls of dark green holly-like foliage. H 5m (15ft) S 4m (12ft).
Aspect: sun or semi-shade
Hardiness: ❊❊❊ Zones: 7–8

Mahonia x media 'Lionel Fortescue'

Dense cluster of scented bright yellow flowers are produced from late autumn to early spring on upright spikes above dark green, holly-like leaves. H 5m (16ft) S 4m (13ft).
Aspect: sun or semi-shade
Hardiness: ❊❊❊ Zones: 7–8

MYRTUS
Myrtle

A genus of just two species, including the common myrtle featured here, that are grown for their sweetly scented summer flowers and aromatic, glossy, evergreen foliage. It is a useful plant for a mixed or shrub border, but it can also make an unusual, informal flowering hedge.

Cultivation Grow in any moisture-retentive, well-drained garden soil that is reasonably fertile and in full sun. Grow against a warm, sunny wall in colder areas. Mulch in spring and insulate from cold, drying winds in winter.

Pruning No routine pruning is required. Any frost-damaged growth should be removed in spring.

Propagation Take semi-ripe cuttings in late summer.

Myrtus communis

A handsome upright and bushy evergreen shrub with very aromatic leaves. It bears fragrant, cup-shaped white flowers, each with prominent fluffy tufts of stamens in the centre, during mid-summer and late summer, followed by purple-black berries. H 3m (10ft) S 3m (10ft).
Named varieties: subsp. *tarentina* (syn. *M.* 'Jenny Reitenbach', *M.* 'Microphylla', *M.* 'Nana'), a compact variety with smaller leaves and flowers, followed by white berries. H 1.5m (5ft) S 1.5m (5ft).
Aspect: sun
Hardiness: ❊❊ Zones: 7–8

NANDINA

A genus of just one species of evergreen shrubs, grown for their handsome foliage and long-lasting autumn tints and berries. This bamboo lookalike is an excellent choice for winter interest.

Cultivation Grow in any moisture-retentive, well-drained garden soil that is reasonably fertile and in full sun, but sheltered from cold winds. Grow against a warm, sunny wall in colder areas.

Pruning No routine pruning is required. Neglected specimens can be rejuvenated by cutting back one stem in three to near ground level in mid-spring, starting with the oldest stems.

Propagation Divide the clump in early spring as you would a perennial, or take semi-ripe cuttings in mid-summer.

Nandina domestica 'Fire Power'
Heavenly bamboo

The handsome, bamboo-like leaves of this compact evergreen

Myrtus communis

Mahonia x media 'Charity'

Nandina domestica 'Fire Power'

take on fiery shades of orange and red in autumn. Clusters of tiny starry flowers are produced in mid-summer, followed by arching sprays of long-lasting bright red fruit. H 45cm (18in) S 60cm (24in).
Aspect: sun
Hardiness: ❊❊ Zones: 7–8

NERIUM
Oleander
A genus of just two species of tender evergreen flowering shrubs, grown for their colourful late summer blooms. In warm regions they make wonderful freestanding specimens, are valuable border fillers and can be grown as an informal flowering hedge. However, elsewhere they are best grown as wall shrubs where there are no winter frosts. In colder regions they can be planted in containers on the patio and moved undercover when the temperature threatens to fall below 5°C (41°F).
Cultivation Grow in any moisture-retentive, well-drained, reasonably fertile soil in full sun. Shelter from cold winds. In frost-prone areas, grow in pots and protect. Use a soil-based compost (soil mix), feed monthly and water as necessary. Stop feeding and water sparingly in winter.
Pruning Cut back flowering shoots by half as the flowers fade. Cut back non-flowering shoots to 10cm (4in) of the framework.
Propagation Air layer in mid-spring or take semi-ripe cuttings in mid-summer.

Nerium oleander
Rose bay
A spreading evergreen shrub with slender grey-green leaves that bears clusters of pink, red or white tubular flowers from early summer to mid-autumn. H 3m (10ft) S 2m (6ft).
Aspect: sun
Hardiness: tender Zones: 10+

OLEARIA
Daisy bush
This genus of about 130 species includes the evergreen summer-flowering shrubs featured here. All of those mentioned make useful border fillers and good hedges or windbreaks for coastal gardens, as they can tolerate strong winds and salt-laden air.
Cultivation These shrubs can be grown in any reasonably well-drained garden soil in full sun, but they need sheltering from cold winds.
Pruning No routine pruning is necessary. Cut back any dead shoots in mid-spring.
Propagation Take semi-ripe cuttings in mid-summer.

Olearia x haastii
During mid-summer and late summer masses of yellow-centred daisy-like flowers smother the branches of this dense, compact evergreen with glossy dark green leaves. H 2m (6ft) S 3m (10ft).
Aspect: sun
Hardiness: ❊❊❊ Zones: 7–8

Nerium oleander

Olearia ilicifolia
Mountain holly
A spreading bushy shrub with leathery, holly-like, grey-green leaves, that is covered in scented daisy-like white flowers during early summer. Borderline hardy. H 3m (10ft) S 3m (10ft).
Aspect: sun
Hardiness: ❊❊❊ Zones: 7–8

Olearia macrodonta
A vigorous upright shrub with holly-like glossy dark green leaves that are silvery underneath. During mid-summer and late summer the branches are smothered in masses of red-centred, daisy-like white flowers. Borderline hardy. H 6m (20ft) S 5m (16ft).
Aspect: sun
Hardiness: ❊❊❊ Zones: 7–8

OSMANTHUS
(syn. x *Osmarea*)
This genus of over 15 species, including the featured evergreen summer-flowering shrubs here, are grown for their highly scented, jasmine-like blooms. Plant them next to an entrance or path so that you can appreciate their early summer fragrance. Alternatively, smaller-growing osmanthus can be grown in a permanent container on the patio. They can even be grown as informal flowering hedges and trained as topiary.
Cultivation In the garden, grow in any well-drained garden soil that

Olearia x haastii

Osmanthus heterophyllus 'Tricolor'

is reasonably fertile and in full sun or dappled shade, sheltered from cold winds. When grown in containers, use a soil-based compost (soil mix), feed monthly and water as necessary during the growing season. Stop feeding and water sparingly in winter.
Pruning No routine pruning necessary.
Propagation Take semi-ripe cuttings in mid-summer or layer suitable shoots in mid-spring.

Osmanthus delavayi (syn. *Siphonosmanthus delavayi*)
A rounded evergreen with lustrous, dark grey-green, sharply toothed leaves covered in masses of scented white jasmine-like flowers during mid-spring and late spring. Good for hedging. H 6m (20ft) S 4m (13ft).
Aspect: sun or semi-shade
Hardiness: ❊❊❊ Zones: 7–8

Osmanthus heterophyllus 'Tricolor' (syn. *O. heterophyllus 'Goshiki'*)
An attractive evergreen with glossy, dark green, holly-like leaves that are a mottled creamy-yellow and pink as they emerge. From mid-summer to early autumn it bears a succession of delicate and fragrant white flowers. Plant in the shelter of a sunny wall in cold areas. Because of its small and compact shape, this shrub makes an excellent container plant. H 1.5m (5ft) S 1m (3ft).
Aspect: sun or semi-shade
Hardiness: ❊❊ Zones: 8–9

Pachysandra terminalis

Paeonia delavayi

PACHYSANDRA

A genus of about five species, including the low-growing, evergreen sub-shrub featured here, grown for their handsome foliage and pretty early summer flowers. It is a useful ground cover plant between shrubs and trees as well as the difficult areas by hedges.

Cultivation Grow in any well-drained garden soil that is reasonably fertile in dappled shade to deep shade.

Pruning No routine pruning is necessary. Rejuvenate neglected plants by cutting back to about 5cm (2in) off the ground in early spring.

Propagation Divide clumps as you would a perennial. Take softwood cuttings in early summer.

Pachysandra terminalis

The handsome, coarsely toothed, glossy dark green leaves of this spreading, evergreen sub-shrub are the perfect foil for the clusters of tiny white flowers produced during late spring and early summer. H 20cm (8in) S indefinite.

Aspect: semi-shade or deep shade
Hardiness: ❈❈❈ Zones: 7–8

PAEONIA
Peony

This genus contains over 30 species, including the woody-stemmed tree peonies featured here, grown for their showy late-spring flowers and attractive foliage. They make a spectacular seasonal focal point in a mixed border or shrubbery.

Cultivation Grow in any moisture-retentive, well-drained garden soil that is reasonably fertile in full sun or dappled shade, but shelter from cold winds and morning sun.

Pruning No routine pruning is necessary. Overgrown plants can be rejuvenated by cutting back one stem in three to near ground level during mid-spring, starting with the oldest stems.

Propagation Take semi-ripe cuttings in mid-summer. Air layer or layer suitable stems in early spring.

Paeonia delavayi

An upright shrub that bears single, cup-shaped, blood-red flowers from mid-spring to early summer above dark green leaves that emerge red-tinged in spring. H 2m (6ft) S 1.2m (4ft).

Aspect: sun or semi-shade
Hardiness: ❈❈❈ Zones: 7–8

Paeonia lutea var. ludlowii (syn P. delavayi var. ludlowii)

The large, bright yellow flowers of this upright tree peony are produced during mid-spring and late spring against lush apple-green foliage that emerges bronze-tinted in spring. H 2.5m (8ft) S 2.5m (8ft).

Aspect: sun or semi-shade
Hardiness: ❈❈❈ Zones: 7–8

Paeonia suffruticosa 'Duchess of Kent'

Tulip-shaped buds open to reveal deep rose-pink, semi-double, cup-shaped flowers. This plant flowers well from a young age.

H 2.2m (7ft) S 2.2m (7ft).
Aspect: sun or semi-shade
Hardiness: ❈❈❈ Zones: 7–8

Paeonia suffruticosa 'Duchess of Marlborough'

This shrub has huge, double, pale pink flowers with crinkle-edged petals that fade to silvery-white at the margins. H 2.2m (7ft) S 2.2m (7ft).

Aspect: sun or semi-shade
Hardiness: ❈❈❈ Zones: 7–8

Paeonia suffruticosa 'Mrs William Kelway'

This shrub has double white flowers with crinkle-edged petals and contrasting yellow anthers in the centre. H 2.2m (7ft) S 2.2m (7ft).

Aspect: sun or semi-shade
Hardiness: ❈❈❈ Zones: 7–8

Paeonia suffruticosa 'Reine Elisabeth'

An upright tree peony with dark green foliage tinged with blue underneath. Bears double, salmon-pink, frilly-edged blooms. H 2.2m (7ft) S 2.2m (7ft).

Aspect: sun or semi-shade
Hardiness: ❈❈❈ Zones: 7–8

PARROTIA

A genus of just one species of deciduous shrub that eventually develops a clear trunk to form a small tree. They are mainly grown for their dramatic, fiery autumn tints, but their handsome foliage, peeling bark and early spring

Parrotia persica

flowers make them year-round specimens for mixed borders, shrubberies or as a seasonal focal point.

Cultivation Grow in a moisture-retentive, well-drained acid soil in sun or dappled shade. Add plenty of organic matter (but not alkaline mushroom compost/soil mix) to the soil before planting. Although it will grow in neutral and even slightly alkaline soils, the autumn colour will not be as good.

Pruning No routine pruning is necessary. Remove damaged or misplaced branches in early spring.

Propagation Sow seed in early autumn or layer a suitable low branch during early autumn.

Parrotia persica
Persian ironwood

Attractive glossy green leaves transform in autumn as they take on fiery autumn tints in shades of amber, crimson, purple and gold. Established plants will produce curious, spidery-looking red flowers on bare stems during late autumn and early winter that complement the attractive peeling bark. H 8m (26ft) S 10m (33ft).

Named varieties: 'Pendula', weeping and compact so suitable for small gardens. H 1.5m (5ft) S 3m (10ft).

Aspect: sun or semi-shade
Hardiness: ❈❈❈ Zones: 7–8

PHILADELPHUS
Mock orange

A genus of about 40 species, including the deciduous shrubs featured here, grown for their orange blossom-scented early summer flowers and attractive foliage. They are also a good choice for town and coastal gardens as they tolerate urban pollution and salt-laden air.

Cultivation Grow in any well-drained garden soil that is reasonably fertile and in full sun or dappled shade.

Pruning For the best flowering, cut out one in three of the stems that have flowered – cutting back to a younger side branch – starting with the oldest stems. The young shoots that did not flower this year will flower next year.

Philadelphus 'Belle Etoile'

Propagation Take semi-ripe cuttings in early summer or take hardwood cuttings in late autumn.

Philadelphus 'Beauclerk'
A stiffly arching deciduous shrub that bears scented, cup-shaped, single white flowers that are flushed pink in the centre during early summer and mid-summer. H 2.5m (8ft) S 2.5m (8ft).
Aspect: sun or semi-shade
Hardiness: ❋❋❋ Zones: 7–8

Philadelphus 'Belle Etoile'
Very fragrant, single, cup-shaped white flowers with contrasting pinky-purple centres are carried throughout early summer and mid-summer on arching branches. H 1.2m (4ft) S 2.5m (8ft).
Aspect: sun or semi-shade
Hardiness: ❋❋❋ Zones: 7–8

Philadelphus coronarius 'Aureus'
Single, fragrant, creamy-white, cup-shaped flowers are carried throughout early summer on upright stems with golden-yellow leaves that become greenish-yellow in summer. Grow in dappled shade. H 2.5m (8ft) S 1.5m (5ft).
Aspect: semi-shade
Hardiness: ❋❋❋ Zones: 7–8

Philadelphus coronarius 'Variegatus'
Pure white, fragrant, cup-shaped flowers are carried throughout early summer on upright stems with white-edged, apple-green variegated foliage.

H 2.5m (8ft) S 2m (6ft).
Aspect: sun or semi-shade
Hardiness: ❋❋❋ Zones: 7–8

Philadelphus x *lemoinei* 'Lemoinei'
The arching branches of this upright mock orange are covered by masses of very fragrant clusters of single, cup-shaped white flowers throughout early summer and mid-summer. H 1.5m (5ft) S 1.5m (5ft).
Aspect: sun or semi-shade
Hardiness: ❋❋❋ Zones: 7–8

Philadelphus 'Manteau d'Hermine'
Elegantly arching shoots are festooned with very fragrant, double, creamy-white flowers throughout early summer and mid-summer on this compact, bushy, deciduous shrub. An ideal choice for a small garden. H 75cm (30in) S 150cm (60in).
Aspect: sun or semi-shade
Hardiness: ❋❋❋ Zones: 7–8

Philadelphus microphyllus
Single, white, fragrant, flowers are carried in clusters throughout early summer and mid-summer against a backdrop of glossy green leaves on this compact plant. H 1m (3ft) S 1m (3ft).
Aspect: sun or semi-shade
Hardiness: ❋❋❋ Zones: 7–8

Philadelphus 'Virginal'
Fully double, white, fragrant flowers festoon upright branches

throughout early summer and mid-summer on this vigorous mock orange. Its dark green leaves go yellow in autumn. H 3m (10ft) S 2.5m (8ft).
Aspect: sun or semi-shade
Hardiness: ❋❋❋

PHLOMIS
A genus of about 100 species, grown for their unusual tiered summer flowers on upright stems and woolly grey foliage.
Cultivation Grow in any well-drained garden soil that is reasonably fertile and in full sun. Grow in the protection of a sunny wall in colder areas.
Pruning In spring, cut back the previous year's growth to about 10cm (4in) of the ground as new shoots emerge from the base.
Propagation Take softwood cuttings in early summer, or semi-ripe cuttings in early autumn.

Phlomis fruticosa
A spreading evergreen shrub, with sage-like, aromatic, grey-green leaves that throws up vertical spikes that carry whorls of hooded, golden-yellow flowers in tiers throughout early summer and mid-summer. Borderline hardy. H 1m (3ft) S 1.5m (5ft).
Aspect: sun
Hardiness: ❋❋❋ Zones: 7–8

Phlomis italica
Upright spikes carry whorls of hooded lilac-pink flowers during early summer and mid-summer

above this compact evergreen shrub with silvery-grey woolly leaves. H 30cm (12in) S 60cm (24in).
Aspect: sun
Hardiness: ❋❋ Zone: 9

PHOENIX
A genus of over 15 species, including the tender miniature date palm featured here, grown for their handsome foliage. Ideal border plant in milder areas or for an exotic touch to the patio.
Cultivation Grow in a reasonably fertile, moisture-retentive, well-drained soil in full sun. In pots, use a soil-based compost, water regularly and feed monthly in the growing season. Water sparingly in winter. Needs protection if the temperature falls below 10°C (50°F) and water sparingly.
Pruning No routine pruning is necessary.
Propagation Sow seed in mid-spring.

Phoenix roebelenii
Miniature date palm
This stemless palm has narrow, dark green leaflets that are grey-green when young. Mature plants carry clusters of cream flowers in early summer and mid-summer, followed by edible black fruit. Move to a heated greenhouse or conservatory in cold areas (min 10°C/50°F) over winter. H 2m (6ft) S 2.5m (8ft).
Aspect: sun
Hardiness: tender Zones: 10+

Philadelphus 'Manteau d'Hermine'

Phlomis italica

Phoenix roebelenii

Photinia x *fraseri* 'Birmingham'

PHOTINIA

A genus of about 60 species grown for their colourful new shoots in spring. It is useful for adding much-needed colour to mixed borders and shrubberies early in the year and for providing an attractive foil at other times.

Cultivation Grow in any moisture-retentive, well-drained soil that is reasonably fertile and in full sun. Train against a sheltered, sunny wall in colder areas.

Pruning No routine pruning is necessary. Cut back straggly plants by about one-third to rejuvenate them and encourage more foliage.

Propagation Take semi-ripe cuttings in mid-summer.

Photinia x *fraseri* 'Birmingham'
Eye-catching purple-red young foliage is the main feature of this handsome evergreen shrub.

Photinia x *fraseri* 'Red Robin'

Clusters of insignificant white flowers are carried in mid-spring and late spring, followed by red berries. H 5m (16ft) S 5m (16ft).
Aspect: sun
Hardiness: ❄❄ Zone: 9

Photinia x *fraseri* 'Red Robin'
A compact evergreen shrub with brilliant red glossy young foliage and clusters of insignificant white flowers carried in mid-spring and late spring, followed by red berries. H 5m (16ft) S 5m (16ft).
Aspect: sun
Hardiness: ❄❄ Zone: 9

PHYGELIUS

A genus of just two species, grown for their elegant summer flowers. A good choice for adding late colour in borders.

Cultivation Grow in any reasonably fertile, moisture-retentive, well-drained soil in full sun. Shelter from cold winds and apply a mulch in autumn.

Pruning No routine pruning is necessary. Deadhead for the best flowering displays. In cold areas, cut back to near ground level in early spring.

Propagation Take softwood cuttings in late spring.

Phygelius aequalis 'Yellow Trumpet'
An upright, suckering evergreen shrub that bears clusters of pale creamy-yellow tubular flowers on slender stems from early summer to late summer.

Phygelius x *rectus* 'Moonraker'

H 90cm (36in) S 90cm (36in).
Aspect: sun
Hardiness: ❄❄ Zone: 9

Phygelius x *rectus*
Tubular pale red flowers are produced in loose open sprays on the slender stems of this upright, suckering evergreen shrub from early summer to late summer on this shrub. H 1.2m (4ft) S 1.5m (5ft).
Named varieties: 'African Queen', red and orange flowers, H 1m (3ft) S 1.2m (4ft). 'Devil's Tears', red flowers, H 1m (3ft) S 1.2m (4ft). 'Moonraker', cream-coloured flowers, H 1m (3ft) S 1.2m (4ft). 'Pink Elf', pink flowers, H 75cm (30in) S 90cm (36in). 'Salmon Leap', pale orange flowers, H 1.2m (4ft) S 1.5m (5ft).
Aspect: sun
Hardiness: ❄❄ Zone: 9

PIERIS

A genus of over five species, including the evergreen shrubs featured here, grown for their fragrant clusters of lily-of-the-valley-like spring flowers and colourful new foliage. They make excellent border fillers, while some compact varieties are also suitable for growing in large containers.

Cultivation In the garden, grow in any well-drained acid soil in dappled shade, but in colder areas shelter from cold winds. Add plenty of organic matter (but not alkaline mushroom compost/soil mix) to the soil before planting. In containers, grow in ericaceous soil mix and keep well watered.

Pruning No routine pruning is necessary. Remove any frost-damaged stems in early summer.

Propagation Take semi-ripe cuttings in late summer, or layer low branches in mid-autumn.

Pieris formosa var. *forrestii* 'Wakehurst'
An upright, evergreen shrub that bears pendent clusters of fragrant, white, urn-shaped flowers during mid-spring and late spring when the glossy, brilliant red young foliage emerges. H 5m (16ft) S 4m (13ft).
Aspect: semi-shade
Hardiness: ❄❄❄ Zones: 7–8

Pieris 'Forest Flame'
The fiery red new foliage of this upright evergreen turns pink and cream before maturing to dark green. Clusters of white, urn-

Pieris 'Forest Flame'

shaped flowers festoon the shrub during mid-spring and late spring. H 4m (13ft) S 2m (6ft).
Aspect: semi-shade
Hardiness: ❀❀❀ Zones: 7–8

Pieris japonica 'Purity'
Clusters of white, urn-shaped flowers are borne in abundance during mid-spring and late spring and stand out against the lustrous young, pale green foliage that darkens with age on this compact evergreen. H 1m (3ft) S 1m (3ft).
Aspect: semi-shade
Hardiness: ❀❀❀ Zones: 7–8

Pieris japonica 'Valley Valentine'
An early and long-flowering compact variety that produces dark pink flowers from early spring until late spring against lustrous dark green leaves. H 4m (13ft) S 3m (10ft).
Aspect: semi-shade
Hardiness: ❀❀❀ Zones: 7–8

Pieris japonica 'Variegata'
New foliage is flushed pink, maturing to green with white margins on this variegated variety. Clusters of white, bell-shaped flowers are produced throughout mid-spring and late spring. H 80cm (32in) S 80cm (32in).
Aspect: semi-shade
Hardiness: ❀❀❀ Zones: 7–8

PITTOSPORUM
A genus of around 200 species, including the handsome, bushy evergreens featured here. They make good border fillers or specimens with year-round interest and can be trimmed into an attractive hedge in mild areas.
Cultivation Grow in reasonably fertile, moisture-retentive, well-drained soil in full sun or dappled shade. Grow against a sheltered, sunny wall in colder areas.
Pruning No routine pruning is necessary. Shrubs can be clipped to keep them compact during mid-spring. Trim hedges in mid-spring and early summer.
Propagation Take semi-ripe cuttings in mid-autumn.

Pittosporum 'Garnettii'
Half-hardy variegated evergreen with pink-spotted grey-green leaves that have creamy-white, wavy edges. Purple, bell-shaped flowers are borne in late spring and early summer. H 4m (13ft) S 3m (10ft).
Aspect: sun or semi-shade
Hardiness: ❀ Zone: 10

Pittosporum tenuifolium 'Silver Queen'
This is a large, ornamental shrub that has handsome, white-variegated, wavy-edged, grey-green leaves that appear on contrasting near-black young stems. Honey-scented dark purple flowers are sometimes produced during late spring and early summer. H 4m (13ft) S 2m (6ft).
Aspect: sun or semi-shade
Hardiness: ❀❀ Zones: 9

Pittosporum tenuifolium 'Tom Thumb'
As its names suggests, this is a compact, rounded evergreen with wavy-edged, purple-bronze leaves and near-black young stems. Honey-scented dark purple flowers are sometimes produced during late spring and early summer. H 90cm (36in) S 60cm (24in).
Aspect: sun or semi-shade
Hardiness: ❀❀ Zone: 9

Pittosporum tenuifolium 'Variegatum'
A large bushy evergreen with creamy-white, variegated, wavy-edged, grey-green leaves on near-black young stems. It makes an attractive, variegated windbreak or hedge in mild coastal areas.

H 4m (13ft) S 2m (6ft).
Aspect: sun or semi-shade
Hardiness: ❀❀ Zone: 9

POTENTILLA
Cinquefoil
A large genus of over 500 species, including the summer-flowering, deciduous shrubs featured here. Smaller, compact varieties are useful for adding summer-long colour in confined spaces and all can be grown on poor soils. Ideal for rock gardens, sunny banks or the sunny base of hedges.
Cultivation Grow in any well-drained soil in full sun.
Pruning For good flowering, trim new growth by one-third each mid-spring. Rejuvenate neglected plants by cutting the plant back to ground level in mid-spring.
Propagation Take semi-ripe cuttings in early autumn.

Potentilla fruticosa 'Abbotswood'
Compact, bushy, deciduous shrub with blue-green foliage that bears masses of brilliant white flowers from late spring to mid-autumn. H 75cm (30in) S 120cm (48in).
Aspect: sun
Hardiness: ❀❀❀ Zones: 7–8

Potentilla fruticosa 'Goldfinger'
Large, bright yellow flowers are produced in abundance from late spring to mid-autumn against a backdrop of small, dark green leaves on this mound-forming deciduous shrub. H 1m (3ft) S 1.5m (5ft).
Aspect: sun
Hardiness: ❀❀❀ Zones: 7–8

Potentilla fruticosa 'Primrose Beauty'
Primrose-yellow flowers resembling wild roses appear from late spring to mid-autumn above a compact mound of deciduous grey-green leaves. Pest- and disease-free, it tolerates partial shade but flowers best in full sun. H 1m (3ft) S 1.5m (5ft).
Aspect: sun
Hardiness: ❀❀❀ Zones: 7–8

Potentilla fruticosa 'Red Ace'
Vermilion-red flowers each with a yellow centre and undersides are borne *en masse* from late spring to mid-autumn and stand out against the dark green leaves. H 1m (3ft) S 1.5m (5ft).
Aspect: sun
Hardiness: ❀❀❀ Zones: 7–8

Potentilla fruticosa 'Royal Flush'
Masses of rich pink flowers, each with a yellow centre that fades to white with age, cover this compact, busy, deciduous shrub from late spring to mid-autumn. H 45cm (18in) S 75cm (30in).
Aspect: sun
Hardiness: ❀❀❀ Zones: 7–8

Potentilla fruticosa 'Sunset'
The unusual, burnt-orange flowers that appear on this shrub are produced in succession from late spring to mid-autumn and appear above a mound of dark green deciduous foliage. H 1m (3ft) S 1m (3ft).
Aspect: sun
Hardiness: ❀❀❀ Zones: 7–8

Pittosporum tenuifolium 'Variegatum'

Potentilla fruticosa 'Abbotswood'

Prostanthera cuneata

Prunus 'Hirtipes'

PROSTANTHERA
Mint bush

A genus of some 50 species, including the bushy evergreen shrub featured here, grown for their eye-catching summer flowers. It is a useful front-of-the-border filler and for adding continuity to the garden display.
Cultivation Grow in any moisture-retentive, well-drained soil that is reasonably fertile and in full sun. Grow against a sheltered, sunny wall in colder areas.
Pruning No routine pruning is necessary. Deadhead to keep neat and help prolong flowering. Trim lightly after flowering to keep compact.
Propagation Take semi-ripe cuttings in mid-summer.

Prostanthera cuneata
Alpine mint bush

Tubular white flowers with distinctive purple and yellow flecks in the throat are produced in clusters from early summer to late summer on this small, bushy, evergreen shrub. H 1m (3ft) S 1m (3ft).
Aspect: sun
Hardiness: ❊❊ Zone: 9

PRUNUS

A large and varied genus of over 200 species, including the bushy evergreen shrubs featured here, grown for their handsome foliage and spring flowers, as well as deciduous shrubs grown for their spring blossom. Plant spring-flowering varieties as seasonal focal points where they will be appreciated most; evergreen types make excellent border fillers, ground cover and hedges, depending on the variety.
Cultivation Grow in any moisture-retentive, well-drained soil that is reasonably fertile and in full sun, dappled shade, even deep shade.
Pruning No routine pruning is necessary. Formal evergreen hedges and screens can be trimmed during early spring and late summer. Neglected or straggly evergreen shrubs can be cut back hard into old wood during early spring. Deciduous shrubs can be kept compact and flowering well by cutting back one stem in three during early summer, starting with the oldest.
Propagation Take semi-ripe cuttings in early autumn.

Prunus laurocerasus 'Otto Luyken'

A compact, bushy, evergreen shrub with narrow, pointed, dark green leaves. Candle-like spikes of small white flowers appear during mid-spring, followed by cherry-red berries. Good ground cover. H 1m (3ft) S 1.5m (5ft).
Aspect: sun, semi-shade to deep shade
Hardiness: ❊❊❊ Zones: 7–8

Prunus laurocerasus 'Rotundifolia'

A large, dense and bushy evergreen shrub with big, glossy, dark green leaves. Candle-like spikes of small white flowers are produced during mid-spring, followed by cherry-red berries. Good hedging plant.
H 5m (16ft) S 4m (13ft).
Aspect: sun, semi-shade to deep shade
Hardiness: ❊❊❊ Zones: 7–8

Prunus laurocerasus 'Zabeliana'

A low-growing, spreading, evergreen shrub with very narrow, pointed, dark green leaves. Candle-like spikes of small white flowers are produced during mid-spring, followed by cherry-red berries. Good ground cover. H 1m (3ft) S 2.5m (8ft).
Aspect: sun, semi-shade to deep shade
Hardiness: ❊❊❊ Zones: 7–8

Prunus lusitanica
Portugal laurel

A large, dense, evergreen shrub with dark green leaves that have red stalks. Candle-like spikes of small white flowers are produced during mid-spring, followed by red berries that mature to purple. Good hedging plant and can tolerate chalky soils. H 20m (70ft) S 20m (70ft).
Aspect: sun, semi-shade to deep shade
Hardiness: ❊❊❊ Zones: 7–8

Prunus tenella 'Fire Hill'
Dwarf Russian almond

An upright-growing, compact and bushy deciduous shrub with narrow, glossy, dark green leaves. The bare stems are smothered with bright pink blossom-like flowers during early spring and mid-spring as the leaves emerge, followed by velvety fruits.
H 1.5m (5ft) S 1.5m (5ft).
Aspect: sun or semi-shade
Hardiness: ❊❊❊ Zones: 7–8

Prunus triloba
Flowering almond

Peach-pink, blossom-like flowers are borne on the bare stems of this dense, twiggy, deciduous shrub during early spring and mid-spring as the leaves emerge, followed by red berries. H 3m (10ft) S 3m (10ft).
Aspect: sun or semi-shade
Hardiness: ❊❊❊ Zones: 7–8

PYRACANTHA

A genus of over five species, including the spreading, spiny evergreen shrubs featured here, grown for their intruder-resistant properties, spring flowers and colourful autumn fruit that are loved by birds. They can be used as freestanding shrubs or hedges or be trained against a wall or fence. They make useful town garden plants, as they are very tolerant of urban pollution.
Cultivation Grow in any well-drained soil that is reasonably fertile in full sun or dappled shade, sheltered from cold winds. Grow less hardy varieties against a sunny wall in colder areas.
Pruning No routine pruning is necessary. Hedges and screens can be trimmed between late spring and mid-summer to keep in shape. Wall-trained specimens should be trimmed back at this time in summer. Cut back all the new shoots after they have flowered, to expose the developing berries.
Propagation Take semi-ripe cuttings in early autumn.

Pyracantha 'Golden Charmer'

A vigorous and bushy shrub that produces masses of small white flowers on arching branches during early summer, followed by clusters of dark orange berries that are resistant to disease.
H 3m (10ft) S 3m (10ft).
Aspect: sun or semi-shade
Hardiness: ❊❊❊ Zones: 7–8

Pyracantha 'Mohave'

Masses of small white flowers are produced in clusters during early summer, followed by clusters of long-lasting bright red berries on this vigorous, bushy shrub. H 4m (13ft) S 5m (16ft).

Pyracantha 'Saphyr Orange'

Aspect: sun or semi-shade
Hardiness: ✿✿ Zone: 9

Pyracantha 'Orange Glow'
Clusters of small white flowers
are produced in late spring against
lustrous, dark green leaves,
followed by brilliant orange
berries that last well into winter
on this open, spreading shrub.
H 3m (10ft) S 3m (10ft).
Aspect: sun or semi-shade
Hardiness: ✿✿✿ Zones: 7–8

Pyracantha 'Saphyr Orange'
This vigorous, evergreen shrub is
a recent introduction that bears
sprays of small white flowers
during early summer, followed by
clusters of disease-resistant,
orange berries that last well into
winter against a backdrop of
glossy, dark green leaves.
Pyracantha 'Saphyr Rouge' is
similar but bears carmine-red
berries that mature to orange.
H 4m (13ft) S 3m (10ft).
Aspect: sun or semi-shade
Hardiness: ✿✿✿ Zones: 7–8

Pyracantha 'Soleil d'Or'
Large clusters of long-lasting,
disease-resistant, golden-yellow
berries follow masses of white
flowers produced in early summer
on red-tinged spiny shoots of this
upright evergreen shrub. H 3m
(10ft) S 2.5m (8ft).
Aspect: sun or semi-shade
Hardiness: ✿✿✿ Zones: 7–8

RHAMNUS
A genus of around 125 species,
including the variegated evergreen

shrub featured here, grown for
their handsome foliage. It makes
an attractive freestanding shrub or
hedge, but in cold areas it is best
trained against a large sunny wall
or fence. It also makes an
excellent permanent container
shrub that provides year-round
interest.
Cultivation In the garden, grow in
any garden soil that is reasonably
fertile and in full sun. In colder
regions, grow in a sheltered
position, protected from cold
winds. In containers, use a soil-
based compost, feed monthly and
water as necessary.
Pruning No routine pruning is
necessary.
Propagation Take semi-ripe
cuttings in mid-summer.

Rhamnus alaternus 'Argenteovariegata' (syn. R. alaternus 'Variegata')
A variegated evergreen shrub,
grown for its white-edged grey-
green leaves. Small, insignificant
mustard-coloured flowers are
produced in late spring and early
summer, followed by red fruits
that ripen to black. H 5m (16ft)
S 4m (13ft).
Aspect: sun
Hardiness: ✿✿ Zones: 7–8

RHAPIS
A genus of over ten species of
multi-stemmed palms, including
the miniature fan palm featured
here, that will add a tropical touch
to mild gardens or can be grown
as a house plant in colder regions.
Cultivation Grow in a well-drained

soil that is reasonably fertile in
dappled shade. In containers, use
a soil-based compost (soil mix),
water regularly and feed monthly
during the growing season. Move
to a warm spot undercover when
the temperature falls below 10°C
(50°F) and water sparingly
throughout the winter.
Pruning No routine pruning is
necessary.
Propagation Sow seed or divide
large clumps in mid-spring.

Rhapis excelsa (syn. R. flabelliformis)
Miniature fan palm
A tender dwarf palm that forms a
clump of bamboo-like stems with
large, deeply lobed, matt green,
palm-like leaves. Insignificant
cream flowers are produced in
early summer and mid-summer.
H 1.5m (5ft) S 5m (16ft).
Aspect: semi-shade
Hardiness: tender Zones: 10+

RHODODENDRON
(including azalea)
A huge genus of nearly 1,000
species, including the medium-
sized and dwarf forms of
evergreen azaleas and
rhododendrons and the deciduous
azaleas featured here, all grown
for their spectacular flowering
displays. Use according to their
size: all make wonderful seasonal
focal points, with smaller varieties
best suited at the front or middle
of borders, while bigger forms
with larger, eye-catching flowers
can be best accommodated
towards the back of the scheme.
Compact varieties also make
excellent permanent container
plants.
Cultivation Shallow-plant in any
well-drained acid soil in dappled
shade, but in colder areas provide
shelter and plant where it gets
afternoon sun. Some varieties are
best grown in full sun. Add plenty
of organic matter to the soil
before planting. In containers,
grow in ericaceous compost and
keep well watered. Wherever the
shrub is planted, bear in mind
that the flowers are susceptible to
damage by a frost that is followed
by rapid thaw, so avoid
positioning in east-facing areas
that get early morning spring sun.

Pruning Deadhead after flowering.
Prune straggly branches of
established plants to maintain the
overall shape during late winter or
early spring.
Propagation Layer low branches in
early spring or take semi-ripe
cuttings in late summer.

EVERGREEN RHODODENDRONS
Rhododendron 'Blue Diamond'
Violet-blue funnel-shaped flowers
that age to lavender-blue are
borne during mid-spring and early
spring. It has small, aromatic,
dark, evergreen leaves. Best in full
sun. H 1.5m (5ft) S 1.5m (5ft).
Aspect: sun
Hardiness: ✿✿✿ Zones: 7–8

Rhododendron 'Blue Peter'
Frilly edged, lavender-blue flowers
with purple markings are
produced in clusters throughout
early summer. Large, dark,
evergreen leaves. H 3m (10ft)
S 3m (10ft).
Aspect: semi-shade
Hardiness: ✿✿✿ Zones: 7–8

Rhododendron 'Cilpinense'
Clusters of pale pink, funnel-
shaped flowers are produced in
profusion during early spring on
this compact evergreen
rhododendron, which has small,
dark leaves. H 1.1m (3½ft)
S 1.1m (3½ft).
Aspect: sun or semi-shade
Hardiness: ✿✿✿ Zones: 7–8

Rhododendron 'Cunningham's White'
Trusses of white, funnel-shaped
flowers with brown or purple
markings are produced
throughout late spring. Compact
evergreen with dark green leaves.
H 2.2m (7ft) S 2.2m (7ft).
Aspect: semi-shade
Hardiness: ✿✿✿ Zones: 7–8

Rhododendron 'Dopey'
Masses of long-lasting, glossy,
red, bell-shaped flowers, spotted
dark-brown inside, are produced
throughout late spring on this
compact evergreen rhododendron.
H 2m (6ft) S 2m (6ft).
Aspect: semi-shade
Hardiness: ✿✿✿ Zones: 7–8

Rhamnus alaternus 'Argenteovariegata'

Rhapis excelsa

Rhododrendron 'Dopey'

Rhododendron 'Grumpy'
Funnel-shaped, pink-flushed, cream flowers are produced in flat-topped trusses during mid-spring and late spring. The glossy, dark green leaves are woolly underneath. H 1.2m (4ft) S 1m (3ft).
Aspect: semi-shade
Hardiness: ❁❁❁ Zones: 7–8

Rhododendron 'Lord Roberts'
Dark crimson, funnel-shaped flowers with black markings are produced in clusters during early summer. Compact evergreen with dark green leaves. H 1.5m (5ft) S 1.5m (5ft).
Aspect: semi-shade
Hardiness: ❁❁❁ Zones: 7–8

Rhododendron 'Pink Drift'
Funnel-shaped, rose-lavender flowers are produced *en masse* throughout mid-spring and late spring on this very compact, dwarf evergreen rhododendron, which has small, pale green leaves. Good choice for small gardens. H 50cm (20in) S 50cm (20in).
Aspect: semi-shade
Hardiness: ❁❁❁ Zones: 7–8

Rhododendron 'Pink Pearl'
White-edged, soft-pink, funnel-shaped flowers that age to white are produced during mid-spring and late spring. Large, pale, evergreen leaves. H 4m (13ft) S 4m (13ft).
Aspect: sun
Hardiness: ❁❁❁ Zones: 7–8

Rhododendron 'Purple Splendor'
Frilly edged, funnel-shaped, deep purple flowers, each with a blackish-purple throat, are produced during late spring and early summer on this late-flowering variety. H 3m (10ft) S 3m (10ft).
Aspect: semi-shade
Hardiness: ❁❁❁ Zones: 7–8

Rhododendron 'Sapphire'
Masses of small, pale blue, funnel-shaped flowers are produced *en masse* during mid-spring and late spring on this compact evergreen, which has small, dark leaves. H 50cm (20in) S 50cm (20in).
Aspect: semi-shade
Hardiness: ❁❁❁ Zones: 7–8

Rhododendron 'Scarlet Wonder'
Wavy-margined, ruby-red, funnel-shaped flowers are produced *en masse* throughout mid-spring on this compact evergreen, which has small, dark leaves. H 2m (6ft) S 2m (6ft).
Aspect: semi-shade
Hardiness: ❁❁❁ Zones: 7–8

DECIDUOUS AZALEAS
Rhododendron luteum
Sweetly scented, the yellow, funnel-shaped blooms appear throughout late spring and early summer on this vigorous-growing deciduous azalea. Mid-green leaves turn fiery shades in autumn.
H 4m (13ft) S 4m (13ft).

Aspect: sun or semi-shade
Hardiness: ❁❁❁ Zones: 7–8

Rhododendron 'Debutante'
Pink, funnel-shaped flowers with orange markings are produced en masse throughout late spring. Mid-green leaves turn fiery shades in autumn. H 2m (6ft) S 2m (6ft).
Aspect: semi-shade
Hardiness: ❁❁❁ Zones: 7–8

Rhododendron 'Gibraltar'
Frilly, bright orange, funnel-shaped flowers appear in late spring on this deciduous azalea. A useful pot specimen on the patio. H 1.5m (5ft) S 1.5m (5ft).
Aspect: sun or semi-shade
Hardiness: ❁❁❁ Zones: 7–8

Rhododendron 'Glowing Embers'
Flaming reddish-orange, funnel-shaped flowers are produced in conical clusters during mid-spring and late spring. H 2m (6ft) S 2m (6ft).
Aspect: semi-shade
Hardiness: ❁❁❁ Zones: 7–8

Rhododendron 'Homebush'
Pretty pink, semi-double, funnel-shaped flowers are borne throughout late spring. A good pink variety for small gardens. H 1.5m (5ft) S 1.5m (5ft).
Aspect: semi-shade
Hardiness: ❁❁❁ Zones: 7–8

Rhododendron 'Klondyke'
Coppery-red flower buds open to reveal flaming red-flushed, golden-orange, funnel-shaped

flowers throughout late spring. The mid-green leaves turn fiery shades in autumn. H 2m (6ft) S 2m (6ft).
Aspect: semi-shade
Hardiness: ❁❁❁ Zones: 7–8

Rhododendron 'Koster's Brilliant Red'
Vivid, orange-red, funnel-shaped flowers are produced during mid-spring and late spring on this early-flowering variety. Mid-green leaves turn fiery shades in autumn. H 2m (6ft) S 2m (6ft).
Aspect: semi-shade
Hardiness: ❁❁❁ Zones: 7–8

Rhododendron 'Persil'
Large clusters of orange-flushed, white funnel-shaped flowers are borne throughout April (mid-spring) on this bushy, deciduous azalea. The mid-green leaves turn fiery shades in autumn.
H 2m (6ft) S 2m (6ft).
Aspect: semi-shade
Hardiness: ❁❁❁ Zones: 7–8

EVERGREEN AZALEAS
Rhododendron 'Blue Danube'
Clusters of small, funnel-shaped, violet-blue flowers are produced *en masse* during late spring and early summer on this compact evergreen azalea. Very hardy. H 80cm (32in) S 100cm (36in).
Aspect: semi-shade
Hardiness: ❁❁❁ Zones: 7–8

Rhododendron 'Geisha Red'
Masses of small, funnel-shaped, pillar-box-red flowers are produced during late spring and

Rhododendron 'Persil'

Rhododendron luteum

early summer on this compact evergreen azalea. It makes a useful container specimen on the patio. H 60cm (24in) S 100cm (36in). Aspect: semi-shade Hardiness: ✱✱✱

Rhododendron 'Gumpo White'
Wavy-edged, funnel-shaped, white flowers are produced *en masse* throughout early summer on this dwarf, evergreen azalea. It makes a useful container specimen on the patio. H 1m (3ft) S 1m (3ft). Aspect: semi-shade Hardiness: ✱✱✱ Zones: 7–8

Rhododendron 'Mother's Day'
Small, funnel-shaped, semi-double, rose-red flowers are produced in profusion during late

spring and early summer. H 80cm (32in) S 100cm (36in). Aspect: semi-shade Hardiness: ✱✱✱ Zones: 7–8

RHUS
A large genus of over 200 species, including the upright, suckering shrub featured here, grown for their handsome foliage that turns fiery shades in autumn. They make spectacular specimen plants for a sunny shrub or mixed border, providing an ever-changing year-round point of interest.
Cultivation Grow in a moisture-retentive, well-drained garden soil that is reasonably fertile and in full sun or dappled shade. Grow in full sun for the best autumn tints. Remove suckers by digging

a hole to expose their point of origin and ripping them from the root. Do not prune off as this will just exacerbate the problem.
Pruning No routine pruning is necessary. Neglected plants can be cut back hard in mid-spring.
Propagation Take semi-ripe cuttings in mid-summer.

Rhus typhina
Stag's horn sumach
The velvet-covered red winter shoots gave rise to the common name, but it is the finely cut dark green foliage, which turns fiery shades of orange-red in autumn, that is the highlight. Mustard flowers on conical spikes appear in early summer and mid-summer, followed by dark red autumn fruits on female shrubs that make a useful food source for birds in winter. Prone to throwing up suckers, so avoid planting next to a lawn or driveway, or restrict its spread with a sucker-proof barrier. Named varieties: 'Dissecta' (syn. *R. typhina* 'Laciniata') has more finely cut leaves and rarely produces suckers. H 2m (6ft) S 3m (10ft). Aspect: sun or semi-shade Hardiness: ✱✱✱ Zones: 7–8

RIBES
Flowering currants
A genus of some 150 species, including the deciduous, quick-growing shrubs here, are grown for their spring flowers and autumn fruit. Useful shrubs for filling gaps and for providing quick results in new gardens.

Cultivation Grow in any reasonably fertile, well-drained soil in full sun or dappled shade.
Pruning Encourage better flowering by pruning annually, cutting out one stem in three after flowering in late spring.
Propagation Take hardwood cuttings in mid-autumn.

Ribes sanguineum 'Brocklebankii'
A compact and upright deciduous shrub, with aromatic, golden-yellow leaves, that carries clusters of pink flowers during mid-spring, followed by blue-black fruit in autumn. Hot midday sun can scorch the foliage. H 1.2m (4ft) S 1.2m (4ft). Aspect: semi-shade Hardiness: ✱✱✱ Zones: 7–8

Ribes sanguineum 'King Edward VII'
Clusters of dark red flowers in mid-spring are followed by blue-black fruit during the autumn on this upright deciduous shrub with aromatic dark green leaves. H 2m (6ft) S 2m (6ft). Aspect: sun Hardiness: ✱✱✱ Zones: 7–8

Ribes sanguineum 'Pulborough Scarlet'
Clusters of white-centred red flowers appear in mid-spring, followed by blue-black fruit in autumn, on this vigorous shrub with dark green leaves. H 3m (10ft) S 2.5m (18ft). Aspect: sun Hardiness: ✱✱✱ Zones: 7–8

Rhododendron 'Pink Pearl'

Rhus typhina

Ribes sanguineum

Rosa 'Alec's Red'

ROSA
Rose

A large genus of over 150 species that includes the varied collection of popular, deciduous, summer-flowering shrubs featured here. Grow roses in traditional blocks to provide a stunning display, or use single specimens in between other shrubs and flowers for a summer-long splash of colour. Combine different varieties to get a succession of flowers and hips.

Cultivation Grow in any garden soil that is reasonably fertile and in full sun. They prefer the soil to remain moist in summer, so incorporate plenty of organic matter before planting. Avoid siting new rose plants in soil that has recently been used for growing other roses.

Pruning To keep neat, open and healthy, prune annually by cutting back the previous season's growth to within 10–15cm (4–6in) of a permanent twiggy framework before new growth starts in late winter or early spring. Traditionally, this was carried out using secateurs (pruners), but recent trials have shown rough pruning with a hedge trimmer to be equally effective. The sizes for individual varieties given here assume regular pruning. Ground-cover roses should have unwanted stems cut back to an outward-facing bud. In containers, use a soil-based compost (soil mix), water regularly and feed monthly during the growing season. Water as necessary during the winter months.

Propagation Take hardwood cuttings in mid-autumn.
Aspect: sun
Hardiness: ❁❁❁ Zones: 7–8

LARGE-FLOWERED BUSH ROSE
Includes the long-flowering hybrid tea roses with large, shapely blooms on long stems and attractive foliage that make them ideal for cutting.

Rosa 'Alec's Red'
Large, double, sweetly fragrant, crimson flowers are borne in succession from mid-summer to early autumn. Glossy, mid-green leaves. H 1m (3ft) S 60cm (24in).

Rosa 'Alexander'
Double, slightly fragrant, vermilion-red flowers with scalloped petals are produced from mid-summer to early autumn. Lustrous, dark green leaves. H 2m (72in) S 80cm (32in).

Rosa 'Blessings'
Double, slightly fragrant, coral-pink flowers are borne in succession from mid-summer to early autumn. Glossy, dark green leaves. H 110cm (42in) S 75cm (30in).

Rosa 'Congratulations'
Double, slightly fragrant, rose-pink flowers on long stems are borne from mid-summer to early autumn. Glossy, mid-green leaves. H 1.5m (5ft) S 1m (3ft).

Rosa 'Fragrant Cloud'
Strongly fragrant, double, deep-scarlet flowers are produced from mid-summer to early autumn. Lustrous, dark green leaves. H 75cm (30in) S 60cm (24in).

Rosa 'Ice Cream'
Large, fragrant, ivory-white flowers are borne in succession from mid-summer to early autumn. Lustrous, bronze-tinted, dark green leaves. H 1m (3ft) S 70cm (28in).

Rosa 'Ingrid Bergman'
Fragrant, double, deep red flowers are borne from mid-summer to

Rosa 'Ingrid Bergman'

early autumn. Lustrous, dark green leaves. H 80cm (32in) S 65cm (26in).

Rosa 'Just Joey'
Fragrant, double, coppery-red flowers with wavy-margined petals are borne from mid-summer to early autumn. Matt, dark-green leaves. H 75cm (30in) S 70cm (28in).

Rosa 'Loving Memory'
Double, slightly scented, dark red flowers are borne in succession from mid-summer to early autumn. Matt, dark-green leaves. H 110cm (42in) S 75cm (30in).

Rosa 'Peace'
Double, pink-flushed, deep yellow, slightly fragrant flowers are borne from mid-summer to early autumn. Glossy, dark green leaves. H 1.2m (4ft) S 1m (3ft).

Rosa 'Just Joey'

Rosa 'Peace'

Rosa 'Polar Star'
Large, double, white flowers are borne in succession from mid-summer to early autumn. Matt, dark green leaves. H 1m (3ft) S 70cm (28in).

Rosa 'Remember Me'
Large, fragrant, double, coppery-orange, flushed-yellow flowers are borne from mid-summer to early autumn. Glossy, dark green leaves. H 1m (3ft) S 60cm (24in).

Rosa 'Royal William'
Double, deep-crimson flowers with a spicy fragrance are borne from mid-summer to early autumn. Matt, dark green leaves. H 1m (3ft) S 75cm (30in).

Rosa 'Ruby Wedding'
Slightly fragrant, double, ruby-red flowers are borne in succession from mid-summer to early autumn. Glossy, dark green leaves. H 75cm (30in) S 70cm (28in).

Rosa 'Silver Jubilee'
Fragrant, double, rose-pink flowers flushed salmon-pink are borne from mid-summer to early autumn. Matt, dark green leaves. H 1m (3ft) S 60cm (24in).

CLUSTER-FLOWERED BUSH ROSE
Including floribunda roses, which produce masses of flowers throughout the summer and autumn. They tend to be hardier and more disease-resistant than large-flowered varieties.

Rosa 'Amber Queen'
Fragrant, double, amber-yellow flowers are borne in succession from mid-summer to early autumn. Glossy, leathery, dark green leaves emerge reddish-green. H 50cm (20in) S 60cm (24in).

Rosa 'Arthur Bell'
Large, semi-double, very fragrant, golden-yellow flowers are borne from mid-summer to early autumn. Glossy, mid-green leaves. H 1m (3ft) S 60cm (24in).

Rosa 'Chinatown'
Fragrant, double, pink-edged yellow flowers are produced by 'Chinatown' from mid-summer to early autumn. Glossy, dark green leaves. H 1.2m (4ft) S 1m (3ft).

Rosa 'Golden Wedding'
Double, slightly fragrant, golden-yellow flowers are produced from mid-summer to early autumn. Glossy, dark green leaves. H 75cm (30in) S 60cm (24in).

Rosa 'Iceberg'
Double, slightly fragrant, white flowers are produced from mid-summer to early autumn. Glossy, mid-green leaves. H 80cm (32in) S 65cm (26in).

Rosa 'Many Happy Returns'
Cup-shaped, fragrant, semi-double, pale pink flowers are borne in succession from mid-summer to early autumn. Glossy, mid-green leaves. H 75cm (30in) S 75cm (30in).

Rosa 'Mountbatten'

Rosa 'Masquerade'
Lightly fragrant, semi-double, yellow flowers that age to salmon-pink and red are borne from mid-summer to early autumn. Glossy, dark green leaves. H 80cm (32in) S 60cm (24in).

Rosa 'Mountbatten'
Large, fragrant, double, golden-yellow flowers are produced from mid-summer to early autumn. Glossy, mid-green leaves. H 1.2m (4ft) S 75cm (30in).

Rosa 'Queen Elizabeth'
Double, slightly fragrant, pale pink flowers are produced in succession and appear from mid-summer to early autumn. Glossy, dark-green leaves. H 2.2m (7ft) S 1m (3ft).

Rosa 'Ruby Anniversary'
Double, slightly scented, ruby-red flowers are produced in succession from mid-summer to early autumn. Glossy, mid-green leaves. H 60cm (24in) S 45cm (18in).

Rosa 'Southampton'
Large, double, slightly scented, red-flushed apricot flowers with ruffled petals from mid-summer to early autumn. Glossy, dark green leaves. H 1m (3ft) S 70cm (28in).

Rosa 'The Times Rose'
Double, slightly fragrant, dark crimson flowers are produced in succession from mid-summer to early autumn.

Glossy, purplish-tinged green leaves. H 60cm (24in) S 75cm (30in).

SHRUB ROSE
A varied collection of roses that grow in bushy, informal plants with spectacular displays of flowers. Many are sweetly scented and some have hips. All are useful for growing in a mixed border with other shrubs. Many old varieties and species roses bloom only in early summer but most modern varieties repeat bloom.

Rosa 'Ballerina'
Slightly scented, white-centred, pale pink flowers are produced from mid-summer to early autumn. Mid-green leaves. H 1.5m (5ft) S 1.2m (48in).

Rosa 'Blanche Double de Coubert'
Large semi-double, very fragrant, white flowers are borne from mid-summer to early autumn, followed by red rose-hips. H 1.5m (5ft) S 1.2m (4ft).

Rosa 'Bonica'
Small semi-double, slightly fragrant, rose-pink flowers are borne from mid-summer to early autumn. Glossy, dark green leaves. H 85cm (34in) S 110cm (42in).

Rosa 'Boule de Neige'
Pink-tinged buds open to produce fragrant, double, white flowers from mid-summer to early autumn. Matt, dark green foliage. H 1.5m (5ft) S 1.2m (4ft).

Rosa 'Buff Beauty'
Double, fragrant, pale apricot-yellow flowers are borne from mid-summer to early autumn. Purple-tinged, dark green leaves. H 1.2m (4ft) S 1.2m (4ft).

Rosa 'Cardinal de Richelieu'
Fragrant, double, deep purple flowers are borne in clusters during early summer and mid-summer. Lustrous, dark green leaves. H 1m (3ft) S 1.2m (4ft).

Rosa 'Charles de Mills'
Double, fragrant, magenta-pink flowers are produced in a single flush during mid-summer. Mid-green leaves. H 1m (3ft) S 1.2m (4ft).

Rosa 'Cornelia'
Very fragrant, double, apricot-pink flowers are produced from early summer to early autumn. Matt, dark green leaves. H 1.5m (5ft) S 1.5m (5ft).

Rosa 'Fantin-Latour'
Slightly fragrant, double, pale pink flowers are produced throughout early summer and mid-summer. Glossy, dark green leaves. H 1.5m (5ft) S 1.2m (4ft).

Rosa 'Felicia'
Sweetly fragrant, double, apricot-yellow flowers that are flushed with pale pink from early summer to early autumn. Matt, mid-green leaves. H 1.5m (5ft) S 2.2m (7ft).

Rosa 'Arthur Bell'

Rosa 'Iceberg'

Rosa 'Felicia'

Rosa 'Fru Dagmar Hastrup'
Clove-scented, single, light-pink flowers are produced in succession from mid-summer to early autumn, followed by dark red autumn hips. Matt, dark green leaves. H 1m (3ft) S 1.2m (4ft).

Rosa glauca
Clusters of single, cerise-pink flowers with pale-pink centres are produced during early summer and mid-summer on almost thornless stems, followed by spherical red rosehips. H 2m (6ft) S 1.5m (5ft).

Rosa 'Graham Thomas'
Double, fragrant, yellow flowers are produced in succession from mid-summer to early autumn. Matt, bright green leaves. H 1.5m (5ft) S 1.2m (4ft).

Rosa 'Heritage'
Cup-shaped, fragrant, double, pale pink flowers that age to white are produced from mid-summer to early autumn. Matt, dark green leaves. H 1.2m (4ft) S 1.2m (4ft).

Rosa 'L.D. Braithwaite'
Large, double, fragrant, bright-crimson flowers are produced in succession from mid-summer to early autumn. Matt, grey-green leaves. H 1m (3ft) S 1.2m (4ft).

Rosa 'Louise Odier'
Fragrant, double, mauve-tinged pink flowers are borne from mid-summer to early autumn. Matt, pale green leaves. H 2m (6ft) S 1.2m (4ft).

Rosa 'Mary Rose'
Cup-shaped, double, fragrant, rose-pink flowers are borne in succession from mid-summer to early autumn. Matt, mid-green leaves. H 1.2m (4ft) S 1m (3ft).

Rosa 'Madame Pierre Oger'
Very fragrant, double, pale silvery-pink flowers are produced in succession from mid-summer to early autumn. Matt, pale green leaves. H 2m (6ft) S 1.2m (4ft).

Rosa moyesii 'Geranium'
Scented, single, cream-centred, bright red flowers are produced during late spring and early summer. Matt, dark-green leaves. H 2.5m (8ft) S 1.5m (5ft).

Rosa 'Penelope'
Semi-double, fragrant, pale creamy-pink flowers are produced from early summer to early autumn. Matt, dark green, bronze-tinged leaves. H 1m (3ft) S 1m (3ft).

Rosa 'Queen of Denmark'
Double, very fragrant, deep to light pink flowers in a single flush appear in mid-summer. Matt, grey-green foliage. H 1.5 (5ft) S 1.2m (4ft).

Rosa 'Rose de Rescht'
Double, mauve-red flowers that age to magenta-pink are produced in a single flush in mid-summer. Matt, mid-green leaves. H 90cm (32in) S 75cm (30in).

Rosa 'Roseraie de l'Haÿ'
Strongly fragrant, double, red-purple flowers are borne in succession from mid-summer to early autumn. H 2.2m (7ft) S 2m (6ft).

Rosa rugosa 'Rubra'
Fragrant, single, yellow-centred, purple-red flowers are produced in succession from mid-summer to early autumn, followed by attractive red or orange-red rosehips. H 2.5m (8ft) S 2.5m (8ft).

Rosa 'Sharifa Asma'
Rose-pink, fragrant, double flowers are borne from mid-summer to early autumn. Matt, mid-green leaves. H 1m (3ft) S 75cm (30in).

Rosa 'William Lobb'
Fragrant, semi-double, purple-magenta flowers that age to lavender are produced during early summer and mid-summer. Matt, dark green leaves. H 2m (6ft) S 2m (6ft).

Rosa 'Winchester Cathedral'
Double, cup-shaped, white flowers are produced in succession from mid-summer to early autumn. Matt, mid-green leaves. H 1.2m (4ft) S 1.2m (4ft).

Rosa xanthina 'Canary Bird'
Musk-scented, single, yellow flowers are produced in a single flush during late spring. Matt, fern-like, grey-green leaves. H 3m (10ft) S 4m (13ft).

PATIO ROSE
These are compact floribunda roses that produce masses of flowers throughout the summer and autumn months and can be used at the front of the border or in containers.

Rosa 'Golden Anniversary'
Large, semi-double, fragrant, apricot-pink flowers are produced from mid-summer to early autumn. Glossy, mid-green leaves. H 45cm (18in) S 45cm (18in).

Rosa 'Happy Anniversary'
Sweetly fragrant, deep-pink flowers appear in succession from mid-summer to early autumn. Glossy, dark green leaves. H 80cm (32in) S 75cm (30in).

Rosa 'Happy Birthday'
Double, creamy-white flowers are produced in succession from mid-summer to early autumn and Glossy, mid-green leaves. H 45cm (18in) S 45cm (18in).

Rosa 'Pearl Anniversary'
Semi-double, pearl-pink flowers are produced in succession from mid-summer to early autumn. Glossy, mid-green leaves. H 60cm (24in) S 60cm (24in).

Rosa 'Queen Mother'
Cup-shaped, semi-double, pink flowers appear in succession from mid-summer to early autumn. Glossy, mid-green leaves. H 40cm (16in) S 60cm (24in).

Rosa 'Sweet Dream'
Fragrant, cup-shaped, double, peach-apricot flowers are produced in succession from mid-summer to early autumn. Glossy, dark-green leaves. H 40cm (16in) S 35cm (14in).

GROUND-COVER ROSE
These are low-growing and spreading roses that produce masses of small blooms and offer good disease resistance. As this category name suggests, they are very useful for covering the ground and also preventing weeds.

Rosa 'Kent'
Slightly fragrant, semi-double, white flowers appear from mid-summer to early autumn, followed by small red hips. H 45cm (18in) S 1m (3ft).

Rosa 'Oxfordshire'
Slightly fragrant, semi-double, pale pink flowers are produced in succession from mid-summer to early autumn. H 60cm (24in) S 1.5m (5ft).

Rosa 'Suffolk'
Single, slightly fragrant, golden-centred, deep-scarlet flowers are borne in succession from

Rosa 'Queen Mother'

mid-summer to early autumn, followed by orange-red rosehips. H 45cm (18in) S 1m (3ft).

Rosa 'Surrey'

The cup-shaped, fragrant, double rose-pink flowers of 'Surrey' are produced in succession from mid-summer to early autumn. Matt, dark green leaves. H 80cm (32in) S 1.2m (4ft).

Rosa 'Sussex'

The slightly fragrant, double, apricot flowers of 'Sussex' are borne in succession from mid-summer to early autumn. The flowers are borne above, mid-green leaves. H 60cm (24in) S 1m (3ft).

ROSMARINIUS
Rosemary

A small genus of just two species, grown for their early summer flowers and aromatic foliage. Widely used in culinary dishes. Good for a sunny border or can be trimmed into a dense hedge.
Cultivation Grow in any well-drained garden soil that is poor or reasonably fertile and in full sun. In colder areas, choose a sunny spot that is sheltered from cold winds or grow in a pot. Use a soil-based compost. Feed monthly during the growing season and water as necessary.
Pruning To keep neat and bushy, cut back the previous year's growth to within 10cm (4in) of the main framework or the ground during mid-spring. Trim hedges after flowering.
Propagation Take semi-ripe cuttings in mid-summer or late summer.

Rosmarinus officinalis
Common rosemary

An evergreen culinary herb that forms a dense and rounded bush bearing purple-blue flowers during late spring and early summer along the stems of evergreen, strongly aromatic, dark green leaves. Good choice for growing as a hedge. H 1.5m (5ft) S 1.5m (5ft).
Named varieties: 'Miss Jessopp's Upright', vigorous, upright-growing rosemary, purple-blue flowers. H 2m (6ft) S 2m (6ft). 'Majorca Pink', compact, pale pink flowers. H 1m (3ft) S 1m (3ft). 'Severn Sea', arching stems carry bright blue flowers. H 1m (3ft) S 1.5m (5ft).
Aspect: sun
Hardiness: ✻✻ Zone: 9

RUBUS

A genus of about 250 species, including the tough, thicket-forming deciduous shrubs here, grown for their summer flowers and striking winter stems.
Cultivation Grow in any well-drained, reasonably fertile soil in full sun or dappled shade. Site those grown for winter stems where they will catch winter sun.

Pruning For the best flowering and stems cut back one in three stems near to ground level during early spring. Rejuvenate neglected plants by cutting back stems to near ground level in early spring.
Propagation Layer shoots or dig up rooted suckers in mid-spring.

Rubus biflorus

A prickly-stemmed, deciduous shrub with a brilliant white bloom when young. Small white flowers appear during late summer and early autumn, followed by yellow fruits. H 3m (10ft) S 3m (10ft).
Aspect: sun
Hardiness: ✻✻✻ Zones: 7–8

Rubus cockburnianus

Thicket-forming deciduous shrub with prickly purple stems that have a brilliant white bloom when young. Insignificant purple flowers are produced during late summer and early autumn, followed by black, inedible fruits. H 2.5m (8ft) S 2.5m (8ft).
Aspect: sun
Hardiness: ✻✻✻ Zones: 7–8

Rubus odoratus
Flowering raspberry

Fragrant, rose-pink, cup-shaped flowers appear from early summer to early autumn on this vigorous thicket-forming, deciduous shrub. H 2.5m (8ft) S 2.5m (8ft).
Aspect: sun or semi-shade
Hardiness: ✻✻✻ Zones: 7–8

Rosa 'Sussex'

Rosmarinus officinalis

Rubus odoratus

Ruta

RUTA
Rue

A genus of over five species that includes the evergreen shrub featured here, grown for their summer flowers and feathery aromatic foliage. An ideal choice for a sunny mixed border or can be trimmed to make a low hedge.
Cultivation Grow in any reasonably fertile, well-drained garden soil in full sun or dappled shade. Wear gloves and long sleeves when working with rue, as contact with the leaves can cause painful skin blistering in sunlight.
Pruning To keep plants neat and compact, cut back hard during mid-spring. Trim hedges after flowering.
Propagation Sow seed in early spring. Take semi-ripe cuttings in late summer.

Ruta graveolens 'Jackman's Blue'
This compact, rounded form has aromatic, steel-blue feathery leaves and tiny, mustard-coloured flowers from early summer to late summer). H 60cm (24in) S 75cm (30in).
Aspect: sun or semi-shade
Hardiness: ❀❀❀ Zones: 7–8

SALIX
Willow

This is a large and varied genus of some 300 species, including the low-growing deciduous shrubs featured here. They are grown for their silvery catkins and colourful bark. Compact and slow-growing varieties make excellent specimen plants for a small, sunny garden.

Willow trees to grow as shrubs

A few willow trees can be kept to shrub-like proportions by annual pruning. Cut all stems to near-ground level in early spring every year.

Salix alba 'Chermesina'
Bright red winter stems. H 3m (10ft) S 3m (10ft).

Salix alba subsp. *vitellina* 'Britzensis'

Fiery orange-red winter stems. H 3m (10ft) S 3m (10ft).

Salix daphnoides
Violet-purple young stems with a white bloom. H 3m (10ft) S 3m (10ft).

Salix irrorata
Purple young stems with a white bloom. H 3m (10ft) S 3m (10ft).

Cultivation Grow in any moisture-retentive, well-drained garden soil in full sun.
Pruning No routine pruning is necessary other than removing wayward or damaged stems in early spring.
Propagation Take hardwood cuttings in late winter.

Salix hastata 'Wehrhahnii'
A neat, slow-growing shrub with dark purple shoots and bright green leaves that turn yellow in autumn. Large, silvery catkins appear in early spring on bare stems before the leaves emerge. H 1m (3ft) S 1m (3ft).
Aspect: sun
Hardiness: ❀❀❀ Zones: 7–8

Salix lanata
Woolly willow
This compact, slow-growing and bushy shrub produces stumpy shoots that are white and woolly when young. Small yellow catkins are borne in mid-spring as the leaves emerge. H 1m (3ft) S 1.5m (5ft).
Aspect: sun
Hardiness: ❀❀❀ Zones: 7–8

SALVIA
Sage

This huge genus of around 900 species, includes the evergreen sub-shrubs featured here, are grown for their handsome aromatic foliage and widely used in cooking. Grow in a mixed or herb border or in a container on a sunny patio.
Cultivation In the garden, grow in a moisture-retentive, well-drained soil that is reasonably fertile and in full sun or dappled shade. In pots, grow in any general-purpose compost (soil mix).
Pruning To keep plants neat and compact, cut back hard to near ground level during mid-spring.

Salix vitellina 'Britzensis'

Salvia officinalis

Replace neglected plants.
Propagation Sow seed in early spring. Take semi-ripe cuttings in early autumn.

Salvia officinalis
Common sage
An evergreen culinary herb with grey-green aromatic foliage that carries spikes of lilac-blue flowers borne from late spring to mid-summer. H 80cm (32in) S 100cm (36in).
Named varieties: 'Icterina', variegated form with yellow-edged green leaves, mauve-blue flowers. H 80cm (32in) S 1m (3ft). 'Purpurascens', bright purple young leaves age to grey-green, mauve-blue flowers. H 80cm (32in) S 1m (3ft). 'Tricolor', grey-green leaves, splashed with cream and reddish-purple, mauve-blue flowers.
H 80cm (32in) S 1m (3ft).
Aspect: sun or semi-shade
Hardiness: ❀❀❀ Zones: 7–8

SAMBUCUS
Elder

A genus of about 25 species grown for their handsome foliage and summer flowers. Useful back-of-the-border plants. They are ideal for filling gaps.
Cultivation Grow in a moisture-retentive, well-drained garden soil that is reasonably fertile in full sun or dappled shade.
Pruning To get the best foliage displays, cut back hard to near ground level during early spring each year. For flowers and berries, cut back one stem in three during the dormant season, starting with the oldest.
Propagation Take hardwood cuttings in late winter.

Sambucus nigra 'Black Beauty'
A new variety with near-black, darkest burgundy foliage that contrasts with the flat heads of lemon-scented pale-pink flowers during early summer, followed by purple-black berries in autumn. H 3m (10ft) S 3m (10ft).
Aspect: sun or semi-shade
Hardiness: ❀❀❀ Zones: 7–8

Sambucus nigra 'Black Lace'
An exciting recent introduction with near-black, finely cut foliage

Sambucus racemosa 'Plumosa Aurea'

that provides a foil for the flat heads of pale-pink flowers that open from cream-coloured buds during late spring and early summer. Good choice for small gardens. H 3m (10ft) S 2m (6ft).
Aspect: sun or semi-shade
Hardiness: ❋❋❋ Zones: 7–8

Sambucus racemosa 'Plumosa Aurea'
Emerging bronze-tinted, the deeply cut, almost feathery, foliage turns golden yellow as it matures. Arching shoots bear conical clusters of creamy-yellow flowers during mid-spring. Grow in dappled shade to avoid scorching the delicate foliage. H 3m (10ft) S 3m (10ft).
Aspect: sun or semi-shade
Hardiness: ❋❋❋ Zones: 7–8

Sambucus racemosa 'Sutherland Gold'
The deeply cut, almost feathery, foliage emerges bronze-tinted before turning golden yellow with age. Conical clusters of creamy-yellow flowers during mid-spring are followed by glossy red fruits. H 3m (10ft) S 3m (10ft).
Aspect: sun or semi-shade
Hardiness: ❋❋❋ Zones: 7–8

SANTOLINA
A genus of nearly 20 species, including the compact evergreen

shrubs featured here, grown for their grey, aromatic foliage and button-like summer flowers. Ideal for a hot spot, such as sunny banks and gravel gardens, or edging sunny borders. They can even make an attractive low, informal flowering hedge or garden divider.
Cultivation Grow in any well-drained garden soil that is poor to reasonably fertile and in full sun, but sheltered from cold winds.
Pruning To keep plants neat and compact, cut back to 5cm (2in) off ground level during mid-spring before new growth emerges. Neglected plants can be rejuvenated by cutting back hard into old wood during mid-spring

Santolina pinnata

to encourage new growth from lower down. Deadhead edging plants and hedges to keep neat all summer.
Propagation Take semi-ripe cuttings in early autumn.

Santolina chamaecyparissus var. nana
Cotton lavender
Feathery, greyish-white, aromatic leaves set off the masses of tiny, lemon-yellow button-like flowers throughout mid-summer and late summer on this dense and rounded evergreen shrub.
H 30cm (12in) S 45cm (18in).
Aspect: sun
Hardiness: ❋❋ Zones: 7–8

Santolina chamaecyparissus 'Lambrook Silver'
Cotton lavender
The silvery mound of finely dissected woolly leaves that this shrub produces are the perfect foil for the tiny lemon-yellow and button-like flowers that are borne during mid-summer and late summer. H 30cm (12in) S 45cm (18in).
Aspect: sun
Hardiness: ❋❋ Zone: 9

SARCOCOCCA
Sweet box
A genus of around 15 species, including the dense-growing, evergreen shrubs featured here, grown for their neat habit and sweet vanilla-scented winter flowers. An ideal choice for a dark, shady corner where nothing else will grow. Well suited to

Santolina chamaecyparissus var. nana

Sarcococca confusa

urban gardens as it is pollution tolerant.
Cultivation Grow in a moisture-retentive, well-drained garden soil that is reasonably fertile and in dappled or deep shade.
Pruning No routine pruning is necessary. Remove any damaged growth in mid-spring.
Propagation Take hardwood cuttings in mid-autumn.

Sarcococca confusa
A dense, evergreen shrub with glossy, dark green leaves that bears clusters of sweetly scented white flowers from early winter to early spring. H 2m (6ft) S 1m (3ft).
Aspect: semi-shade to deep shade
Hardiness: ❋❋❋ Zones: 6–9

Sarcococca hookeriana var. digyna
A thicket-forming shrub with slender, pointed, dark green leaves and small creamy-white or pink-tinged flowers that are produced in clusters from early winter to early spring. H 1.5m (5ft) S 2m (6ft).
Aspect: semi-shade to deep shade
Hardiness: ❋❋❋ 6–9

Sarcococca hookeriana var. humilis (syn. S. humilis)
Compact, clump-forming evergreen shrub with slender dark green leaves and small, creamy-white or pink-tinged flowers produced in clusters from early winter to early spring. H 60cm (24in) S 1m (3ft).
Aspect: semi-shade to deep shade
Hardiness: ❋❋❋ 6–9

Skimmia japonica 'Rubella'

SKIMMIA

A small genus of just four species, including the compact evergreen shrubs featured here, grown for their fragrant flowers, neat foliage and long-lasting colourful autumn berries. They make useful border fillers in shade. Compact forms make excellent winter pots.

Cultivation Grow in a moisture-retentive, well-drained garden soil that is reasonably fertile and in dappled or deep shade. In containers, grow in any general-purpose compost (soil mix). To be sure of berries, grow both male and female forms.

Pruning No routine pruning is necessary. Remove any damaged growth in mid-spring.

Propagation Take semi-ripe cuttings in early autumn.

Skimmia japonica 'Rubella' (male form)

A compact shrub with handsome, red-margined, dark green leaves and dense clusters of deep red flower-buds in autumn that do not open until early spring to reveal fragrant white flowers. H 1.5m (5ft) S 1.5m (5ft).
Aspect: semi-shade to deep shade
Hardiness: ✿✿✿ Zones: 7–8

Skimmia japonica subsp. reevesiana (hermaphrodite form)

A large, spreading, evergreen shrub with narrow, tapered, dark green leaves and clusters of white flowers during mid-spring and late spring, followed by bright red berries. H 7m (23ft) S 1m (3ft).
Named varieties: 'Robert Fortune', dark-edged, pale green leaves, white flowers, followed by bright red berries. H 7m (23ft) S 1m (3ft).
Aspect: semi-shade to deep shade
Hardiness: ✿✿✿ Zones: 7–8

Skimmia x confusa 'Kew Green' (male form)

Dome-shaped, compact, evergreen shrub with aromatic, pointed, leaves that set off the dense clusters of sweetly scented, cream-coloured flowers produced during mid-spring and late spring. H 3m (10ft) S 1.5m (5ft).
Aspect: semi-shade to deep shade
Hardiness: ✿✿✿ Zones: 7–8

SOPHORA

A genus of about 50 species, including the evergreen shrubs featured here, grown for their clusters of bell-shaped flowers that hang from zigzag shoots covered in symmetrical leaves that are tiny, oval, dark green leaflets. Good seasonal specimens for a sunny border, or can be trained against a wall or fence.

Cultivation Grow in any well-drained garden soil in full sun. Grow against a sunny wall in colder areas.

Pruning No routine pruning is necessary. Remove any wayward or damaged growth in mid-spring.

Propagation Sow seed in early spring.

Sophora microphylla (syn. Edwardia microphylla)

Open, spreading, frost-hardy evergreen shrub that carries pendent clusters of pea-shaped yellow flowers from arching branches during mid-spring and late spring. H 8m (26ft) S 8m (26ft).
Named varieties: 'Sun King', a recent fully hardy introduction that forms a more compact, but still open, bushy shrub with drooping clusters of bell-shaped

Sophora microphylla

yellow flowers during early spring and mid-spring. H 3m (10ft) S 3m (10ft).
Aspect: sun
Hardiness: ✿✿ or ✿✿✿
Zones: 7–9

SPARTIUM
Spanish broom

A genus of just one species of deciduous shrubs grown for their long-lasting and fragrant golden summer flowers. Good border filler or back-of-the-border shrub for a sunny spot. Pollution- and salt-tolerant, they are therefore well-suited for growing in town and coastal gardens.

Cultivation Grow in any well-drained, reasonably fertile, garden soil in full sun. Grow by a sunny wall in colder areas.

Pruning Prevent it going woody at the base and encourage flowering by trimming new growth lightly directly after flowering.

Propagation Sow seed in early spring.

Spartium junceum

A slender shrub with dark green shoots that carries masses of pea-like flowers in succession from early summer to late summer, followed by dark brown seed-pods. H 3m (10ft) S 3m (10ft).
Aspect: sun
Hardiness: ✿✿ Zone: 9

SPIRAEA

A genus of about 80 species, including the easy-to-grow, deciduous, summer-flowering shrubs featured here, some of

Spartium junceum

which are grown mainly for their eye-catching foliage. A useful border filler in sun or can be grown as an informal low hedge.
Cultivation Grow in a moisture-retentive, well-drained, reasonably fertile soil in full sun.
Pruning Varieties that flower on the previous season's growth need no routine pruning. Otherwise, cut out one stem in three during early spring, starting with the oldest. Informal hedges should be trimmed after flowering. Remove all-green reverted shoots on variegated varieties as soon as they appear.
Propagation Take semi-ripe cuttings in mid-summer, or hardwood cuttings in late autumn.

Spiraea 'Arguta'
Bridal wreath
Beautiful arching sprays of tiny, saucer-shaped, white flowers dominate this dense, rounded shrub during mid-spring and late spring. H 2.5m (8ft) S 2.5m (8ft).
Aspect: sun
Hardiness: ❂❂❂ Zones: 7–8

Spiraea japonica 'Anthony Waterer'
Emerging bronze-tinted, the sharply toothed foliage matures to

dark green with pink and cream margins. Flat heads of rose-pink flowers appear from mid-summer to late summer. Good informal hedge. H 1.5m (5ft) S 1.5m (5ft).
Aspect: sun
Hardiness: ❂❂❂ Zones 7–8

Spiraea japonica 'Goldflame'
Bronze-red emerging foliage turns bright yellow and then ages to luminous green on this compact shrub. Dark pink flowers are borne in clusters during mid-summer and late summer. Good informal hedge. H 75cm (30in) S 75cm (30in).
Aspect: sun
Hardiness: ❂❂❂ Zones: 7–8

Spiraea japonica 'Golden Princess'
The foliage emerges bronze-red on this clump-forming shrub before turning bright yellow then red in autumn. Purplish-pink flowers are produced in clusters during mid-summer and late summer. H 2m (6ft) S 1.5m (5ft).
Aspect: sun
Hardiness: ❂❂❂ Zones: 7–8

Spiraea nipponica 'Snowmound' (syn. S. nipponica var. tosaensis)
The rounded, dark green leaves of

Stephandra incisa 'Crispa'

this spreading deciduous shrub make the perfect backdrop for the arching sprays of cup-shaped white flowers that are produced throughout early summer and mid-summer. H 2.5m (8ft) S 2.5m (8ft).
Aspect: sun
Hardiness: ❂❂❂ Zones: 7–8

Spiraea prunifolia (syn. S. prunifolia 'Plena')
Finely toothed, bright green leaves that are silvery beneath, cover this deciduous shrub, which has arching stems that are wreathed in double white flowers throughout early spring and mid-spring.
H 2m (6ft) S 2m (6ft).
Aspect: sun
Hardiness: ❂❂❂ Zones: 7–8

Spiraea thunbergii
From mid-spring to early summer, arching sprays of tiny, saucer-shaped, white flowers cover this dense and bushy deciduous shrub. The pale green leaves turn yellow in autumn. H 1.5m (5ft) S 2m (6ft).
Aspect: sun
Hardiness: ❂❂❂ Zones: 7–8

STEPHANANDRA
This is a small genus comprising just four species, including the deciduous early summer-flowering shrubs featured here. These plants make useful front-of-the-border fillers when planted in sun or

dappled shade. They can also be used for edging or ground cover.
Cultivation Grow in a moisture-retentive, well-drained garden soil that is reasonably fertile in full sun or dappled shade.
Pruning Prune out one stem in three during early spring, starting with the oldest.
Propagation Take semi-ripe cuttings in mid-summer or hardwood cuttings in late autumn.

Stephanandra incisa 'Crispa'
The deeply lobed and wavy-edged leaves cover this thicket-forming, low-growing shrub and turn orange-yellow in autumn before they fall to reveal rich brown stems. This shrub makes a good edging and ground cover plant. H 60cm (24in) S 3m (10ft).
Aspect: sun or semi-shade
Hardiness: ❂❂❂ Zones: 7–8

Stephanandra tanakae
This is a thicket-forming, bushy shrub that has striking bright orange-brown stems that are revealed during the winter. The arching shoots are covered in toothed green leaves at other times before turning shades of yellow and orange in autumn. Bears greenish-yellow flowers throughout the summer.
H 3m (10ft) S 3m (10ft).
Aspect: sun or semi-shade
Hardiness: ❂❂❂ Zones: 7–8

Spirea 'Arguta'

Symphoricarpos x doorenbosii 'Mother of Pearl'

SYMPHORICARPOS
Snowberry

A genus of over 15 species, including the deciduous thicket-forming shrubs featured here, grown mainly for their handsome foliage or long-lasting, marble-sized, autumn berries. Useful border fillers in sun or dappled shade. They make attractive informal low hedges.
Cultivation Grow in any reasonably fertile, well-drained soil in full sun or dappled shade.
Pruning For brightly coloured foliage displays, prune out one stem in three during early spring, starting with the oldest. Informal hedges can be trimmed every couple of months during the summer to keep neat.
Propagation Take semi-ripe cuttings in early summer or hardwood cuttings in late autumn.

Symphoricarpos x chenaultii 'Hancock'
Low-growing and spreading snowberry that has green leaves that turn orange-red in autumn. Small bell-shaped flowers are produced in late summer, followed by conspicuous dark pink berries. H 3m (10ft) S 3m (10ft).
Aspect: sun or semi-shade
Hardiness: ✼✼✼ Zones: 7–8

Symphoricarpos x doorenbosii 'Mother of Pearl'
A thicket-forming shrub with dark green leaves and arching stems that carry small, bell-shaped flowers during mid-summer, followed by conspicuous pearl-like pink-flushed white berries from early autumn. The best fruiting variety. H 2m (6ft) S indefinite.
Aspect: sun or semi-shade
Hardiness: ✼✼✼ Zones: 7–8

Symphoricarpos orbiculatus 'Albovariegatus'
A compact, thicket-forming shrub with variegated white and green leaves on a dense and busy shrub. Few berries are produced.
H 2m (6ft) S 2m (6ft).
Aspect: sun or semi-shade
Hardiness: ✼✼✼ Zones: 7–8

SYRINGA
Lilac

A genus of about 20 species including the large, spreading deciduous shrubs featured here, grown for their highly fragrant spring flowers. They make useful seasonal specimens and can be trained into attractive multi-stemmed trees.
Cultivation Grow in a moisture-retentive, well-drained neutral to alkaline soil that is reasonably fertile and in full sun.
Pruning After flowering, cut back the fading flowering shoots to the first leaves below the flower cluster. In the dormant season thin out overcrowded branches and rejuvenate neglected shrubs by cutting the whole shrub back to within 1m (3ft) of the ground. Create a multi-stemmed tree by selecting three, four or five of the strongest stems, removing all others and cutting off side branches in successive seasons to raise the height of the canopy. All major pruning should be carried out during the dormant season (early winter to early spring).
Propagation Bud named varieties during mid-summer.

Syringa meyeri var. spontanea 'Palibin'
Fragrant, purple-pink flowers are produced in dense clusters throughout late spring and early summer on this slow-growing Korean lilac. Ideal for small gardens. H 2m (10ft) S 1.5m (5ft).
Aspect: sun
Hardiness: ✼✼✼ Zones: 7–8

Syringa pubescens subsp. microphylla 'Superba'
The oval green leaves provide a backdrop for the rose-pink fragrant flowers that are borne in dense clusters during mid-spring and late spring and intermittently thereafter until mid-autumn.
H 6m (20ft) S 6m (20ft).
Aspect: sun
Hardiness: ✼✼✼ Zones: 7–8

Syringa vulgaris 'Charles Joly'
A spreading shrub with heart-shaped, dark green leaves and dense, cone-shaped clusters of double, dark purple flowers in late spring and early summer.
H 7m (23ft) S 7m (23ft).
Aspect: sun
Hardiness: ✼✼✼ Zones: 7–8

Syringa vulgaris 'Katherine Havemeyer'
Dense, cone-shaped clusters of purple buds open during late spring and early summer to reveal strongly scented, double, lavender-purple flowers above heart-shaped leaves. H 7m (23ft) S 7m (23ft).
Aspect: sun
Hardiness: ✼✼✼ Zones: 7–8

Syringa vulgaris 'Madame Lemoine'
This elegant white lilac produces dense, cone-shaped clusters of very fragrant, double, white flowers during late spring and early summer above heart-shaped, apple-green leaves. H 7m (23ft) S 7m (23ft).
Aspect: sun
Hardiness: ✼✼✼ Zones: 7–8

Syringa protolaciniata

Syringa x josiflexa

Syringa vulgaris 'Michel Buchner'
A spreading shrub with heart-shaped, dark green leaves and large, cone-shaped clusters of fragrant, double, rose-mauve flowers with white centres during late spring and early summer.
H 7m (23ft) S 7m (23ft).
Aspect: sun
Hardiness: ✼✼✼ Zones: 7–8

TAMARIX
Tamarisk

A genus of over 50 species, including the deciduous shrubs featured here, grown for their feathery, late-summer flowerheads. A good back-of-the-border shrub that makes an excellent windbreak in mild coastal gardens.
Cultivation Grow in any well-drained garden soil in full sun, but sheltered from cold winds.
Pruning To keep in shape, prune flowering stems in early spring, removing half to two-thirds of the previous year's growth.
Propagation Take hardwood cuttings in mid-autumn.

Tamarix ramosissima (syn. T. pentandra)
A vigorous shrub with graceful, arching, red-brown stems that carry airy, plume-like, pale pink flowers in dense clusters during late summer and early autumn.
H 5m (16ft) S 5m (16ft).
Named varieties: 'Pink Cascade',

Tamarix 'Rubra'

plumes of tiny, rich pink flowers.
H 5m (16ft) S 5m (16ft).
Aspect: sun
Hardiness: ❀❀❀ Zones: 7–8

Tamarix 'Rubra'

A vigorous shrub with graceful,
arching stems that carry airy,
plume-like, purple-pink flowers in
dense clusters during late summer
and early autumn. H 5m (16ft)
S 5m (16ft).
Aspect: sun
Hardiness: ❀❀❀ Zones: 7–8

TIBOUCHINA

A large genus of over 350 species,
including the spreading tender
evergreen shrub featured here,
grown for its exotic summer

Tibouchina semi-decandra

flowers. An attractive border filler
in warm gardens. Grow in a
container in cooler areas.
Cultivation Grow in a moisture-
retentive, well-drained garden soil
in full sun. In containers, grow in
a soil-based compost (soil mix).
Feed every month throughout the
growing season and water as
necessary. Move to a warm spot
undercover when the temperature
falls below 5°C (41°F) and water
sparingly throughout the winter.
Pruning No routine pruning is
necessary.
Propagation Take softwood
cuttings in mid-spring or semi-
ripe cuttings in mid-summer.

Tibouchina urvilleana (syn. *Pleroma macrantha. T. semidecandra*)
Brazilian spider flower

A tall, spreading shrub with
velvety, dark green leaves that are
distinctively veined. Large saucer-
shaped rich purple flowers with a
satin finish are borne from mid-
summer to late autumn. H 4m
(12ft) S 5m (16ft).
Aspect: sun
Hardiness: tender Zones: 10+

VIBURNUM

A varied genus of over 150
species, including the deciduous
and evergreen shrubs featured
here, grown for their clusters of
winter or spring flowers or eye-

catching autumn berries. Most are
good border fillers, with many
coping well with a partly shady
shrub border or woodland-edge
planting scheme. The winter-
flowering deciduous varieties and
fruiting evergreen forms are
useful for adding interest during
the coldest months.
Cultivation Grow in a moisture-
retentive, well-drained garden soil
that is reasonably fertile and in
full sun or dappled shade.
Pruning Evergreen varieties require
no routine pruning. Damaged or
misplaced shoots can be removed
in late spring. If required,
deciduous varieties can be thinned
by removing one stem in three,
starting with the oldest. Prune
winter-flowering varieties during
mid-spring and summer-flowering
varieties in early summer.
Propagation Layer deciduous
shrubs in mid-spring. Take
hardwood cuttings in mid-autumn
or semi-ripe cuttings of evergreen
varieties in early autumn.

EVERGREEN VIBURNUMS
Viburnum davidii

A compact, evergreen shrub with
prominently veined, dark green
leaves that bears small flat heads
of white flowers during late
spring followed by eyecatching
metallic, turquoise-blue berries.
H 1.5m (5ft) S 1.5m (5ft).
Aspect: sun or semi-shade
Hardiness: ❀❀❀ Zones: 7–8

Viburnum x burkwoodii

Clusters of pink buds open on
this lovely viburnum during mid-

Viburnum tinus 'Eve Price'

spring and late spring to expose
deliciously fragrant white flowers
that are followed by red fruit.
H 2.5m (8ft) S 2.5m (8ft).
Aspect: sun or semi-shade
Hardiness: ❀❀❀ Zones: 7–8

Viburnum 'Eskimo'

This is a compact, semi-evergreen
viburnum that produces lovely
round clusters of pink-tinged,
cream buds that open during mid-
spring and late spring to show off
its white tubular flowers against
glossy, dark green leaves.
H 1.5m (5ft) S 1.5m (5ft).
Aspect: sun or semi-shade
Hardiness: ❀❀❀ Zones: 7–8

Viburnum rhytidophyllum

This is a spreading, evergreen
viburnum that bears flat clusters
of cream-coloured flowers
throughout late spring. They are
produced at the ends of arching
shoots of wavy-edged, dark green
leaves. Red berries follow in
autumn. H 3m (10ft)
S 4m (12ft).
Aspect: sun or semi-shade
Hardiness: ❀❀❀ Zones: 7–8

Viburnum tinus 'Eve Price'

Small flatheads of carmine-pink
buds reveal pinkish-white flowers
from early winter to mid-spring
and are followed by dark blue-
black berries. H 3m (10ft)
S 3m (10ft).
Aspect: sun or semi-shade
Hardiness: ❀❀❀ Zones: 7–8

Viburnum tinus 'French White'

This viburnum produces flat
heads of rosy-red buds open in
succession from early winter to
mid-spring to reveal white flowers
that are followed by dark blue-
black berries. H 3m (10ft)
S 3m (10ft).
Aspect: sun or semi-shade
Hardiness: ❀❀❀ Zones: 7–8

Viburnum tinus 'Gwenllian'

Masses of dark pink buds open in
succession on this shrub from
early winter to mid-spring to
reveal pink-flushed white flowers,
that are followed by a profusion
of dark, blue-black berries.
H 3m (10ft) S 3m (10ft).
Aspect: sun or semi-shade
Hardiness: ❀❀❀ Zones: 7–8

Viburnum opulus 'Roseum'

DECIDUOUS VIBURNUMS
Viburnum x bodnantense 'Dawn'
An upright deciduous shrub that carries dense clusters of fragrant dark pink flowers on bare stems from late autumn to early spring. H 3m (10ft) S 2m (6ft).
Aspect: sun or semi-shade
Hardiness: ✿✿✿ Zones: 7–8

Viburnum x bodnantense 'Charles Lamont'
Strongly scented, bright pink flowers are carried in dense clusters on bare stems from late autumn to early spring on this upright deciduous shrub. H 3m (10ft) S 2m (6ft).
Aspect: sun or semi-shade
Hardiness: ✿✿✿ Zones: 7–8

Viburnum carlesii

Viburnum x carlcephalum
Rounded clusters of pink buds open during mid-spring and late spring to reveal fragrant white flowers against heart-shaped, dark-green leaves, that turn red in autumn. H 3m (10ft) S 3m (10ft).
Aspect: sun or semi-shade
Hardiness: ✿✿✿ Zones: 7–8

Viburnum carlesii
Dense clusters of pink buds open throughout mid-spring and late spring into fragrant white or pink-flushed white flowers. The dark green leaves take on red-purple tints in autumn.
H 2m (6ft) S 2m (6ft).
Aspect: sun or semi-shade
Hardiness: ✿✿✿ Zones: 7–8

Viburnum x juddii
Pink buds in rounded clusters open during mid-spring and late spring to reveal fragrant pink-tinted white flowers. The oval, dark green leaves take on red-purple tints in autumn.
H 1.2m (4ft) S 1.5m (5ft).
Aspect: sun or semi-shade
Hardiness: ✿✿✿ Zones: 7–8

Viburnum opulus 'Roseum' (syn. V. 'Sterile')
Snowball tree
Rounded, snowball-like clusters of white flowers are produced during late spring and early summer against a backdrop of dark green leaves that become purple-tinted in autumn. H 4m (12ft) S 4m (13ft).
Aspect: sun or semi-shade
Hardiness: ✿✿✿ Zones: 7–8

Viburnum plicatum 'Mariesii'

Viburnum plicatum 'Mariesii'
Japanese snowball bush
Tiered branches carry white, lacecap-like flowers throughout late spring over toothed, prominently veined, dark-green leaves that turn red-purple in autumn. H 3m (10ft) S 4m (13ft).
Aspect: sun or semi-shade
Hardiness: ✿✿✿ Zones: 7–8

Viburnum plicatum 'Pink Beauty'
Horizontal, tiered branches of this deciduous shrub show off the white, lacecap-like flowers in late spring that age to pink. The toothed, prominently veined, dark green leaves turn red-purple in autumn. H 3m (10ft) S 4m (13ft).
Aspect: sun or semi-shade
Hardiness: ✿✿✿ Zones: 7–8

VINCA
Periwinkle
This genus of seven species includes the low-growing sub-shrubs featured here, grown for their colourful spring flowers and their weed-smothering carpet of attractive foliage. It makes excellent ground cover in sun or shade as well as a useful addition to winter containers.
Cultivation Grow in a moisture-retentive, well-drained soil that is reasonably fertile and in full sun or dappled shade. Grow in sun for better flowering displays. In containers, grow in any general-purpose compost (soil mix).
Pruning No routine pruning is necessary, other than to keep it within bounds. Neglected plants can be rejuvenated by cutting all stems back to near ground level during late winter.
Propagation Lift and divide clumps as for perennials or separate and pot-up rooted layers.

Vinca major
Greater periwinkle
This is a fast-growing, sprawling, evergreen sub-shrub with large, violet-blue flowers that are

Vinca minor 'Aureovariegata'

Vinca major

produced in succession from mid-spring to early autumn above dark green leaves. This shrub makes excellent ground cover between deciduous trees and shrubs. H 45cm (18in) S indefinite.
Aspect: sun or semi-shade
Hardiness: ❋❋❋ Zones: 7–8

Vinca minor
Lesser periwinkle
This is a less invasive version of the periwinkle, which has evergreen, lance-shaped, dark green leaves and pale blue flowers borne from mid-spring to early autumn. Good ground cover choice for small areas or for softening the edges of raised beds and containers. H 20cm (8in) S indefinite.
Named varieties: 'Aureovariegata', variegated form with deep purple flowers. H 20cm (18in) S indefinite. 'Gertrude Jekyll', white flowers. H 20cm (8in) S indefinite.
Aspect: sun or semi-shade
Hardiness: ❋❋❋ Zones: 7–8

Vinca minor 'Illumination'
This is a recent introduction that has glossy golden, green-edged leaves on sprawling stems. Light blue flowers are carried in succession from mid-spring to early autumn. Ideal for use in containers or even for trailing over the edge of a hanging basket. H 15m (50ft) S 1m (3ft).
Aspect: sun or semi-shade
Hardiness: ❋❋❋ Zones: 7–8

WEIGELA
A genus of over 10 species, including the summer-flowering deciduous shrubs featured here. These plants can be used all around the garden filling gaps and boosting early summer displays.
Cultivation Grow in any well-drained garden soil that is reasonably fertile and in full sun or dappled shade.
Pruning To keep established shrubs flowering well, cut back one stem in three to near ground level after flowering, starting with the oldest stems.
Propagation Take semi-ripe cuttings in mid-summer or hardwood cuttings in mid-autumn.

Weigela 'Bristol Ruby'
An upright-growing shrub with dark green leaves that is covered in clusters of purple buds. These open into bell-shaped, ruby-red flowers throughout late spring and early summer. H 2.5m (8ft) S 2m (6ft).
Aspect: sun or semi-shade
Hardiness: ❋❋❋ Zones: 7–8

Weigela florida 'Foliis Purpureis'
A deciduous shrub with bronze-green leaves that carries clusters of funnel-shaped, deep pink flowers on arching stems during late spring and early summer. H 1m (3ft) S 5m (16ft).
Aspect: sun or semi-shade
Hardiness: ❋❋❋ Zones: 7–8

Weigela 'Florida Variegata'
Clusters of pale pink funnel-shaped flowers are borne on arching stems throughout late spring and early summer against a

Weigela 'Apple Blossom'

Weigela 'Candida'

backdrop of greyish-green leaves that are edged with white. H 2.5m (8ft) S 2.5m (8ft).
Aspect: sun or semi-shade
Hardiness: ❋❋❋ Zones: 7–8

YUCCA
This genus of about 40 species includes the spiky, evergreen shrubs with sword-shaped leaves featured here. Ideal focal points in a mixed border in sun or shade and provide architectural interest throughout the year.
Cultivation Grow in any well-drained, reasonably fertile soil in full sun or dappled shade. Mulch with gravel to protect the crown.
Pruning Pruning is unnecessary. Remove dead or damaged leaves in mid-spring.
Propagation Separate young offshoots during mid-spring.

Yucca filamentosa
Adam's needle
Spiky clumps of stiff, dark green, sword-shaped leaves provide year-round interest, with the bonus of towering spikes of white, bell-shaped flowers during mid-summer and late summer. H 75cm (30in) S 150cm (60in).
Aspect: sun or semi-shade
Hardiness: ❋❋❋ Zones: 7–8

Yucca flaccida 'Ivory'
Impressive clumps of dark, blue-green, sword-shaped leaves look good all year round, with tall spikes of green-tinged, creamy-white flowers produced in mid-summer and late summer. H 1.5m (5ft) S 1.5m (5ft).
Aspect: sun or semi-shade
Hardiness: ❋❋❋ Zones: 7–8

Yucca flaccida 'Golden Sword'
Clumps of spiky, yellow-striped, sword-shaped, blue-green leaves with green-tinged, creamy-white flowers appearing in mid-summer and late summer. H 55cm (22in) S 150cm (60in).
Aspect: sun or semi-shade
Hardiness: ❋❋❋ Zones: 7–8

Yucca gloriosa 'Variegata'
Spiky clumps of stiff yellow-edged, sword-shaped, dark green leaves are joined by white bell-shaped flowers on vertical spikes from late summer to early autumn. H 2m (6ft) S 2m (6ft).
Aspect: sun or semi-shade
Hardiness: ❋❋❋ Zones: 7–8

Yucca filamentosa

A directory of climbers

This section provides a highly illustrated listing of popular climbers that are available. It demonstrates very clearly just how versatile these plants can be – providing every conceivable colour of bloom, growth achievements and types of foliage. Bearing these factors in mind will enable you to create wonderful effects in any style or size of garden. Increasingly, plants are becoming known by their Latin (botanical) names, so these are given throughout, together with their English (common) names.

The hardiness zones given in the text refer only to the selected main plants featured and not to the whole genus. The height and spread given for each of the plants is an indication only. The dimensions will vary, depending on the growing conditions and the vigour of the individual plants – as well as your ability to care for them. The spread is particularly difficult to predict, as many plants go on increasing their width throughout their lives.

This magnificent climber, *Clematis montana* var. *rubens* 'Elizabeth', tumbles over a wall in full bloom to display its magnificent flowers. It is a prime example of how climbers can enhance any structure in the garden.

Actinidia kolomikta

ACTINIDIA

A genus of about 40 species, including the deciduous, twining climber featured here, which is grown for its seemingly paint-dipped foliage. Useful for adding interest to sunny walls and fences and will quickly cover trellis and arbours. Fast growing, it is an ideal choice for a quick cover-up, too, with a single plant able to smother about two standard fence panels in five years.

Cultivation Grow in any well-drained garden soil that is reasonably fertile and in full sun, but sheltered from strong winds.

Pruning No routine pruning is necessary. Thin out over-crowded stems in late winter. For a quick cover-up, train stems 20cm (8in) apart across the screen and tie in new shoots as necessary. When the screen is complete, cut back new growth to within 15cm (6in) of the established framework of stems in late winter. Neglected plants can be rejuvenated by cutting the oldest stems back to a younger side shoot lower down in late winter.

Propagation Take semi-ripe nodal cuttings in mid-summer.

Actinidia kolomikta
Kolomikta vine

A deciduous climber with dark green, heart-shaped leaves that are splashed pink and white as if the tips had been dipped in paint. Clusters of fragrant white flowers are produced in early summer. H 5m (16ft) S 4m (13ft).
Aspect: sun
Hardiness: ✿✿✿ Zone: Min. 7

AKEBIA
Chocolate vine

A genus of around five species, including the semi-evergreen vigorous twining climber featured here, grown for its fragrant chocolate-coloured spring flowers. Good for growing up screens and walls next to an entrance, where its fragrance can be appreciated. It is fairly fast-growing, with a single plant covering one standard fence panel in five years.

Akebia quinata

Cultivation Grow in a moisture-retentive, well-drained garden soil that is reasonably fertile and in full sun or dappled shade.

Pruning No routine pruning is necessary. Encourage dense growth and keep tidy by trimming in mid-spring. Neglected plants can be rejuvenated by cutting back the oldest stems to a younger side shoot lower down in late winter.

Propagation Take semi-ripe nodal cuttings in late summer or layer suitable stems in mid-autumn.

Akebia quinata

Pendent clusters of maroon-chocolate flowers that have a sweet and spicy fragrance are produced from early to late spring. The lobed dark green foliage becomes purple-tinged in winter. In long, warm summers, large, sausage-shaped fruit can form. H 10m (33ft) S 10m (33ft).
Aspect: sun or semi-shade
Hardiness: ✿✿✿ Zone: Min. 7

AMPELOPSIS

A genus of about 25 species, including the deciduous self-clinging climbers featured here, grown for their unusual flowers, fruit and autumn tints. They make useful and unusual climbers for walls or fences. If grown over a pergola or other similar open support, they can be trained to create an attractive, hanging curtain-effect of foliage.

Cultivation Grow in a moisture-retentive, well-drained garden soil that is reasonably fertile and in full sun or dappled shade. Grow in full sun for best fruit production.

Pruning No routine pruning is necessary. Thin out over-crowded stems in late winter. For a curtain effect, cut back all new growth to within a couple of buds from the main horizontal framework overhead in late winter.

Propagation Take softwood cuttings in mid-summer.

Ampelopsis aconitifolia (syn. Vitis aconitifolia)

This luxuriant vine will cloak any garden structure effortlessly, creating a highly textured curtain of attractively lush foliage. This is a vigorous climber, with palmate dark green leaves, that carries insignificant green flowers during early and mid-summer, followed by showy bunches of orange-red berries. H 12m (40ft) S 10m (33ft).
Aspect: sun or semi-shade
Hardiness: ✿✿✿ Zone: Min. 7

Ampelopsis glandulosa var. brevipedunculata (syn A. brevipedunculata)

This plant produces miniature birds' egg-like speckled fruit that change from cream to pink to clear blue as they ripen on this vigorous climber. The fruit follow insignificant green flowers produced during early and mid-summer. H 5m (16ft) S 6m (20ft).
Aspect: sun or semi-shade
Hardiness: ✿✿✿ Zone: Min. 7

Ampelopsis brevipedunculata elegans

Aristolochia littoralis

Ampelopsis megalophylla

A vigorous twining climber with deeply cut foliage that bears insignificant green flowers during early summer, followed by unusual black fruit. H 10m (33ft) S 10m (33ft).
Aspect: sun or semi-shade
Hardiness: ❋❋❋ Zone: Min. 7

ARISTOLOCHIA
Dutchman's pipe

A very large genus of over 300 species, including the tender twining deciduous and evergreen climbers featured here, grown for their intriguing, pipe-shaped summer flowers. In warm gardens they will quickly cover supports with a cloak of handsome foliage to disguise eyesores. Elsewhere, they make an exotic choice for a frost-free conservatory.
Cultivation In the garden, grow in any well-drained garden soil that is reasonably fertile in full sun or dappled shade, but protected from cold winds. In containers, grow in a soil-based compost (soil mix). Feed every month throughout the growing season and water as necessary. Tender plants should be moved to a warm spot undercover when the temperature falls below 7°C (45°F) and watered sparingly during winter.
Pruning No routine pruning is necessary. Cut back wayward stems after flowering.
Propagation Take softwood cuttings in early spring for tender species indoors and in mid-summer for hardy species outside.

Berberidopsis corallina

Aristolochia littoralis
(syn. *A. elegans*)

A tender climber with evergreen kidney-shaped, pale green leaves. During early summer and mid-summer it bears unusual rounded purple flowers, spotted with white. H 10m (33ft) S 10m (33ft).
Aspect: sun or semi-shade
Hardiness: tender Zones: 10–12

Aristolochia macrophylla
(syn. *A. durior, A. sipho*)

A robust, twining, deciduous climber, with dark green, heart-shaped leaves, that bears unusual rounded, green flowers, spotted with yellow, purple and brown, during early summer. H 10m (33ft) S 10m (33ft).
Aspect: sun or semi-shade
Hardiness: ❋❋ Zones: Min. 7

BERBERIDOPSIS

A genus of just one species of evergreen climbers, grown for their eye-catching pendent summer flowers. Useful for adding colour to shady structures.
Cultivation Grow in a moisture-retentive, well-drained neutral to acid soil that is fertile and in dappled shade, but protected from cold winds. In colder regions, apply an insulating mulch in autumn to protect the crown.
Pruning No routine pruning is necessary. Cut back wayward stems in mid-spring.
Propagation Take semi-ripe cuttings in late summer.

Berberidopsis corallina
Coral plant

A twining climber with spiny-edged, dark green, heart-shaped leaves that are lighter beneath.

Strings of dark red flowers hang from shoot tips from early to late summer. 5m (16ft) S 6m (20ft).
Aspect: semi-shade
Hardiness: ❋❋ Zones: Min. 7

BILLARDIERA

This comprises a genus of over five species, including the evergreen climber featured here, which are grown mainly for their colourful fruit. This plant makes an unusual climber for screens and fences and will grow over many different structures, such as fences, arbours, trellis or walls.
Cultivation Grow in a moisture-retentive, well-drained neutral to acid soil that is reasonably fertile and in full sun or dappled shade, but protected from cold winds.
Pruning No routine pruning is necessary.
Propagation Take semi-ripe cuttings in late summer or layer suitable stems in mid-spring.

Billardiera longiflora
Climbing blueberry

This is a twining climber, with lance-shaped, dark green leaves, that bears pale green flowers during early and mid-summer, followed by plum-shaped, violet-purple, red, white or pink fruit. H 2.5m (8ft) S 1m (3ft). The purple colour of the fruit gives it its blueberry common name.
Aspect: sun or semi-shade
Hardiness: ❋❋ Zones: Min. 7

Billardiera longifolia

Bougainvillea

BOUGAINVILLEA

This genus of about 15 species, including the evergreen climbers featured here, is grown for their long-lasting displays of colourful petal-like bracts. All produce stiff thorny stems. It can be grown in gardens where the weather is mild and will quickly cover a large wall. Alternatively, it can be allowed to scramble over the ground. Elsewhere, grow in containers on the patio and give winter protection – they are a good choice for a large, cool conservatory that is frost-free.
Cultivation In the garden, grow in any well-drained soil that is reasonably fertile in full sun. If growing in containers, use a soil-based compost (soil mix). Feed every month throughout the growing season and water as necessary. Move to a cool but frost-free undercover spot when

the temperature falls below 3°C (37°F) and water sparingly throughout the winter.
Pruning No routine pruning is necessary, other than to keep it in within bounds.
Propagation Take softwood cuttings in early spring or semi-ripe cuttings stems in early summer.

Bougainvillea glabra
This is a vigorous evergreen climber with lustrous, dark green leaves, which bears spectacularly attractive sprays of delicate-looking white, pink and red floral bracts from early summer to mid-autumn. It is borderline half-hardy. H 6m (20ft) S 3m (10ft). Named varieties: 'Snow White', sprays of brilliant white floral bracts. H 6m (20ft) S 3m (10ft). 'Variegata' (syn. B. 'Sanderiana'), cream-edged

grey-green leaves and sprays of purple floral bracts. H 6m (20ft) S 3m (10ft).
Aspect: sun
Hardiness: ✼ (borderline)
Zone: Min. 5

Bougainvillea 'Miss Manila' (syn. *B.* 'Tango')
Spectacular displays of sugar-pink floral bracts are produced in sprays from early summer to mid-autumn against the rounded, lustrous green leaves on this vigorous climber. Borderline half-hardy. H 10m (33ft) S 10m (33ft).
Aspect: sun
Hardiness: ✼ (borderline)
Zone: Min. 5

Bougainvillea 'Raspberry Ice' (syn. *B.* 'Tropical Rainbow')
Luminescent, cerise-pink, flowering bracts shine out from early summer to mid-autumn on this vigorous-growing bougainvillea. The eye-catching cream-splashed dark green leaves provide year-round interest. Borderline half-hardy. H 10m (33ft) S 10m (33ft).
Aspect: sun
Hardiness: ✼ (borderline)
Zone: Min. 5

Bougainvillea 'Scarlett O'Hara' (syn. *B.* 'Hawaiian Scarlet')
This vigorous evergreen climber produces sprays of red floral bracts from early summer to

mid-autumn against lustrous dark green leaves. Borderline half-hardy. H 10m (33ft) S 10m (33ft).
Aspect: sun
Hardiness: ✼ (borderline)
Zone: Min. 5

CAMPSIS
Trumpet vine
A genus of just two species, including the vigorous deciduous climber featured here, grown for its startling, trumpet-shaped, late-summer flowers. It is an ideal choice as a scrambling plant over a sunny wall or fence, with a single plant covering about two standard fence panels in five years. The tendrils of this vigorous climber can damage old masonry, so make sure the pointing is sound before planting.
Cultivation Grow in a moisture-retentive, well-drained soil that is reasonably fertile in full sun, but sheltered from cold winds. In colder areas, grow by a sunny wall.
Pruning Keep this fast-growing climber within bounds by cutting new growth back hard to within a couple of buds from the main framework during late winter.
Propagation Take semi-ripe nodal cuttings in mid-summer or hardwood cuttings in mid-autumn.

Campsis grandiflora (syn. *Bignonia grandiflora, C. chinensis, Tecoma grandiflora*)
Chinese trumpet vine
Reddish-orange, funnel-shaped

Campsis radicans

flowers appear in succession from late summer to early autumn on this vigorous climber, which has dark green leaves. H 10m (33ft) S 10m (33ft).
Aspect: sun
Hardiness: ❀❀ Zone: Min. 7

Campsis radicans 'Flamenco'
Eye-catching trumpet-shaped, yellow flowers appear in succession from late summer to early autumn and stand out against the dark green leaves of this vigorous climber. H 10m (33ft) S 10m (33ft).
Aspect: sun
Hardiness: ❀❀ Zone: Min. 7

Campsis x tagliabuana 'Madame Galen'
This is a vigorous climber that bears trumpet-shaped, salmon-red flowers throughout late summer and early autumn highlighted against its dark green leaves. H 10m (33ft) S 10m (33ft).
Aspect: sun
Hardiness: ❀❀

CELASTRUS
Staff vine
A genus of about 30 species, including the vigorous deciduous climber featured here, which is grown for its bead-like yellow berries. It provides quick cover for eyesores such as an old stump or dilapidated shed, but it also makes an attractive climber for walls and fences – one plant covers about three standard fence panels in five years. The twining stems can be constricting, so avoid planting through young trees and shrubs.
Cultivation Grow in any well-drained soil that is reasonably fertile in full sun or dappled shade.
Pruning No routine pruning is necessary. Thin out over-crowded stems in late winter.
Propagation Take semi-ripe nodal cuttings in mid-summer.

Celastrus orbiculatus (syn. C. articulatus) Oriental bittersweet
This is a vigorous, deciduous climber with scalloped green leaves that turn yellow in autumn. Clusters of insignificant green flowers in mid-summer are followed by yellow berries that split to reveal their contrasting red seeds. H 14m (46ft) S 6m (20ft).
Aspect: sun or semi-shade
Hardiness: ❀❀❀ Zone: Min. 7

Cissus rhombifolia

CISSUS
This large genus of over 350 species includes the tender evergreen climbers featured here. They are mainly grown as house plants because of their handsome foliage. Outside in warm areas, a single plant will quickly cover several standard fence panels or can be left to scramble over the ground and up banks. Elsewhere, they are an ideal choice for a shady but warm conservatory and, as they are very pollution tolerant, they make a good choice for smoke-filled rooms, too.
Cultivation In the garden, grow in a moisture-retentive, well-drained garden soil in full sun or dappled shade. In containers, grow in a soil-based compost (soil mix). Feed every month throughout the growing season and water as necessary. Move to a warm spot undercover when the temperature falls below 5°C (41°F) and water sparingly throughout the winter.
Pruning No routine pruning is necessary. Thin out overcrowded stems in late winter.
Propagation Take semi-ripe cuttings in mid-summer.

Cissus antarctica Kangaroo vine
This is a woody, tendril climber with toothed, polished green, leathery leaves, which bears insignificant green flowers from early summer to late summer, followed by black fruit. H 5m (16ft) S 3m (10ft).
Aspect: sun or semi-shade
Hardiness: tender Zones: 10–12

Cissus rhombifolia (syn. Rhoicissus rhombifolia) Grape ivy
This is a coarsely toothed, woody, tendril climber, with attractive trifoliate evergreen leaves, which bears insignificant green flowers from early summer to late summer, followed by blue-black fruit. H 3m (10ft) S 2m (6ft).
Aspect: sun or semi-shade
Hardiness: tender Zones: 10–12

Celastrus orbiculatus

Clematis alpina

CLEMATIS
Old man's beard

This is a large and varied genus of over 200 species that includes the deciduous and evergreen climbers featured here, mainly grown for their spectacular flowers. Clematis makes a coverall climber that can be used on all types of structures, established trees and shrubs, as well as scrambling across the ground. Vigorous varieties are ideal for covering eyesores and will cloak up to three standard fence panels within five years. Combine different varieties to give a succession of colour throughout the year.

Cultivation Grow in a moisture-retentive, fertile, well-drained soil in full sun or dappled shade, with their roots shaded from hot sun.

Pruning Clematis can be divided into three groups: those that produce all their flowers on old wood (Pruning Group 1); those that produce blooms on both old wood and new growth (Group 2); and those that flower on new growth only (Group 3). Pruning Group 1 requires no routine pruning other than the removal of dead, damaged or diseased stems. Pruning Group 2 should be thinned to avoid congestion by pruning back unwanted stems to a pair of plump buds lower down or at their point of origin. Pruning Group 3 should have all stems cut back to the lowest pair of buds during late winter. Plant deep, burying about 10cm (4in) of the stem, to help recovery in case of clematis wilt.

Propagation Take double-leaf bud cuttings in early summer.

SPRING-FLOWERING CLEMATIS
Clematis alpina
Alpine clematis

Small, bell-shaped, lavender-blue flowers with creamy-white centres are produced during mid- and late spring, followed by fluffy seed heads. Pruning Group 1.
H 3m (10ft) S 1.5m (5ft).
Aspect: semi-shade
Hardiness: ❀❀❀ Zones: 4–11

Clematis alpina 'Frances Rivis'
Nodding, bell-shaped, blue flowers are borne in profusion during mid- and late spring, followed by fluffy seed-heads. Pruning Group 1.
H 3m (10ft) S 1.5m (5ft).
Aspect: semi-shade
Hardiness: ❀❀❀ Zones: 4–11

Clematis alpina 'Frankie'
Double, nodding, bell-shaped, blue flowers are produced during mid- and late spring, followed by fluffy seed-heads. Pruning Group 1.
H 3m (10ft) S 1.5m (5ft).
Aspect: sun or semi-shade
Hardiness: ❀❀❀ Zones: 4–9

Clematis armandii 'Apple Blossom'
Almond-scented, pale pink flowers are produced during early and mid-spring against leathery evergreen leaves that are bronze-tinted when young. Pruning Group 1.
H 5m (16ft) S 3m (10ft).
Aspect: sun or semi-shade
Hardiness: ❀❀❀ Zones: 8–11

Clematis 'Early Sensation'
Masses of small, green-centred, white, bowl-shaped flowers are produced in a single flush during mid- and late spring. Pruning Group 1. H 4m (13ft) S 2m (6ft).
Aspect: sun
Hardiness: ❀❀❀ Zones: 8–11

Clematis macropetala 'Markham's Pink'
Semi-double, clear pink flowers with creamy-yellow centres are produced throughout mid- and late spring, followed by silvery seed-heads. Pruning Group 1.
H 3m (10ft) S 1.5m (5ft).
Aspect: sun or partial shade
Hardiness: ❀❀❀ Zones: 4–9

EARLY SUMMER-FLOWERING CLEMATIS
Clematis 'Barbara Jackman'
Large, pale purple flowers with a distinctive red stripe are produced during late spring and early summer and again in early autumn. Pruning Group 2.
H 3m (10ft) S 1m (3ft).
Aspect: sun or partial shade
Hardiness: ❀❀❀ Zones: 4–11

Clematis 'Bees' Jubilee'
A compact variety that bears large dark pink flowers with darker pink bars during late spring and early summer and again in early autumn. Pruning Group 2.
H 2.5m (8ft) S 1m (3ft).
Aspect: sun or partial shade (zones 4–9); partial shade (zones 10–11)
Hardiness: ❀❀❀ Zones: 4–11

Clematis 'Mrs Cholmondeley'

Clematis 'Belle of Woking'
Large, double, silvery-mauve flowers with creamy-white centres are produced during late spring and early summer and again in early autumn. Pruning Group 2. H 2.5m (8ft) S 1m (3ft).
Aspect: partial shade
Hardiness: ❀❀❀ Zones: 4–11

Clematis 'Doctor Ruppel'
A compact variety that bears large, dark pink flowers with darker bars in succession during late spring and early summer and then again in early autumn. Pruning Group 2. H 2.5m (8ft) S 1m (3ft).
Aspect: sun or partial shade (zones 4–9); partial shade (zones 10–11)
Hardiness: ❀❀❀ Zones: 4–11

Clematis armandii 'Apple Blossom'

Clematis 'Lasurstern'

Clematis 'Duchess of Edinburgh'

Yellow-centred, double white flowers are produced in succession during late spring and early summer with a second flush occasionally produced during early autumn. Pruning Group 2. H 4m (13ft) S 2m (6ft).
Aspect: partial shade
Hardiness: ✿✿✿ Zones: 4–11

Clematis 'Fireworks'

Large purple flowers with red bars and crimped petals are borne in succession during late spring and early summer and then again in early autumn. Pruning Group 2. H 4m (13ft) S 2m (6ft).
Aspect: sun or partial shade
Hardiness: ✿✿✿ Zones: 4–11

Clematis 'Gillian Blades'

Large, mauve-flushed, white flowers that age to white with golden-yellow centres are produced in succession through late spring and early summer, with a second flush produced in early autumn. Pruning Group 2. H 2.5m (8ft) S 1m (3ft).
Aspect: sun or partial shade
Hardiness: ✿✿✿ Zones: 4–11

Clematis 'Lasurstern'

Large, cream-centred, purple-blue flowers with wavy-edged petals that fade in full sun are borne throughout late spring and early summer and again in early autumn. Pruning Group 2. H 2.5m (8ft) S 1m (3ft).
Aspect: sun or partial shade
Hardiness: ✿✿✿ Zones: 4–11

Clematis 'Miss Bateman'

Green-striped white flowers that age to white with chocolate centres are produced during late spring and early summer, with a second flush in late summer. Pruning Group 2. H 2.5m (8ft) S 1m (3ft).
Aspect: sun or partial shade
Hardiness: ✿✿✿ Zones: 4–11

Clematis montana var. *rubens* 'Elizabeth'

Masses of fragrant, pale pink flowers with golden-yellow centres are produced during late spring and early summer, against purple-flushed, green foliage on this vigorous clematis. Pruning Group 1. H 7m (23ft) S 3m (10ft).
Aspect: sun or partial shade
Hardiness: ✿✿✿ Zones: 4–11

Clematis montana var. *rubens* 'Pink Perfection'

A vigorous variety of clematis that bears fragrant pink flowers that appear during late spring and early summer against a backdrop of purple-flushed foliage. Pruning Group 1. H 7m (23ft) S 3m (10ft).
Aspect: sun or partial shade
Hardiness: ✿✿✿ Zones: 4–11

Clematis 'Mrs Cholmondeley'

Chocolate-centred, lavender-blue flowers with darker veins appear in succession from late spring to early autumn. Pruning Group 2. H 3m (10ft) S 1m (3ft).
Aspect: sun or partial shade
Hardiness: ✿✿✿ Zones: 4–11

Clematis 'The President'

Clematis 'Multi Blue'

Large, double, pale-centred, dark blue flowers appear in late spring, early summer, late summer and early autumn. Pruning Group 2. H 4m (13ft) S 2m (6ft).
Aspect: sun or partial shade
Hardiness: ✿✿✿ Zones: 4–11

Clematis 'Nelly Moser'

One of the most commonly found clematis in gardens, chocolate-centred pink flowers with darker stripes fading in full sun appear in late spring and early summer with a second flush in early autumn. Pruning Group 2. H 4m (13ft) S 2m (6ft).
Aspect: partial shade
Hardiness: ✿✿✿ Zones: 4–11

Clematis 'The President'

Large, red-centred, purple flowers with pointed petals that are silvery underneath appear from early summer to early autumn. Foliage on 'The President' is bronze-tinted when young. Pruning Group 2. H 3m (10ft) S 1m (3ft).
Aspect: Sun or partial shade
Hardiness: ✿✿✿ Zones: 4–11

Clematis 'Vyvyan Pennell'

Double, golden-centred, mauve, violet and purple flowers appear in late spring and early summer and again in early autumn. This clematis is fully hardy. Pruning Group 2. H 3m (10ft) S 1m (3ft).
Aspect: sun or partial shade
Hardiness: ✿✿✿ Zones: 4–11

Clematis montana var. *rubens* 'Elizabeth'

Clematis 'Bill MacKenzie'

Clematis florida var. sieboldiana

LATE SUMMER-FLOWERING CLEMATIS

Clematis 'Alba Luxurians'
Bell-shaped, green-tipped, white flowers with purple centres are produced from mid-summer to early autumn against grey-green leaves. Wind and wilt tolerant. Pruning Group 3. H 4m (13ft) S 1.5m (5ft).
Aspect: sun or partial shade
Hardiness: ✿✿✿ Zones: 4–11

Clematis 'Betty Corning'
Nodding, bell-shaped and fragrant creamy-white flowers edged and flushed with lilac-blue, are produced in succession from mid-summer to early autumn. This variety is wind and wilt-tolerant. Pruning Group 3. H 2m (6ft) S 1m (3ft).
Aspect: sun or partial shade
Hardiness: ✿✿✿ Zones: 4–11

Clematis 'Bill MacKenzie'
Butter-yellow, bell-shaped flowers are produced in succession from mid-summer to early autumn against ferny mid-green leaves, followed by large, fluffy seed-heads. Pruning Group 3. H 7m (23ft) S 3m (10ft).
Aspect: sun or partial shade
Hardiness: ✿✿✿ Zones: 4–11

Clematis 'Comtesse de Bouchaud'
A popular variety that bears masses of large, yellow-centred, mauve-pink flowers in succession from mid-summer to early autumn. Pruning Group 3. H 3m (10ft) S 1m (3ft).
Hardiness: ✿✿✿ Zones: 4–11

Clematis 'Ernest Markham'
Large, cream-centred, purple-red flowers are produced in succession from mid-summer to mid-autumn. Pruning Group 3. H 4m (13ft) S 1m (3ft).
Aspect: sun
Hardiness: ✿✿✿ Zones: 4–11

Clematis 'Etoile Violette'
A vigorous clematis that produces masses of yellow-centred, dark purple flowers in succession from mid-summer to early autumn. Wind and wilt resistant. Pruning Group 3. H 5m (16ft) S 1.5m (5ft).
Aspect: sun or partial shade
Hardiness: ✿✿✿ Zones: 4–11

Clematis flammula
Fragrant, starry white flowers are produced *en masse* from mid-summer to mid-autumn on this vigorous clematis, followed by shimmering seed-heads. Pruning Group 3. H 6m (20ft) S 1m (3ft).
Aspect: sun or partial shade
Hardiness: ✿✿✿ Zones: 4–9

Clematis florida var. sieboldiana
This is an unusual passion flower-like plant that produces creamy-white flowers with dark purple centres that appear in succession from early summer to early autumn, followed by shimmering seed-heads. Pruning Group 2. H 2.5m (8ft) S 1m (3ft).
Aspect: sun or partial shade
Hardiness: ✿✿✿ Zones: 4–11

Clematis 'General Sikorski'
Easy-to-grow clematis with large, yellow-centred, purple-blue flowers produced in succession from early summer to early autumn. Fully hardy. Pruning Group 2. H 3m (10ft) S 1m (3ft).
Aspect: sun or partial shade
Hardiness: ✿✿✿ Zones: 4–11

Clematis 'Gipsy Queen'
Red-centred, bright purple flowers are produced in succession from mid-summer to early autumn. Pruning Group 3. H 3m (10ft) S 1m (3ft).
Aspect: sun or partial shade
Hardiness: ✿✿✿ Zones: 4–11

Clematis 'Hagley Hybrid'
Cup-shaped, mauve-pink flowers with red centres that fade in the sun are produced in succession from mid-summer to early autumn. Pruning Group 3. H 2m (6ft) S 1m (3ft).
Aspect: sun or partial shade
Hardiness: ✿✿✿ Zones: 4–11

Clematis 'Henryi'
Attractive large white flowers with chocolate centres are produced in succession from mid-summer to early autumn. Pruning Group 2. H 3m (10ft) S 1m (3ft).
Aspect: sun or partial shade
Hardiness: ✿✿✿ Zones: 4–11

Clematis 'Huldine'
Attractive and large, cup-shaped, yellow-centred, silvery-white flowers with pale lilac undersides appear from mid-summer to early autumn. Pruning Group 3. H 5m (16ft) S 2m (6ft).
Aspect: sun
Hardiness: ✿✿✿ Zones: 4–11

Clematis 'Comtesse de Bouchaud'

Clematis 'Jackmanii'

Clematis 'Marie Boisselot'

Clematis 'Rouge Cardinal'

Clematis viticella 'Purpurea Plena Elegans'

Clematis 'Jackmanii'
Large, green-centred, purple flowers are produced in succession from mid-summer to early autumn. Pruning Group 3. H 3m (10ft) S 1m (3ft). Aspect: sun or partial shade Hardiness: ❀❀❀ Zones: 4–11

Clematis 'Jackmanii Superba'
Red-flushed, dark purple flowers with cream-coloured centres are produced in succession from mid-summer to early autumn. Ideal for a north-facing site. Pruning Group 3. H 3m (10ft) S 1m (3ft). Aspect: sun or partial shade Hardiness: ❀❀❀ Zones: 4–11

Clematis 'Marie Boisselot'
Large white flowers with golden centres and overlapping petals are produced in succession from early summer to early autumn. Pruning Group 2. H 3m (10ft) S 1m (3ft). Aspect: sun or partial shade Hardiness: ❀❀❀ Zones: 4–11

Clematis 'Niobe'
Golden-centred, dark ruby-red flowers are produced in succession from mid-summer to early autumn. Pruning Group 3.

H 3m (10ft) S 1m (3ft). Aspect: sun or partial shade Hardiness: ❀❀❀ Zones: 4–11

Clematis 'Perle d'Azur'
Yellow-centred, lilac-blue flowers of medium size, that are pink-tinged at the base, are produced in succession from mid-summer to early autumn. Pruning Group 3. H 3m (10ft) S 1m (3ft). Aspect: sun or partial shade Hardiness: ❀❀❀ Zones: 4–9

Clematis 'Perle d'Azur'

Clematis 'Polish Spirit'
Red-centred and rich purple saucer-shaped flowers are produced in succession from mid-summer to early autumn on this vigorous variety. Pruning Group 3. H 5m (16ft) S 2m (6ft). Aspect: sun or partial shade Hardiness: ❀❀❀ Zones: 4–11

Clematis 'Prince Charles'
Pale mauve-blue flowers with green centres are produced in succession from mid-summer to early autumn. Pruning Group 3. H 2.5m (8ft) S 1.5m (5ft). Aspect: sun or partial shade Hardiness: ❀❀❀ Zones: 4–11

Clematis 'Princess Diana'
Clear pink, cream-centred, tulip-like flowers are produced in succession from late summer to mid-autumn. Pruning Group 3.

Clematis tangutica

H 2.5m (8ft) S 1m (3ft). Aspect: sun Hardiness: ❀❀❀ Zones: 4–11

Clematis 'Rouge Cardinal'
Rich velvet-crimson flowers appear during mid-summer to early autumn. Pruning Group 3. H 3m (10ft) S 1m (3ft). Aspect: sun or partial shade Hardiness: ❀❀❀ Zones: 4–9

WINTER-FLOWERING CLEMATIS
Clematis cirrhosa 'Jingle Bells'
From early to late winter the large, creamy-coloured, bell-shaped flowers stand out against the dark evergreen leaves. Pruning Group 1. H 3m (10ft) S 1.5m (5ft). Aspect: sun Hardiness: ❀❀❀ Zones: 7–9

Clematis cirrhosa var. balearica
Fragrant, creamy-white, bell-shaped and waxy-looking flowers blotched with maroon inside are produced from early to late winter against glossy bronze-tinted leaves. Pruning Group 1. H 3m (10ft) S 1.5m (5ft). Aspect: sun Hardiness: ❀❀❀ Zones 7–9

Clematis cirrhosa 'Wisley Cream'
Bronze-tinted leaves in winter set off the small, creamy, bell-shaped, waxy-looking flowers borne from early to late winter. Frost hardy. Pruning Group 1. H 3m (10ft) S 1.5m (5ft). Aspect: sun Hardiness: ❀❀❀ Zones 7–9

Clerodendrum thomsoniae

Clianthus puniceus 'Roseus'

Cobaea scandens

CLERODENDRUM

This large genus of over 400 species includes the tender, twining, evergreen climber featured here, which is grown for its clusters of bell-shaped summer flowers. In warm gardens it can reach 3m (10ft) or more and can also be trained to make an attractive standard. Elsewhere, it makes an ideal plant for adding an exotic touch to a heated conservatory.
Cultivation In the garden, grow in any well-drained, moisture-retentive soil that is reasonably fertile. Site in full sun, but protected from wind. If grown in containers, use a soil-based compost (soil mix). Feed every month throughout the growing season and water as necessary. Move to a warm spot undercover when the temperature falls below 10°C (50°) and water sparingly throughout the winter.
Pruning No routine pruning is necessary. Cut back wayward stems, shortening shoots by about two-thirds of their length, in mid-spring.
Propagation Take softwood cuttings in mid-spring.

Clerodendrum thomsoniae
Glory bower
This is a woody-stemmed, evergreen, twining climber that during early summer to early autumn bears clusters of bi-coloured flowers made up of a white lantern-shaped calyx and a crimson star-shaped corolla, against large green leaves.

H 4m (13ft) S 2m (6ft).
Aspect: sun
Hardiness: tender Zones: 10–12

CLIANTHUS

This comprises a genus of just two species, including the evergreen climber featured here, which are grown for their unusual lobster-claw or beak-like flowers that appear in early summer. It makes an interesting choice for sunny and sheltered screens and fences or can be left unsupported to form a sprawling shrub.
Cultivation Grow in any well-drained soil that is reasonably fertile in full sun, but protected from wind. In very cold areas, grow in a cool conservatory.
Pruning No routine pruning is necessary. Cut back wayward stems and thin congested growth during early summer.
Propagation Sow seeds in early spring or take semi-ripe cuttings in early summer.

Clianthus puniceus
Lobster claw, Parrot's bill
This is a sprawling evergreen climber, with dark green leaves, which bears dramatic and unusual lobster-claw-like scarlet flowers in clusters during late spring and early summer. If not left to sprawl, it requires tying into its support. H 4m (13ft) S 2m (6ft).
Named varieties: 'Albus', white flowers. H 4m (13ft) S 2m (6ft).
Aspect: sun
Hardiness: ❈❈ Zone: Min. 6

COBAEA

This genus of about 20 species includes the evergreen tendril climber featured here, grown for its spectacular fragrant summer flowers. In warm gardens, it is a good choice for covering a sheltered sunny wall or fence. Elsewhere, grow in a container and move undercover during the winter months, or use it as a permanent addition to a large heated greenhouse or conservatory.
Cultivation In the garden, grow in any well-drained, moisture-retentive soil that is reasonably fertile in full sun, but protected from wind. In containers, grow in a soil-based compost. Feed every month throughout the growing season and water as necessary.

Move to a warm spot under cover when the temperature falls below 5°C (41°F) and water sparingly throughout the winter.
Pruning No routine pruning is necessary. Cut back wayward stems and thin congested growth during early autumn.
Propagation Sow seeds in early spring.

Cobaea scandens
Cathedral bell, cup-and-saucer plant
This is a vigorous tendril climber that bears huge, scented, bell-shaped, creamy-green flowers that age to dark purple from early summer to early autumn, against a backdrop of dark green leaves.
H 20m (70ft) S 3.5m (12ft).
Aspect: sun
Hardiness: tender Zones: 10–12

ECCREMOCARPUS
Chilean glory flower
A genus of some five species, including the vigorous evergreen climber featured here, grown for its succession of unusual and colourful summer flowers. It makes a perfect choice for a fence or screen next to a sunny patio.
Cultivation Grow in any well-drained soil that is reasonably fertile in full sun, but protected from cold wind. Plant out after the last frost in colder areas.
Pruning No routine pruning is necessary. In colder areas, treat as

Eccremocarpus scaber

Hedera canariensis 'Gloire de Marengo'

Hedera colchica 'Dentata Variegata'

a perennial and cut frost-damaged top-growth back during mid-spring.
Propagation Sow seeds in late winter.

Eccremocarpus scaber
A quick-growing, evergreen, tendril climber that produces a profusion of red, pink, orange or yellow flowers in succession from early summer to mid-autumn on slender stems. It requires tying into a support to get it started.
H 5m (16ft) S 5m (16ft).
Aspect: sun
Hardiness: ❋❋ Zone: Min. 7

FALLOPIA
A genus of over five species, including the very vigorous deciduous climber featured here, it is grown for its rapid speed of growth and clouds of late-summer flowers. It makes a useful plant for covering up eyesores and for quick garden makeovers. However, a word of caution is necessary with this climber: a

single plant will smother an area equivalent to about 10 standard fence panels in five years.
Cultivation Grow in a moisture-retentive, well-drained soil that is poor to reasonably fertile in full sun or dappled shade.
Pruning No routine pruning is necessary. Cut back wayward or congested stems in mid-spring.

Fallopia baldschuanica

Propagation Take semi-ripe cuttings in early summer.

Fallopia baldschuanica
(syn. *Bilderdykia baldschuanica, Polygonum baldschuanicum*)
Russian vine, mile-a-minute
Very fast growing and vigorous, this is a woody, deciduous climber that is covered in clouds of tiny, funnel-shaped, white flowers with pink tinges throughout late summer and early autumn.
H 12m (40ft) S 4m (13ft).
Aspect: sun or semi-shade
Hardiness: ❋❋❋ Zone: Min. 7

HEDERA
Ivy
This genus of about 10 species includes many popular, self-clinging, evergreen climbers, some of which are featured here. They are grown for their easy-going nature and handsome foliage. Many of these plants are excellent on shady walls and fences, while others thrive in full sun. A single plant covers one standard fence panel in five years. Some can provide weed-smothering groundcover and a few also make year-round house plants.
Cultivation Although these plants are very tolerant of a wide range of conditions, they grow best in a moisture-retentive, well-drained neutral to alkaline soil that is reasonably fertile. Variegated ivies prefer dappled shade and shelter from cold winds; green-leaved varieties can cope with anything from full sun to deep shade.

Pruning No routine pruning is necessary. Remove frost-damaged growth and all-green reverted stems from variegated varieties in mid-spring.
Propagation Take semi-ripe nodal cuttings in early summer.

Hedera canariensis 'Gloire de Marengo'
Huge, three-lobed, silvery-green glossy leaves, edged with creamy-white, cover this vigorous evergreen climber. Use indoors or outside in sheltered, dappled shade. H 4m (13ft) S 5m (16ft).
Aspect: semi-shade
Hardiness: ❋❋ Zone: Min. 7

Hedera colchica 'Dentata Variegata'
A variegated evergreen ivy with huge, heart-shaped, cream-edged, mottled grey-green leaves. It is useful climber for brightening up semi-shade or for growing as weed-smothering groundcover.
H 5m (16ft) S 5m (16ft).
Aspect: semi-shade
Hardiness: ❋❋❋ Zone: Min. 5

Hedera colchica 'Sulphur Heart'
(syn. *H. colchica* 'Paddy's Pride')
A fast-growing, self-clinging, variegated, evergreen ivy with heart-shaped green leaves splashed with creamy yellow. It is useful for brightening up semi-shade or for growing as weed-smothering groundcover. H 5m (16ft) S 5m (16ft).
Aspect: semi-shade
Hardiness: ❋❋❋ Zone: Min. 5

Hedera helix 'Goldchild'

Hedera helix 'Buttercup'

This is a sun-loving, vigorous, self-clinging, evergreen ivy with lobed bright yellow leaves that turn pale green in shade. Insignificant pale green flowers are borne in mid- to late autumn, followed by spherical black fruit. H 2m (6ft) S 2.5m (8ft).
Aspect: sun
Hardiness: ❀❀❀ Zone: Min. 7

Hedera helix 'Glacier'

Ideal for use as groundcover, this variegated evergreen climber has triangular and lobed grey-green leaves with silver and cream splashes. Pale green flowers appear in mid- to late autumn. H 2m (6ft) S 2m (6ft).
Aspect: semi-shade
Hardiness: ❀❀❀ Zone: Min. 7

Hedera helix 'Goldheart' (syn. H. helix 'Jubilaum Goldhertz', H. helix 'Jubilee Goldheart', H. helix 'Oro di Bogliasco')

Vigorous once established, this fast-growing, variegated, evergreen climber has glossy, three-lobed, dark green leaves splashed with yellow. Insignificant pale green flowers are borne in mid- to late autumn. H 8m (26ft) S 5m (16ft).
Aspect: semi-shade
Hardiness: ❀❀❀ Zone: Min. 7

Hedera helix 'Green Ripple'

A vigorous evergreen climber with large, glossy, bright green leaves that are five-lobed and sharply pointed with distinctive veining. They turn copper-bronze over winter. Insignificant pale green flowers are borne in mid-autumn and late autumn. H 2m (6ft) S 2m (6ft).
Aspect: semi-shade
Hardiness: ❀❀❀ Zone: Min. 7

Hedera helix 'Ivalace' (syn. H. helix 'Mini Green')

Suitable for use indoors and outside, this adaptable ivy has glossy, five-lobed, wavy-edged, dark green leaves. Insignificant pale green flowers are borne in mid- to late autumn.
H 1m (3ft) S 1.2m (4ft).
Aspect: semi-shade
Hardiness: ❀❀❀ Zone: Min. 7

Hedera helix 'Parsley Crested' (syn. H. helix 'Cristata')

The glossy dark green and wavy-edged leaves on this vigorous, self-clinging evergreen climber are ideal for covering a wall or fence in shade. Insignificant pale green flowers are borne in mid- to late autumn. H 2m (6ft) S 1.2m (4ft).
Aspect: semi-shade to deep shade
Hardiness: ❀❀❀ Zone: Min. 7

HIBBERTIA

A genus of around 120 species, including the twining evergreen featured here, grown for their bright yellow flowers. They make useful groundcover in warm gardens, where they also look good trained over arches and pergolas. They are also tolerant of salt-laden air, and so make a good choice for mild coastal gardens. Elsewhere, grow in a container and move under cover during the cold winter months.
Cultivation In the garden, grow in any well-drained, moisture-retentive soil that is reasonably fertile in dappled shade, but protected from wind. In containers, grow in a soil-based compost (soil mix). Feed every month throughout the growing season and water as necessary. Move to a warm spot under cover when the temperature falls below 5°C (41°F) and water sparingly during the winter.
Pruning No routine pruning is necessary. Cut back wayward stems and thin congested growth during early autumn after flowering.
Propagation Sow seeds in early spring.

Hibbertia scandens (syn. H. volubilis)

This is a vigorous, twining evergreen with lustrous, leathery, green leaves that are distinctively veined and notched. The climber has red hairy stems and the leaves are also covered in paler hairs underneath. Saucer-shaped, bright yellow flowers are borne from early summer to late summer.
H 3m (10ft) S 2m (6ft).
Aspect: semi-shade
Hardiness: tender Zones: 10–12

HOYA

This genus of over 200 species includes the epiphytic climber featured here, which is grown for its waxy-looking clusters of night-scented summer flowers and handsome foliage. It is best grown in a container as this promotes flowering. It makes a good choice for a sunny conservatory, greenhouse or porch.
Cultivation Grow in a soil-based compost. Feed every month throughout the growing season and water as necessary. Move to a warm spot under cover when the temperature falls below 5°C (41°F) and water sparingly during the winter.
Pruning No routine pruning is necessary. Pinch out growing tips to promote bushy growth.
Propagation Sow seeds in early spring.

Hoya carnosa
Wax plant

A vigorous evergreen climber with leathery dark green oval leaves that climbs using clinging aerial roots. Large, dense clusters of waxy-looking star-shaped and night-scented white flowers that are pink-flushed, each with a crimson eye, are produced from late spring to early autumn.
H 6m (20ft) S 2m (6ft).
Aspect: sun
Hardiness: tender Zones: 10-12

HUMULUS
Hop

This comprises a genus of just two species, including the vigorous deciduous climber featured here, which is grown for its yellow foliage. It is ideal for growing over sturdy arches and pergolas, or for allowing it to scramble through coloured trellis.

Hibbertia scandens

Hoya carnosa

Humulus lupulus 'Aureus'

Cultivation Grow in any well-drained, moisture-retentive soil that is reasonably fertile in full sun or dappled shade. Choose a sunny site to achieve the best leaf coloration.
Pruning Treat this climber as a perennial in colder areas, cutting back all stems to near ground level in early spring.
Propagation Take leaf-bud cuttings in early summer.

Humulus lupulus 'Aureus'
Golden hop

This climber has striking, bright yellow, deeply lobed leaves that mature to yellow-green on twining stems. Tie these into the support in spring. Green flowering cones are produced in early autumn. H 6m (20ft) S 6m (20ft).
Aspect: sun to semi-shade
Hardiness: ✿✿✿ Zone: Min. 7

HYDRANGEA

A genus of about 80 species, including the deciduous climber featured here, that is grown for its summer flowers and handsome foliage. They are useful for covering large north-facing walls, although they take a few years to get established.
Cultivation Grow in a moisture-retentive, well-drained and reasonably fertile soil in full sun or dappled shade. Before planting, add plenty of organic matter to the soil.
Pruning No routine pruning is necessary. Cut back wayward stems in late winter.

Propagation Take softwood basal cuttings in mid-spring or layer suitable shoots in mid-spring.

Hydrangea anomala subsp. *petiolaris* (syn. *H. petiolaris*)
Climbing hydrangea

Huge flat heads of creamy lace-cap flowers stand out against a backdrop of dark green leaves from late spring to mid-summer on this woody, deciduous climber. The leaves turn butter-yellow in autumn before falling to reveal flaking brown bark. H 1.5m (5ft) S 3m (10ft).
Aspect: sun to shade
Hardiness: ✿✿✿ Zone: Min. 7

JASMINUM

This comprises a genus of over 200 species, including the deciduous and evergreen climbers featured here, which are grown for their sweetly scented summer flowers. It is a good choice for sheltered structures near entrances, paths and patios, covering a standard fence panel in about five years. Others make excellent fragrant house plants.
Cultivation In the garden, grow in any well-drained soil that is reasonably fertile in full sun or dappled shade. Choose a sunny site for the best leaf coloration. In containers, grow in a soil-based compost (soil mix). Feed every month throughout the growing season and water as necessary.
Pruning No routine pruning is necessary. Overcrowded shoots on *Jasminum officinale* can be thinned after flowering.

Hydrangea anomala subsp. *petiolaris*

Propagation Take semi-ripe basal cuttings in mid-summer.

Jasminum beesianum

Fragrant pinkish-red flowers are produced in small clusters throughout early and mid-summer against strap-shaped, dark green leaves on this twining and woody evergreen climber. This plant requires the shelter of a sunny wall or fence. H 5m (16ft) S 5m (16ft).
Aspect: sun
Hardiness: ✿✿ Zone: Min. 7

Jasminum officinale
Common jasmine

A succession of fabulously fragrant white flowers cover this vigorous semi-evergreen, twining climber from early summer to early autumn. H 12m (40ft) S 3m (10ft).
Aspect: sun to semi-shade
Hardiness: ✿✿✿ Zone: Min. 7

Jasminum officinale 'Devon Cream'

A new and very compact variety of common jasmine, this woody and twining deciduous climber bears large, fragrant, creamy-white flowers from mid-summer to early autumn. Give it the shelter of a sunny south- or west-facing wall or fence. H 2m (6ft) S 1m (3ft).
Aspect: sun
Hardiness: ✿✿ Zone: Min. 7

Jasminum officinale 'Fiona Sunrise'

This is a recent introduction that has eyecatching golden foliage and a succession of fragrant white flowers from early summer to early autumn. It is a compact variety that does best in the shelter of a warm, sunny wall or fence. H 3m (10ft) S 2m (6ft).
Aspect: sun
Hardiness: ✿✿ Zone: Min. 7

Jasminum polyanthum

This vigorous and twining evergreen climber is a very popular house plant. It produces fabulously fragrant white flowers that open from pink buds throughout mid-spring and early summer when grown outside. When grown inside, it will fill the house with a lovely scent from late autumn to mid-spring. H 3m (10ft) S 2m (6ft).
Aspect: sun to semi-shade
Hardiness: ✿ Zone: 10+

Jasminum x *stephanense*

Scented pale pink flowers are produced in clusters throughout early and mid-summer on this vigorous and twining deciduous climber. Give it the shelter of a warm sunny wall or fence. H 5m (16ft) S 5m (16ft).
Aspect: sun
Hardiness: ✿✿ Zone: Min. 7

Jasminum officinale 'Fiona Sunrise'

LAPAGERIA

This is a genus of just one species of twining evergreen climber, grown for its exotic and colourful waxy-looking summer flowers. It is ideal for growing against a sheltered sunny wall or fence or on a post in a sheltered garden.
Cultivation In the garden, grow in a moisture-retentive, well-drained neutral to acid soil that is reasonably fertile. Site in dappled shade, but sheltered from cold winds. In containers, grow in an ericaceous compost (soil mix). Feed every month in the growing season and water as necessary.
Pruning No routine pruning is necessary. Wayward shoots can be thinned after flowering.
Propagation Sow seeds or layer suitable stems in mid-spring.

Lapageria rosea
Chilean bellflower
Exotic, elongated, bell-shaped, pink to crimson flowers are produced singly or in small clusters from leaf joints on this twining evergreen climber from mid-summer to mid-autumn. The leathery, lustrous, dark green leaves look good at other times. Borderline frost hardy. H 5m (16ft) S 3m (10ft).
Aspect: semi-shade
Hardiness: ❈❈ (borderline)
Zone: Min. 8

LONICERA
Honeysuckle
A genus of over 180 species, including the deciduous and evergreen twining climbers

Lapageria rosea

featured here, grown for their spidery, often highly fragrant, summer flowers. A coverall climber, it is ideal for screens and fences or for training through established shrubs and trees. A single specimen will cover a standard fence panel in about five years.
Cultivation Grow in a moisture-retentive, well-drained soil that is reasonably fertile in full sun or dappled shade. Add plenty of organic matter to the soil before planting time.
Pruning Honeysuckles that flower on the current year's growth do not need regular pruning; those that flower on the previous season's growth should have old growth that has flowered cut back to a newer shoot produced lower down on the stem. All neglected honeysuckles can be rejuvenated by removing one in three stems, starting with the oldest.
Propagation Take leaf-bud cuttings in early summer or mid-summer, layer suitable shoots in late summer or take hardwood cuttings in mid-autumn.

Lonicera x americana
Very large, fragrant, yellow, tubular flowers that are purple-flushed are produced in succession from early summer to early autumn against a backdrop of oval dark green leaves. H 7m (23ft) S 2m (6ft).
Aspect: sun to semi-shade
Hardiness: ❈❈❈ Zone: Min. 7

Lonicera x brownii 'Dropmore Scarlet'
Long, trumpet-shaped, bright scarlet flowers are produced in succession from mid-summer to early autumn against handsome blue-green foliage, occasionally followed by red berries. H 4m (13ft) S 2m (6ft).
Aspect: sun to semi-shade
Hardiness: ❈❈❈ Zone: Min. 7

Lonicera x heckrottii 'Gold Flame'
A vigorous twining climber that bears very fragrant, orange-yellow tubular flowers that are pink-flushed in succession from early to late summer, occasionally followed by red berries.

Lonicera x brownii 'Dropmore Scarlet'

H 500cm (180in) S 50cm (20in).
Aspect: sun to semi-shade
Hardiness: ❈❈❈ Zone: Min. 7

Lonicera henryi
Scarlet trumpet honeysuckle
Reddish-purple tubular flowers, each with a yellow throat, are produced throughout early and mid-summer against lustrous, dark green leaves on this vigorous evergreen variety. H 10m (33ft) S 1m (3ft).
Aspect: sun to semi-shade
Hardiness: ❈❈❈ (borderline)
Zone: Min. 7

Lonicera japonica 'Halliana'
Fabulously fragrant, tubular, white flowers that age to yellow are borne in succession from mid-spring to late summer, appearing against handsome dark green leaves on this vigorous evergreen variety. H 10m (33ft) S 2m (6ft).
Aspect: sun to semi-shade
Hardiness: ❈❈❈ Zone: Min. 7

Lonicera japonica 'Hall's Prolific'
Tubular white and sweetly fragrant flowers that age to yellow are borne in succession from mid-spring to late summer on this free-flowering vigorous variety

that has dark green foliage. H 4m (13ft) S 3m (10ft).
Aspect: sun to semi-shade
Hardiness: ❈❈❈ Zone: Min. 7

Lonicera japonica var. repens
Very fragrant, tubular, reddish-purple flowers that age to yellow and are white-flushed are borne from mid-spring to late summer on this long-flowering and vigorous variety that has purple-tinged foliage. H 10m (33ft) S 5m (16ft).
Aspect: sun to semi-shade
Hardiness: ❈❈❈ Zone: Min. 7

Lonicera periclymenum 'Graham Thomas'

Mandevilla splendens

Lonicera periclymenum 'Belgica' Early Dutch honeysuckle

Very fragrant, tubular, reddish-purple flowers that are yellow-lipped are produced *en masse* during late spring and early summer on this twining vigorous climber. H 7m (23ft) S 1m (3ft).
Aspect: sun to semi-shade
Hardiness: ❉❉❉ Zone: Min. 7

Lonicera periclymenum 'Graham Thomas'

Large, tubular and sweetly fragrant white flowers that age to yellow are produced from mid-summer to early autumn against a backdrop of oval green leaves on this vigorous deciduous climber. H 7m (23ft) S 1m (3ft).
Aspect: sun to semi-shade
Hardiness: ❉❉❉ Zone: Min. 7

Lonicera periclymenum 'Harlequin'

This is an unusual variegated honeysuckle that is covered in fragrant and tubular reddish-purple and yellow-lipped flowers from early summer to late summer on this twining vigorous climber. H 7m (23ft) S 1m (3ft).
Aspect: sun to semi-shade
Hardiness: ❉❉❉ Zone: Min. 7

Lonicera periclymenum 'Serotina' Late Dutch honeysuckle

Superbly fragrant and tubular creamy-white flowers that are purple-streaked are produced from mid-summer to mid-autumn on this vigorous, late-flowering, deciduous cultivar. It is a good climber to have growing in dappled shade. H 7m (23ft) S 1m (3ft).
Aspect: semi-shade
Hardiness: ❉❉❉ Zone: Min. 7

Lonicera x tellmanniana

Striking-looking, bright orange, tubular flowers open from red-tinged buds from late spring to mid-summer against a backdrop of large, dark green leaves. H 5m (16ft) S 2m (6ft).
Aspect: sun to semi-shade
Hardiness: ❉❉❉ Zone: Min. 7

MANDEVILLA

This genus of about 120 species includes the twining and woody climbers featured here, which are grown for their exotic summer flowers. It is an ideal patio plant in warm gardens as it responds well to being grown in pots, but it can be grown at the back of sheltered borders and used to cover trellis and fences. In cooler areas it can be grown as a houseplant and will add colour to a heated conservatory in colder areas.
Cultivation In the garden, grow in a moisture-retentive, well-drained soil that is reasonably fertile in full sun, but sheltered from cool winds. If grown in containers, grow in a soil-based compost (soil mix). Feed every month throughout the growing season and water as necessary. Move to a warm spot undercover when the temperature falls below 10°C (50°F) and water sparingly in winter.
Pruning Cut back side shoots on established plants to 3 buds of the woody framework after it has flowered.
Propagation Sow seeds in mid-spring or take softwood cuttings in late spring.

Mandevilla x amabilis 'Alice du Pont' (syn. M. x amoena 'Alice du Pont')

Fragrant pink, tubular flowers are produced throughout mid- to late summer against a backdrop of wavy-edged green leaves on this twining and woody climber. H 7m (23ft) S 2m (6ft).
Aspect: sun
Hardiness: tender Zones: 10–12

Mandevilla boliviensis (syn. Dipladenia boliviensis)

White tubular flowers with a yellow eye are carried throughout mid- to late summer against a backdrop of glossy, narrow, green foliage on this twining, woody climber. H 4m (13ft) S 2m (6ft).
Aspect: sun
Hardiness: tender Zones: 10–12

Mandevilla splendens (syn. Dipladenia splendens)

Showy, rose-pink, tubular flowers are borne in succession from mid- to late summer on this twining climber, which has hairy stems and glossy green leaves.
H 5m (16ft) S 2m (6ft).
Aspect: sun
Hardiness: tender Zones: 10–12

MONSTERA

This genus of over 20 species, including the tender evergreen climber featured here, are grown for their handsomely cut, lustrous foliage. It is grown outside in tropical areas but in colder climates it makes an attractive and easy-to-please house plant.
Cultivation Grow in a general-purpose compost (soil mix). Feed every month during the growing season and water as necessary. If kept outside, move to a warm spot undercover when the temperature falls below 15°C (60°F). Water sparingly in winter.
Pruning No routine pruning is necessary.
Propagation Air layer in early autumn.

Monstera deliciosa Swiss cheese plant

Large, deeply notched and sometimes perforated, glossy, dark green, leathery leaves are displayed on arching stems that splay outwards from a vigorous climbing stem supported in part by aerial roots. Mature plants may flower, producing creamy, arum-like spathes from late spring to late summer. H 10m (33ft) S 2m (6ft).
Aspect: semi-shade
Hardiness: tender Zones: 10–12

Monstera deliciosa

Parthenocissus quinquefolia

Passiflora caerulea

PARTHENOCISSUS

Comprising a genus of about ten species, including the vigorous deciduous tendril climbers featured here, they are grown for their handsome foliage and fiery autumn tints. It makes a cover-all climber that is excellent for camouflaging ugly buildings and other eyesores. A single specimen will cloak about two standard fence panels in five years.

Cultivation Grow in any well-drained soil that is reasonably fertile in full sun, dappled shade or full shade.

Pruning No routine pruning is necessary. Keep plants in check by pruning out unwanted stems in late winter.

Propagation Take semi-ripe stem cuttings in late summer; alternatively, take hardwood cuttings in late autumn.

Parthenocissus henryana
(syn. *Vitis henryana*)
Chinese Virginia creeper
The handsome, deeply divided dark green leaves with distinctive white and pink veins turn fiery shades in autumn. It is less vigorous than other varieties. H 10m (33ft) S 5m (16ft).
Aspect: sun, semi-shade to deep shade
Hardiness: ❋❋❋ (borderline)
Zone: Min. 7

Parthenocissus quinquefolia
(syn. *Vitis quinquefolia*)
Virginia creeper
The deeply divided, slightly puckered, green leaves transform in autumn as they take on brilliant shades of crimson and purple on this vigorous deciduous climber. H 15m (50ft) S 5m (16ft).
Aspect: sun, semi-shade to deep shade
Hardiness: ❋❋❋ Zone: Min. 7

Parthenocissus tricuspidata
'**Robusta**'
A very vigorous deciduous climber with large, dark green leaves that are deeply lobed, turning brilliant crimson and purple in autumn. H 20m (70ft) S 10m (33ft).
Aspect: sun, semi-shade to deep shade
Hardiness: ❋❋❋ Zone: Min. 7

Parthenocissus tricuspidata
'**Veitchii**' (syn. *Ampelopsis veitchii*)
Lustrous, deeply lobed, dark green leaves transform in autumn into a spectacular cloak of red and purple on this very vigorous variety. H 20m (70ft) S 10m (33ft).
Aspect: sun, semi-shade to deep shade
Hardiness: ❋❋❋ Zone: Min. 7

PASSIFLORA
Passion flower
This large genus of over 400 species includes the evergreen tendril climbers featured here, which are grown mainly for their distinctive and tropical-looking summer flowers. They are a very good choice for growing up a pergola, arch or open screen, as this allows the flowers and fruit to hang down attractively.

Cultivation In the garden, grow in a moisture-retentive, well-drained soil that is reasonably fertile in full sun or dappled shade, sheltered from cold winds. In containers, grow in a soil-based compost (soil mix). Feed every month in the growing season and water as necessary. Protect from severe frost in cold areas.

Pruning Thin overcrowded plants in early spring. In cold areas, treat as a perennial and cut back all stems to near ground level in mid-autumn then protect the

Parthenocissus tricuspidata

Passiflora 'Amethyst'

Passiflora caerulea 'Constance Elliot'

Philodendron scandens

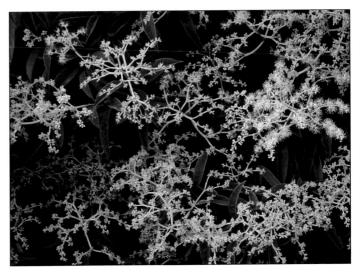

Pileostegia virburnoides

crown with an insulating mulch.
Propagation Take semi-ripe nodal
cuttings in mid-summer.

Passiflora 'Amethyst'

Large, showy purple flowers, each
with a ruff of spiky filaments and
darker eye, are produced in
succession from mid-summer to
early autumn, followed by egg-
shaped yellow-orange fruit.
H 10m (30ft) S 2m (6ft).
Aspect: sun or semi-shade
Hardiness: ❀❀ Zone: 8–9

Passiflora caerulea
Blue passion flower

Exotic, waxy-looking white
flowers, each with a purple, blue
and white ruff of spiky filaments
at the centre, are produced from
mid-summer to early autumn.
Egg-shaped, yellow-orange fruit
follow. H 10m (33ft) S 1m (3ft).
Aspect: sun or semi-shade
Hardiness: ❀❀ Zone: Min. 7

Passiflora caerulea
'Constance Elliot'

A succession of fragrant, waxy-
looking white flowers, each with a
bluish-white ruff of spiky
filaments, are borne from mid-
summer to early autumn, followed
by egg-shaped yellow-orange fruit.
H 10m (33ft) S 2m (6ft).
Aspect: sun or semi-shade
Hardiness: ❀❀ Zone: Min. 7

PHILODENDRON

A large genus of over 500 species,
including the fast-growing, tender,
evergreen climber featured here,

grown for its handsome foliage. It
makes an attractive house plant.
In tropical areas they can be
grown up posts and over sturdy
supports, such as arches.
Cultivation Grow in a fresh,
general-purpose potting compost
(soil mix). Feed every month
throughout the growing season
and water as necessary. Move to a
warm spot undercover when the
temperature falls below 15°C
(60°F) and water sparingly
during the winter.
Pruning No routine pruning is
necessary. Pinch out shoot tips to
encourage bushy growth.
Propagation Take tip cuttings in
late spring or early summer or air
layer in mid-spring.

Philodendron scandens
Heart leaf, sweetheart plant

Slender stems of heart-shaped,
glossy green leaves are sometimes
flushed with purple underneath.
It is able to tolerate low light and
some degree of neglect – and
so this makes it an ideal first-
timer's house plant. H 3m (13ft)
S 2m (6ft).
Aspect: semi-shade
Hardiness: tender Zone: 10+

PILEOSTEGIA

A small genus of just four species,
including the evergreen climber
featured here, which is grown for
its handsome foliage and star-
shaped late-summer flowers. It is
ideal for covering shady walls and
fences, as well as growing through
a well-established tree.

Cultivation Grow in any well-
drained soil that is reasonably
fertile in full sun or dappled
shade. Shelter from cold winds.
Pruning No routine pruning is
necessary. Overgrown plants can
have their stems thinned and
shortened after flowering in
early autumn.
Propagation Take tip cuttings in
mid-spring.

Pileostegia viburnoides (syn.
Schizophragma viburnoides)

Star-shaped, creamy-white flowers
are produced in generous clusters
throughout late summer and early
autumn against a backdrop of
glossy, dark green and leathery
leaves. H 6m (20ft) S 2m (6ft).
Aspect: sun or semi-shade
Hardiness: ❀❀ Zone: Min. 7

PLUMBAGO

This genus contains at least ten
species, including the evergreen
climber featured here, grown for
its summer and autumn flowers.
Ideal for a frost-free, sheltered
and protected spot. In warmer
areas, it can be grown as ground
cover, through shrubs or as an
informal hedge.
Cultivation Grow in any well-
drained soil that is reasonably
fertile in full sun but sheltered
from cold winds. In frost-prone
areas, grow in a container using a
soil-based compost (soil mix).
Feed every month in the growing
season and water as necessary.
Protect in winter by moving it to
a frost-free area.

Pruning Cut back after flowering,
removing around two-thirds of
the new growth.
Propagation Sow seeds in early
spring or take semi-ripe cuttings
in mid-summer.

Plumbago auriculata (syn.
P. capensis)
Cape leadwort

An extremely long-flowering
climber that bears sky-blue
flowers in trusses from early
summer to late autumn against
matt, apple-green leaves.
H 6m (20ft) S 3m (10ft).
Aspect: sun
Hardiness: ❀ Zone: 9+

Plumbago auriculata var. alba

Rosa 'Albertine'

ROSA

A large genus of over 150 species, which includes the varied collections of popular, deciduous, summer-flowering climbers featured here. Use all around the garden, combining varieties that flower at different times to achieve a succession of flowers, autumn colour and winter hips.
Cultivation Grow in any reasonably fertile soil in full sun. Avoid soil that has recently been used for growing roses.
Pruning Cut back flowering stems of ramblers to a new non-flowering side shoot lower down. This can be trained to replace the removed stem. Climbing roses that produce a single flush of blooms should be pruned after flowering by removing one in three stems, starting with the oldest. Cut back near to the base or to a side shoot lower down. Prune repeat-flowering climbing roses in winter to remove the weakest and oldest stems. Trim side shoots on remaining stems to within two or three buds.
Propagation Take hardwood cuttings in mid-autumn.
Aspect: sun
Hardiness: ✷✷✷ Zone: Min. 7

RAMBLER ROSES
Rosa 'Albéric Barbier'
Sprays of fragrant, double, cream-coloured flowers are borne in early and mid-summer against lustrous, dark green leaves. H 5m (16ft) S 3m (10ft).

Rosa 'Albertine'
Strongly fragrant, double, pale salmon-pink flowers are borne on red-green stems during early and mid-summer. This is an excellent rose for cutting. H 5m (16ft) S 4m (13ft).

Rosa 'American Pillar'
Clusters of white-centred, dark pink flowers are produced throughout early and mid-summer against lustrous, fresh green leaves. It is very pliable and so is ideal for growing up arches. H 5m (16ft) S 4m (13ft).

Rosa 'Emily Gray'
Sprays of fragrant, double, yellow flowers are produced in a single flush during mid-summer against glossy, dark green leaves, that emerge bronze-tinted. H 5m (16ft) S 3m (10ft).

Rosa 'Rambling Rector'
A vigorous rambler that bears fragrant, semi-double, creamy-white flowers in large clusters from mid-summer to early autumn, followed by small red rosehips. Ideal for a shady site. H 6m (20ft) S 6m (20ft).

Rosa 'Veilchenblau' (syn. R. 'Blue Rambler', R. 'Violet Blue')
Large clusters of small, fragrant semi-double, white-streaked violet flowers that age to a delicate lilac-grey are borne in early and mid-summer on this vigorous rambler. H 4m (13ft) S 4m (13ft).

Rosa 'Wedding Day'
This is a vigorous rambler that bears huge clusters of fragrant, single, creamy-white flowers that age to the palest pink, during mid- to late summer. H 8m (26ft) S 4m (13ft).

CLIMBING ROSES
Rosa 'Aloha'
Large, double, rose-pink, fragrant flowers are produced in succession from mid-summer to early autumn against leathery, dark green leaves. Rain-resistant blooms. H 3m (13ft) S 2.5m (8ft).

Rosa 'Bantry Bay'
Subtly fragrant clusters of semi-double pink flowers are produced from mid-summer to early autumn. Rain- and disease-resistant. H 4m (13ft) S 2.5m (8ft).

Rosa 'Breath of Life' (syn. R. 'Harquanne')
Strongly fragrant, double, apricot-coloured flowers are produced in succession from mid-summer to early autumn. Excellent for cutting. H 2.5m (8ft) S 2.2m (7ft).

Rosa 'Climbing Iceberg'
Fragrant sprays of double white flowers appear in succession from mid-summer to early autumn. H 3m (10ft) S 2m (6ft).

Rosa 'Compassion' (syn. R. 'Belle de Londres')
Masses of strongly fragrant, double, apricot-flushed, pink flowers are produced in succession from mid-summer to early autumn. H 3m (10ft) S 2.5m (8ft).

Rosa 'Danse du Feu' (syn. R. 'Spectacular')
Subtly fragrant, double, fiery orange-red flowers are produced in succession from mid-summer to early autumn against bronze-tinted, lustrous green leaves. H 2.5m (8ft) S 2.5m (8ft).

Rosa filipes 'Kiftsgate' (syn. R. 'Kiftsgate')
This is a very vigorous climbing rose that bears large sprays of

Rosa 'American Pillar'

Rosa 'Bantry Bay'

Rosa 'Aloha'

Rosa 'New Dawn'

Rosa 'Danse du Feu'

Rosa 'Laura Ford'

fragrant, single, creamy-white flowers during mid- and late summer, followed by bright red hips. H 10m (33ft) S 6m (20ft).

Rosa 'Gloire de Dijon' Old glory rose
Strongly fragrant, double, creamy-yellow flowers are produced in succession from mid-summer to early autumn against lustrous, dark green leaves. H 5m (16ft) S 4m (13ft).

Rosa 'Golden Showers'
Large, double, rich-yellow flowers are produced in succession from mid-summer to early autumn on a compact climber with lustrous, dark green leaves. Ideal for small gardens. H 3m (10ft) S 2m (6ft).

Rosa 'Guinée'
Strongly fragrant, double, red-velvet flowers are produced throughout early to mid-summer against a backdrop of leathery, dark green leaves. H 5m (15ft) S 2.2m (7ft).

Rosa 'Handel'
Subtly fragrant clusters of double, pink-edged, cream flowers are produced in succession from mid-summer to early autumn against lustrous, bronze-tinted, dark green leaves. H 3m (10ft) S 2.2m (7ft).

Rosa 'Laura Ford' (syn. *R.* 'Chewarvel')
Subtly fragrant, semi-double, yellow flowers are borne in

clusters from mid-summer to early autumn against lustrous, pale green leaves. H 2.2m (7ft) S 1.2m (4ft).

Rosa 'Madame Alfred Carrière'
Strongly fragrant, double, white flowers flushed with pink are produced in succession from mid-summer to early autumn. Ideal for a north-facing site. H 5m (16ft) S 3m (10ft).

Rosa 'Madame Grégoire Staechelin' (syn. *R.* 'Spanish Beauty')
Large, blousy, double, crimson-flushed pink flowers, which are strongly fragrant, are produced throughout early summer and mid-summer, followed by large red rosehips. H 6m (20ft) S 4m (12ft).

Rosa 'Maigold'
Clusters of fragrant, semi-double, bronze-yellow flowers on thorny stems are produced from early summer to early autumn. Shade-tolerant. H 2.5m (8ft) S 2.5m (8ft).

Rosa 'Mermaid'
Fragrant, single, primrose-yellow blooms are produced in succession from mid-summer to early autumn. Very hardy. H 6m (20ft) S 6m (20ft).

Rosa 'New Dawn' (syn. *R.* 'The New Dawn')
Fragrant, double, clear pink flowers are borne in clusters from mid-summer to early autumn

against shiny mid-green leaves. Disease resistant and shade tolerant. H 3m (10ft) S 2.5m (8ft).

Rosa 'Paul's Scarlet Climber'
A vigorous climbing rose that is covered with clusters of subtly fragrant, double, bright-red flowers throughout early and mid-summer. H 3m (10ft) S 3m (10ft).

Rosa 'Schoolgirl'
Fragrant, double, coppery-apricot, almost orange, flowers are produced in succession from mid-summer to early autumn. H 3m (10ft) S 2.5m (8ft).

Rosa 'Warm Welcome' (syn. *R.* 'Chewizz')
A compact and long-flowering climber that bears sprays of subtly fragrant, semi-double, orange-red flowers from mid-summer to early autumn. Disease resistant. H 2.2m (7ft) S 2.2m (7ft).

Rosa 'Zéphirine Drouhin' Thornless rose
Double, strongly fragrant, deep pink flowers are produced from early summer to early autumn on thornless stems. This rose is ideal for growing up a north-facing wall or growing as an informal flowering hedge. H 3m (10ft) S 2m (6ft).

Rosa 'Zéphirine Drouhin'

Solanum crispum 'Glasnevin'

SOLANUM

This comprises a huge genus of over 1400 species, including the evergreen climbers featured here, that are grown for their abundant clusters of summer flowers. They are ideal for a sheltered spot where they will cover all types of garden structures. A single specimen will cover an area the size of a standard fence panel in five years.
Cultivation Grow in a moisture-retentive, well-drained neutral to slightly alkaline soil that is reasonably fertile. Grow in full sun, but protected from cold winds. In frost-prone areas, grow half-hardy solanums in containers using a soil-based compost (soil mix). Feed every month during the growing season and water as necessary. Move to a frost-free conservatory or greenhouse in winter.
Pruning Thin out established plants and cut out any frost-damaged shoots in mid-spring. Neglected climbers can be cut back hard to 15cm (6in) of ground level in mid-spring.
Propagation Take basal cuttings in early summer.

Solanum crispum 'Glasnevin' (syn. *S. C.* 'Autumnale') Chilean potato tree
A vigorous climber with dark green leaves that bears fragrant, pale purple flowers from early summer to early autumn, followed by creamy-white fruit.
H 6m (20ft) S 4m (13ft).
Aspect: sun
Hardiness: ❀❀ Zone: Min. 7

Solanum jasminoides 'Album'
Glossy, dark green leaves provide the perfect foil for the clusters of jasmine-scented flowers borne from early summer to early autumn. Each star-shaped white bloom has a yellow eye and is followed by round, purple-black berries. H 6m (20ft) S 6m (20ft).
Aspect: sun
Hardiness: ❀ Zone: Min 9

SOLLYA

A small genus of just three species, grown for its pendent flowers that appear in summer. It can be grown in a sheltered spot in mild gardens, but it will need tying into its support. It is best grown as a conservatory climber in other conditions.
Cultivation Grow in a moisture-retentive, well-drained neutral to slightly alkaline soil that is

Sollya hetrophylla

reasonably fertile in full sun, but protected from midday sun scorch and cold winds. In frost-prone areas, grow in a container using a soil-based compost (soil mix). Feed every month throughout the growing season and water as necessary. Protect in winter by moving it to a frost-free conservatory or greenhouse.
Pruning Thin established plants and cut out any frost-damaged shoots in mid-spring. Neglected climbers can be cut back hard to 15cm (6in) of ground level in mid-spring.
Propagation Take softwood cuttings in mid-spring.

Sollya heterophylla (syn. *S. fusiformis*) Bluebell creeper
From early summer to early autumn, sky blue, bell-shaped flowers hang from this twining climber, which is clothed in lance-shaped, dark green leaves, followed by edible blue berries. Borderline half hardy. H 2m (6ft) S 2m (6ft).
Aspect: sun
Hardiness: ❀ Zone: Min. 5

STEPHANOTIS

This genus of about 10 species includes the long-flowering evergreen climber featured here, grown for its fragrant clusters of waxy-looking flowers. Grow on a sunny wall in warm gardens or, in colder areas, in a heated greenhouse or conservatory.
Cultivation In the garden, grow in a moisture-retentive, well-drained

Stephanotis floribunda

garden soil in full sun but protected from midday sun scorch and cold winds. In containers, grow in a soil-based compost (soil mix). Feed every month throughout the growing season and water as necessary. Move to a warm spot undercover when below 15°C (60°F) and water sparingly in the winter.
Pruning Cut back damaged or weak stems. Lateral shoots on congested plants can be shortened to within 15cm (6in) of the main framework in late winter.
Propagation Take softwood cuttings in mid-spring.

Stephanotis floribunda (syn. *S. jasminoides*) Bridal wreath, Madagascar jasmine
Small cluster of fragrant, waxy-looking, creamy-white flowers are borne from late spring to mid-autumn on this twining evergreen climber that has glossy, leathery, dark green leaves. H 3m (10ft) S 2m (6ft).
Aspect: sun
Hardiness: tender Zones: 10–12

TRACHELOSPERMUM

This genus of about 20 species includes the woody evergreen climbers featured here, grown for their fragrant clusters of summer flowers. Grow against a sheltered, structure or through a well-established tree in a sunny spot or allow it to scramble over the soil as groundcover.
Cultivation Grow in any well-drained soil that is reasonably fertile in full sun or dappled shade that is sheltered from cold winds. In very cold areas, grow in a container using a soil-based compost (soil mix). Feed every month throughout the growing season and water as necessary. Protect against cold in winter.
Pruning No routine pruning is necessary. Wayward shoots can be removed in mid-spring.
Propagation Take semi-ripe cuttings in mid-summer.

Trachelospermum asiaticum Asian jasmine
Jasmine-scented, creamy-white, tubular flowers are produced in clusters throughout mid- and late

Trachelospermum jasminoides

summer and are set off by this twining climber's dark evergreen leaves. H 6m (20ft) S 3m (10ft). Aspect: sun or semi-shade Hardiness: ✤✤ Zone: Min. 7

Trachelospermum jasminoides
Star jasmine
Clusters of jasmine-scented, white, tubular flowers are borne in mid- and late summer on this twining evergreen climber, which has glossy, dark green leaves. H 9m (28ft) S 3m (10ft). Aspect: sun or semi-shade Hardiness: ✤✤ Zone: Min. 7

VITIS
Vine
This genus contains about 65 species, including the deciduous tendril climbers featured here, which are grown mainly for their handsome foliage. This takes on fabulously coloured autumn tints. Vitis are reliable cover-all climbers for walls and fences, but they can also be used to scramble through established trees and hedges, as well as covering the ground in a carpet of foliage. They are very fast-growing and so make an ideal choice if you are looking for a quick cover-up – a single plant will be able to smother about two standard fence panels in five years.
Cultivation Grow in any well-drained neutral to alkaline soil that is reasonably fertile, in full sun or dappled shade. Add plenty of organic matter to the soil before planting.

Pruning No routine pruning is necessary. Keep plants in check by pruning out unwanted stems in early summer.
Propagation Layer suitable shoots in late spring, take semi-ripe cuttings in mid-summer or take take hardwood cuttings in late autumn.

Vitis 'Brant'
This is a vigorous, deciduous, ornamental grape vine with serrated, lobed, apple-green leaves that turn rust-red between the main veins in autumn. Large bunches of edible blue-black grapes are also produced. H 7m (23ft) S 5m (16ft). Aspect: sun or semi-shade Hardiness: ✤✤✤ Zone: Min. 7

Vitis coignetiae
Crimson glory vine
Huge, heart-shaped and lobed, dark green leaves turn fiery shades of red in autumn, accompanied by bunches of small, blue-black, inedible grapes. H 15m (50ft) S 5m (16ft). Aspect: sun or semi-shade Hardiness: ✤✤✤ Zone: Min. 7

Vitis vinifera 'Purpurea'
This is a deciduous tendril climber with lobed, pale green young leaves that mature to claret red, becoming plum purple in autumn, accompanied by bunches of small purple inedible grapes. H 7m (22ft) S 3m (10ft). Aspect: sun or semi-shade Hardiness: ✤✤✤ Zone: Min. 7

Vitis vinifera 'Purpurea'

Wisteria sinensis

WISTERIA
A genus of about ten species, including the twining deciduous climbers featured here, wisterias are grown for their enormous pendent clusters of beautiful early summer flowers. They are ideal for growing up sun-drenched walls and sturdy structures, such as pergolas and arches, where their cascading flowers can be seen at their best.
Cultivation Grow in a moisture-retentive, well-drained soil that is reasonably fertile in full sun or dappled shade. Add plenty of organic matter to the soil before planting time.
Pruning Prune in two stages: cut back all new whippy growth to four or six leaves during late summer. Later, after leaf fall, cut these stumps back to just two or three buds of the main structural framework.
Propagation Take semi-ripe basal cuttings in late summer, or layer suitable shoots in late spring.

Wisteria floribunda
Japanese wisteria
Scented violet-blue to white pea-like flowers hang down in elegant pendent clusters during early summer, followed by felty green pods. The airy, grey-green leaves on this vigorous climber turn yellow in autumn. It is slow to get established and may take several

years to start flowering. H 9m (28ft) S 5m (16ft). Named varieties: 'Alba' (syn. *W.* 'Shiro-Noda'), white flowers. H 9m (28ft) S 5m (16ft). 'Macrobotry' (syn. *W.* 'Kyushaku', *W. multijuga*, *W.* 'Naga Noda'), mauve flowers. H 9m (28ft) S 5m (16ft). 'Royal Purple' (syn. *W.* 'Black Dragon', *W.* 'Kokuryu'), violet-purple flowers. H 9m (28ft) S 5m (16ft). Aspect: sun or semi-shade Hardiness: ✤✤✤ Zone: Min. 7

Wisteria x *formosa*
Fragrant violet-blue and pea-like flowers with white and yellow markings are borne in pendent clusters during late spring and early summer. H 9m (28ft) S 5m (16ft). Aspect: sun or semi-shade Hardiness: ✤✤✤ Zone: Min. 7

Wisteria sinensis (syn. *W. chinensis*)
Chinese wisteria
Clusters of fragrant, mauve, pea-like flowers hang down in pendent clusters during late spring and early summer, often followed by felty green pods. H 9m (28ft) S 5m (16ft). Named varieties: 'Alba', white flowers. H 9m (28ft) S 5m (16ft). Aspect: sun or semi-shade Hardiness: ✤✤✤ Zone: Min. 7

Index

Fuchsia

Camellia williamsii 'Anticipation'

Lavandula stoechas

Plant hardiness zones

Hardiness symbols

✼ = half-hardy (down to 0°C)
✼✼ = frost hardy (down to -5°C)
✼✼✼ = fully hardy (down to -15°C)

Zone numbers

Plant entries in this book have been given zone numbers. These zones relate to their hardiness. The zonal system used (shown below) was developed by the Agricultural Research Service of the US Department of Agriculture. According to this system, there are 11 zones, based on the average annual minimum temperature in a particular geographical zone. When a range of zones is given for a plant, the smaller number indicates the northern-most zone in which a plant can survive the winter. The higher number gives the most southerly in which it will perform consistently. However, this is only a rough indicator, as there are many factors other than temperature that play an important part where hardiness is concerned. These factors vary across the same state and include altitude, wind exposure, proximity to water, soil type, the presence of snow, the existence of shade, night temperature and the amount of water received by the plant. These factors can easily alter a plant's hardiness by several zones.

Zone 1 Below -45°C (-50°F)
Zone 2 -45 to -40°C (-50 to -40°F)
Zone 3 -40 to -34°C (-40 to -30°F)
Zone 4 -34 to -29°C (-30 to -20°F)
Zone 5 -29 to -23°C (-20 to -10°F)
Zone 6 -23 to -18°C (-10 to 0°F)
Zone 7 -18 to -12°C (0 to 10°F)
Zone 8 -12 to -7°C (10 to 20°F)
Zone 9 -7 to -1°C (20 to 30°F)
Zone 10 -1 to 4°C (30 to 40°F)
Zone 11 Above 4°C (40°F)